# Preaching to the Hungers of the Heart

## The Homily on the Feasts and within the Rites

*James A. Wallace, C.Ss.R.*

**THE LITURGICAL PRESS**

Collegeville, Minnesota

www.litpress.org

# Acknowledgments

*The Real Thing* by Tom Stoppard. Copyright © 1983. All rights reserved. Used with permission of Faber and Faber, Ltd., London.

From "The Visitation Journey," by Jessica Powers, *The Selected Poetry of Jessica Powers*, published by ICS Publications, Washington, D.C. All copyrights, Carmelite Monastery, Pewaukee, WI. Used with permission.

From "At Evening with a Child," by Jessica Powers, *The House at Rest*, published by Carmelite Monastery. All copyrights, Carmelite Monastery, Pewaukee, WI. Used with permission.

Cover design by David Manahan, O.S.B. Illustration copyright Marie Docher/PhotoAlto.

The Scripture quotations contained herein are from the New Revised Standard Version Bible, Catholic edition, © 1989 by the Division of Christian Education of the National Council of Churches of Christ in the USA. Used by permission. All rights reserved.

1     2     3     4     5     6     7     8

Library of Congress Cataloging-in-Publication Data

Wallace, James A., 1944–
    Preaching to the hungers of the heart : the homily on the feasts and within the rites / James A. Wallace.
      p. cm.
    Includes bibliographical references and index.
    ISBN 0-8146-1224-5 (alk. paper)
      1. Preaching. 2. Fasts and feasts—Catholic Church. 3. Catholic Church—Liturgy. I. Title.
    BV4211.3. W35 2002
    251—dc21                                    2001038537

In loving memory of my mother
Colette Cecilia Hahn
1922–2000

# Contents

# Preface

Words create and destroy. They create worlds to enter and dwell in. They give us visions of things never before seen and restore memories long forgotten. They have the capacity to reveal the human heart of one person to another and to bind together thousands of people into a community of common purpose. Words also can destroy, strike at the core of long accepted truths and subvert them. They can penetrate and in a few strokes obliterate what we thought was secure and lasting. Words can betray and seduce, defile and deny.

This is a book about words, most particularly it is a book about *the* Word, the living Word of God, found in the Scriptures, and embodied once and for all in the person of Jesus, the Word made flesh. This book has been written for those called to preach the Word of God, and comes out of years of listening to the first efforts of many men and women to be preachers of the gospel of Jesus Christ. It is written from within the world of Roman Catholicism and its liturgical life, a world I was baptized into as a child, and whose riches I have come to appreciate more and more deeply as I come near to the end of my sixth decade. As a professor of homiletics for almost thirty years, I have been preoccupied with words and the Word, and how they interact: sometimes with power, sometimes in tension, and sometimes with little apparent impact.

In 1963 a word was restored to the ordinary vocabulary of Roman Catholics. That word was *homily*. It was not a new word for those who knew the history of preaching. St. Justin Martyr first used it in the second century to refer to the preaching that takes place when the community gathers for worship. The preaching of the Church Fathers, especially during the third, fourth, and fifth centuries, has been called the golden age of the homily, a time when preaching was so very rich in biblical proclamation and exegesis. The homilies that have come down to us from this period are part of the Church's treasury of stored wisdom. But since the Council of Trent in the sixteenth century the preaching that took place in Catholic churches on Sundays had always been called the sermon,[1] sometimes related to the gospel that had been heard, but more often an exposition of some doctrine of the faith, or an instruction on some virtue to be cultivated or vice to be avoided. Then, on December 4, 1963, at the end of the second session of the Second Vatican Council, a document was promulgated that began a new period of reflection on liturgical preaching. In the context of calling for the revision of the rite of the Mass, the Constitution on the Sacred Liturgy (*Sacrosanctum Concilium*) spoke of the important role of the homily and inaugurated a discussion that continues to this day as to its nature and function within the liturgical life of the Church.

I would propose that the understanding of the liturgical homily remains a work in progress, for the Church continues to reflect on what a homily is and does. Furthermore, I would suggest that it is time to enter a new phase in our understanding. Thus far there have been two phases. The first phase tended to see the homily as another word for preaching in general, embracing all the tasks and purposes traditionally assigned to preaching: evangelization, catechesis, exhortation, and witnessing. Phase one would include the reflections found in the Constitution on the Sacred Liturgy which reintroduced the word *homily* to the Catholic community and linked it with both proclamation and catechesis (nos. 35.2 and 52),[2] and the 1975 exhortation of Paul VI, On Evangelization in the Modern World (*Evangelii Nuntiandi* 43), which emphasized the homily as a tool for evangelization, especially in its capacity to witness in a world "sated by talk" (42). In the writings of John Paul II we also find an emphasis on these traditional goals of preaching, especially the catechetical as is evidenced in the 1979 exhortation, On Catechesis in our Time (*Catechesi Tradendae* 48). The homily's embrace, then, in this first phase can be seen to be comprehensive and its task multiple: to proclaim God's wonderful works in the history of salvation, particularly as located in the mystery of Christ, to expound from the Scriptures the

---

1. One can find mention of the *consueta homilia* (i.e., the "accustomed homily") in the 1917 Code of Canon Law, Can. 1344, no.1, to be given on Sundays and certain feasts during the year, especially within the Mass at which the majority of people were present. But in the memory of most Catholics growing up in the middle decades of the last century, preachers gave "sermons" on Sundays and other feast days.

2. Interestingly, the Constitution uses the word "sermon" in no. 35.2 and "homily" in no. 52. For a treatment of the historical and contemporary usage of these two words, see Robert P. Waznak, S.S., *An Introduction to the Homily* (Collegeville: The Liturgical Press, 1998), ch. 1, 1–31.

mysteries of the faith and the guiding principles of the Christian life, and to witness to Christ by expressing in love the faith of the preacher. A worthy, if daunting, agenda for the homily.

Phase two was inaugurated in 1982 by the publication of the U.S. Bishops' document, *Fulfilled In Your Hearing: The Homily in the Sunday Assembly (FIYH)*,[3] and can be characterized as offering a more focused understanding of the nature of the homily and how it functions. Before attending to this understanding, two observations are important. First of all, note that the title of this document limits its concern to the homily *in the Sunday Assembly. FIYH* is not addressing every context for liturgical preaching. Secondly, there is an explicit recognition that the Sunday liturgical homily cannot do everything: "even though the liturgical homily can incorporate instruction and exhortation, it will not be able to carry the whole weight of the Church's preaching" (26), and that there will be a need for special times and occasions for three other kinds of preaching, "sometimes referred to as pre-evangelization, evangelization and catechesis" (26–27). Keeping these two limitations in mind, then, *FIYH* understands the homily as "a scriptural interpretation of human existence which enables a community to recognize God's active presence, to respond to that presence in faith through liturgical word and gesture, and beyond the liturgical assembly, through a life lived in conformity with the Gospel" (29).

What are the implications of this particular understanding of the homily? What communal need does it address? *FIYH* sees the Sunday homilist as one who addresses a "people hungry, sometimes desperately so, for meaning in their lives" (7). The Sunday homily attends to feeding that particular hunger. And in offering the gathered community a word of meaning, "a scriptural interpretation of human existence," it empowers them to be active participants in the Liturgy of the Eucharist and to go forth to live a gospel-influenced life. The homilist here is "a mediator of meaning" (7), enabling people to enter more fully into both liturgy and life. *FIYH*, then, offers a more focused understanding of the homily as feeding the hunger for meaning.

3. Bishops' Committee on Priestly Life and Ministry, National Conference of Catholic Bishops, *Fulfilled In Your Hearing, The Homily in the Sunday Assembly* (Washington, D.C.: USCC, 1982). It is important to note that *FIYH* is the work of a committee. As such it does not have the weight of a council document or papal exhortation. What it does offer is a pastoral approach to preaching attentive to the riches of the Scriptures and our theological tradition and how these can intersect with life as lived in a particular context in a particular time.

The image of the homilist as one who feeds the people is rooted in the 1970 General Instruction of the Roman Missal which speaks of the homily as "a necessary source of nourishment of the Christian life" (41). This same paragraph prescribes that the homily keep in mind "the needs of the particular community." *FIYH*, then, can be seen as building on this image of providing nourishment and directing it toward one particular need of the believing community, the hunger for meaning. The homilist feeds this hunger for "ultimate meaning" by helping the community recognize God's presence and action in its midst, especially in the routine and random events of daily life. The focus of the Sunday homily, then, is the ongoing human existence of the community existing in a particular time and place.

This book proposes that it is time for a third phase in our understanding of the homily and will attempt to offer a more nuanced consideration of the homily as nourishment. It will consider three hungers of the heart and reflect primarily on liturgical contexts other than the ordinary Sunday Eucharist as providing the occasions to satisfy them. These contexts include the solemnities and feasts of the Lord, the sacramental rites other than the Sunday Eucharist, and the feasts of Mary and the saints. Insofar as Sunday celebrations of the Eucharist are taken into account, it is in relation to these other liturgical settings.

Chapter one will consider in greater detail the image of feeding God's people with the word of God, taking into account the ministry of Jesus and the significance of his feeding the people, the biblical understanding of the word of God as food and how this has been carried into the Christian tradition of *lectio divina*, and the homily's role in the Liturgy of the Word as providing nourishment. The main body of the book will then consider three hungers of the human heart and how they might be fed by the liturgical preaching of the Church. Perhaps it might be helpful to think of these hungers as three circles, one within the other. In this way, they are seen as distinct yet related, one flowing into the other, with fluid boundaries that allow for crossover and interchange. Feeding one hunger is not totally disconnected from nourishing another; they are not rigidly separated. But, for heuristic purposes, distinguishing the various hungers allows for a particular emphasis to be recognized and given attention.

Chapter two will consider the innermost hunger of the human person: the hunger for wholeness, that yearning at our deepest level for being complete, fulfilled, "perfect" as Jesus calls his disciples to be. This chapter will look to the preaching that takes place on the great feasts of the Lord, especially the solemnities that celebrate (a) those pivotal events in the life of Jesus: his birth, epiphany, death, resurrection, ascension, and sending of the Holy Spirit and (b) those feasts that celebrate such central doctrinal beliefs as Trinity Sunday, the Body and Blood of Christ, and Christ the King, and how such preaching can nourish this particular hunger for wholeness.

Chapter three will return to the hunger for meaning already mentioned and, building on the contribution of *FIYH*'s understanding of the homily within the Sunday Eucharist, will extend to the other sacramental celebrations the homily's capacity to meet this hunger. While the Sunday Eucharist meets the hunger for meaning by addressing the events of ordinary life, especially those random happenings which can lead a community either to praise God, or to question and even doubt God, there are yet other occasions in life that have their own unique context and invite the skills of a mediator of meaning. Such occasions include those addressed by the various sacramental celebrations of the Church such as baptisms, weddings, funerals, rites of reconciliation and anointing of the sick. These liturgical celebrations invite a word offering a faith perspective to those present, that is, a way of seeing the profound human experiences at the heart of the sacraments in the light of Christ. In this way the hunger for meaning will be addressed not only in the events that occur within our larger world and community, but also during the more personal experiences that invite communal reflection and celebration.

Chapters four and five will present the homily as responding to the hunger to belong, a hunger that often brings us individually to church, to come into contact with a larger community, to be connected with others on the level of shared faith, and to live more fully in a deeper awareness of our communion with all who have gone before us, with whom we remain united in and through Christ. Chapter four will consider the feasts of the saints celebrated in the annual sanctoral cycle, and chapter five will attend to the feasts and solemnities of Mary, Mother of God, as having the potential to respond to this hunger for belonging, allowing the preacher to bring these "friends and prophets of God" into deeper contact with us who continue to struggle to grow in Christ. At first, I intended to have only one chapter, and to include Mary under the general heading of the sanctoral cycle in the liturgical calendar, but the great number of Marian celebrations—fourteen of them!—and the present reappraisal of her ongoing role in the life of today's believing community, along with the difficulty so many preachers have with preaching on the Marian feasts, led to a separate chapter. However, I would include the preaching done on these feasts under the rubric of feeding the hunger for belonging.

The final chapter will consider one other hunger of the heart, unique to the preacher, referred to by John Paul II as "a hunger to preach the gospel" (*Pastores Dabo Vobis* 28). Preachers can stimulate this hunger of the heart by tending to their "love life," specifically, through the cultivation of four particular loves: a love of language, a love of the Scriptures, a love of the people, and a love of Jesus Christ. In deepening these loves, their hunger to preach will increase. By entering more completely into the world of words, especially the words of the Scriptures, and by deepening our understanding of both the hearts of our people and that of the God revealed in Jesus, we will fan the flame that must burn within us in order to preach well, with both fire and light.

I am greatly indebted to my students at the Washington Theological Union where I have been teaching homiletics for the past fifteen years, who have helped me to formulate and refine the ideas presented here. Their recognition of the importance of preaching for the life of the Church has provided an ongoing stimulus for my continued work in this field. I am equally indebted to the people of Holy Trinity parish, Georgetown, Washington, D.C., especially the community of the 11:30 Sunday Eucharist whose faith has been a nourishing force in my life over the last five years. Special words of thanks are owed to Walter J. Burghardt, S.J., John Allyn Melloh, S.M., Donald Heet, O.S.F.S., and, especially, to Daniel Grigassy, O.F.M., whose careful reading and thoughtful comments have helped in the final shaping of this work. Most especially, I want to acknowledge my friend and colleague Robert P. Waznak, S.S., whose support, encouragement, and friendship has been a mainstay in my life for the last fifteen years.

Finally, I am grateful to my religious community, the Redemptorists, for their ongoing support.

James A. Wallace, C.SS.R.

Chapter 1

# Preaching's Task
# in a New Millennium:
# Feeding God's People

*"Everybody's got a hungry heart."*

(Bruce Springsteen)

*"Significantly, the only miracle found in all four gospels is one involving food . . ."*[1]

(Nathan Mitchell)

*"Feed the man dying of hunger, because if you have not fed him you have killed him."*

(The Church in the Modern World, no. 69)

Proclaiming, heralding, witnessing, teaching, interpreting, sowing the seed of God's word, sacred eloquence, sermonizing—all are ways to think about the work of preaching. This book will settle on yet another one. Allow me to begin in a leisurely fashion by bringing a fictional preacher to your attention. Barbara Kingsolver's novel *The Poisonwood Bible* is the story of the Reverend Nathan Price, an evangelical preacher from the South who volunteers to go to the Congo to spend a year at a mission there. He takes his family, which includes his wife Oleanna and their four daughters: Rachel (age 17),

1. Nathan Mitchell, *Real Presence: The Work of Eucharist* (Chicago: Liturgical Training Publications, 1998) 71.

1

Leah and Adah (twins, age 14), and Ruth May (age 5). The year is 1951. The story is mostly told from the perspectives of the four Price daughters, each with a unique voice.

As the narrative begins, the family arrives at the airport to depart for Africa; there they discover that they are limited to forty-four pounds of luggage per person. This had not entered into their calculations when packing; they are sixty-one pounds overweight. Rev. Price walks off and leaves it up to his wife to sort out what needs to be discarded. All things deemed "frivolous" are cast aside, but this in no way solves the problem. Then, someone remembers that the weight limitation does not apply to what they have on their persons. Leah, one of the daughters, tells the reader,

> We struck out for Africa carrying all our excess baggage on our bodies, under our clothes. Also we had clothes under our clothes. My sisters and I left home, wearing six pairs of underdrawers, two half-slips and camisoles, several dresses one on top of the other, with pedal pushers underneath and outside of everything an all weather coat. The other goods, tools, cake-mix boxes and so forth were tucked out of sight in our pockets and under our waistbands, surrounding us in a clanking armor. . . . My father, of course, was bringing the Word of God, which fortunately weighs nothing at all.[2]

Leah's comment set me thinking about the word of God, and what it weighs. How does one estimate the weight of God's word? Does it "weigh nothing at all"? Another Price daughter, Rachel, suggests an answer when she recounts their arrival in Africa and what happens when the family is taken directly to the open-roofed church where the village has prepared a meal for them. When all is ready, the village chief announces: "Reverend and Mrs. Price and your children! . . . You are welcome to our feast. Today we have killed a goat to celebrate your coming" and the half-naked women cooking the meal break into clapping, cheering, and a great clamor ensues. Then, Nathan is invited to offer a word of thanks for the feast. In doing so, he serves up his own meal, choosing a text from Genesis 19 about how "the *emissaries* of mercy *smote* the sinners who had come *heedless* to the sight of God, *heedless in their nakedness*." As he is speaking, Nathan points to one woman at the fire, who like all of the women, is bare breasted. He then builds to his conclusion: "*Nakedness*," Father repeated, "and *dark-*

---

2. Barbara Kingsolver, *The Poisonwood Bible* (New York: Harper Perennial, 1998) 15, 19.

*ness* of the *soul!* For we shall *destroy* this place where the *loud clamor* of the *sinners* is waxen *great* before the *face* of the Lord."[3]

When Nathan concludes, no one cheers or claps or sings anymore. There is certainly no more high-spirited "loud clamor." A few women use their wraparound sarongs to cover their breasts. Some leave to go home without any supper. Nathan has served up the word of God, on this occasion a weighty word; he has provided his own meal, heavy and indigestible. What, then, is the weight of the word of God? I invite you to imagine it in terms of food, the weight of a meal. Depending on how it is presented, it can sometimes be heavy and unappetizing; at other times it might offer little more than insubstantial sound bytes. At its best, however, it can provide substantial sustenance for the human spirit, mind, and heart. God's word then weighs in as nourishment that can build up the body of believers, feeding their deepest hunger. It has the capacity to respond to the existential condition captured in the words of a contemporary troubadour, Bruce Springsteen, who has reminded us: "Everybody's got a hungry heart."

## "You Give Them Something to Eat" (Mark 6:37): A Pericope for Preachers

An event told six times in just over one hundred pages must be an important one. Such is the case with the story of Jesus feeding the crowd in the New Testament. It occurs as two distinct occasions in the first two Gospels and as a single occurrence in the other two: Matthew 14:14-21 and 15:32-38; Mark 6:34-44 and 8:1-9; Luke 9:10-17; and John 6:1-13. Since the two accounts in Mark's Gospel are the earliest, I will use them as the basis for my remarks on the significance of this event in Jesus' ministry for today's Christian life and ministry, especially that of preachers. Mark's telling of the first miracle is set at the beginning of what has been called in Latin the *sectio panis*, "the bread section," which runs from 6:34 to 8:21. This section of the oldest gospel not only includes the two feeding accounts but also many other references to bread and eating.[4] Consider Mark's rendition of the first feeding (6:34-44). You might find it helpful to read it aloud:

3. Ibid., 26–27.
4. I am indebted in this section on the various gospel accounts of the miracle of the loaves to the following works: Francis J. Moloney, S.D.B., *The Gospel of Mark: A Commentary* (Peabody, Mass.: Hendrickson, 2002) and Eugene LaVerdiere, *The Eucharist in*

As he went ashore, he saw a great crowd; and he had compassion for them, because they were like sheep without a shepherd; and he began to teach them many things. When it grew late, his disciples came to him and said, "This is a deserted place, and the hour is now very late; send them away so that they may go into the surrounding country and villages and buy something for themselves to eat." But he answered them, "You give them something to eat." They said to him, "Are we to go and buy two hundred denarii worth of bread, and give it to them to eat?" And he said to them, "How many loaves have you? Go and see." When they had found out, they said, "Five, and two fish." Then he ordered them to get all the people to sit down in groups on the green grass. So they sat down in groups of hundreds and of fifties. Taking the five loaves and the two fish, he looked up to heaven, and blessed and broke the loaves, and gave them to his disciples to set before the people; and he divided the two fish among them all. And all ate and were filled; and they took up twelve baskets full of broken pieces and of the fish. Those who had eaten the loaves numbered five thousand.[5]

Over twenty years ago I heard the British actor Alec McCowen perform Mark's Gospel in its entirety. One of the moments still vivid in my memory is his interpretation of this story. To understand its impact at that time, however, it is important to realize that we had been listening to the first five chapters. Because we rarely hear or read any gospel at one sitting it is easy to be unaware of certain aspects that Mark's Gospel emphasizes. One such characteristic is the amount of movement in this gospel. Jesus is always going somewhere and the crowds are always following and pressing in on him. By the time McCowen came to the events narrated in the sixth chapter of the gospel and Jesus says to his disciples who have just returned from their first mission of preaching and healing, "Come away to a deserted place all by yourselves and rest awhile" (6:31), everyone in the audience was also ready for a little rest. The text itself captures this in its presentation of the disciples' condition as being surrounded by people "coming and going," with the apostles' having "no leisure even to eat." So they all go out in a boat to a deserted place to rest. And what happens? "Many saw them going and recognized

---

the *New Testament and the Early Church* (Collegeville: The Liturgical Press, 1996) especially 52–58, 69–73, 87, and 119–25 and Idem, *The Beginning of the Gospel: Introducing the Gospel According to Mark* Vol. 1 (Collegeville: The Liturgical Press, 1999), 170–77 and 205–10.

5. All excerpts from the Bible will be taken from *The Holy Bible: New Revised Standard Version* (Nashville: Thomas Nelson, 1989).

them, and they hurried there on foot from all the towns and arrived there ahead of them" (6:33). The account above picks up from this point.

McCowen's interpretation brought out the exhaustion, impatience, frustration, and escalating tempers on the part of both Jesus and the disciples. The performer made certain words and phrases stick in the memory:

"a deserted place . . . the hour . . . very late . . ."
"Send them away."
"*You* give them something . . ."
"Are *we* to go and buy *two hundred denarii* worth of bread . . . ?"
"How many loaves . . . ? GO AND SEE."
"Five . . . and two fish." (Spoken through gritted teeth.)

The tension captured in this exchange brings out two different perspectives: that of the disciples and that of Jesus. First, on the part of the disciples, hunger was taken very seriously when out in "a deserted place" at the end of the day. Their solution is to send the people away, so they can go where there is food. In response to this, Jesus says: "You feed them." The disciples then reveal their awareness of their limited capacity to respond to this challenge. In Mark the emphasis is on *how much* is needed to feed them; with a denarii being a day's wage, two hundred days' wages were necessary to feed this crowd. In Matthew, the emphasis is on *how little* they had: "We have nothing here but . . ." In both responses, attention is either on the size of the crowd or on the disciples themselves and their scant resources. To which Jesus responds in three ways: Go and see what's around; bring it here; now distribute it. The key moment, of course, is when he takes the five loaves and two fish from them, blesses, breaks, and gives it to them to distribute.

How we interpret this occasion of the feeding of the crowd depends once again on where we focus. At least three interpretations come to mind. If we focus on the central moment of the narrative with Jesus taking, blessing, breaking, and giving the bread, we are most likely to hear this event primarily for its eucharistic overtones, both the foreshadowing of what happens at the Last Supper when he takes, blesses, breaks and gives the bread to those gathered within him, and what happens at every gathering of the community to celebrate Eucharist. If, however, we focus on Jesus and his response to the crowd and its immediate, physical hunger, we can also hear in this text the command to care for those in need, to feed the hungry and not send them away, to share what resources are available, and to trust that we are not working alone but there is one who works with us who has power and authority. Both of these understandings are clearly grounded in the text itself and its understanding of Jesus. He is described as standing before a people who "were like sheep without a shepherd," calling to mind both Ezekiel 34 where the Lord declares, "I myself will be the shepherd of my sheep," and Psalm 23 whose shepherd brings his flock to green pastures and prepares a table for them. This event also evokes Exodus 16 where Moses feeds God's people in the desert, and the story of Elisha who feeds a group of a hundred men with only twenty barley loaves and still has some left over (2 Kings 4:42-44). It is noteworthy that when Elisha does this, he quotes the Lord as saying, "They shall eat and have some left over." Jesus is not only in the line of the prophets who proclaim God's will that all have sufficient food, especially the poor and destitute, but he is the one on whose authoritative word the people will "eat and have some left over."

The importance of this event for the ministry of the Church is recognized by LaVerdiere who says that the universal mission of the Church is set out in 6:1–8:21 when the Church, represented by the Twelve, is sent to Jews (6:30-44) and Gentiles (8:1-10) for the breaking of the bread. These two accounts "show how the Church fulfills its mission, really and symbolically, when taking bread, blessing (6:41) or giving thanks (8:6), breaking the bread and giving it to the hungry."[6] Both the feeding that is a response to physical hunger and the feeding that occurs when the community gathers to remember the Lord's passion, death, and resurrection are brought together here. In all three Synoptic accounts of this event, the eucharistic words—*took, blessed* (*gave thanks*), *broke,* and *gave* are found, just as the disciples are involved in all three accounts in the task of pastoring the people by distributing the food to them.

But there is a third understanding of this event to be uncovered by attending to Jesus as he is presented later in Mark's extended "bread section" and in the Johannine Bread of Life discourse following the Fourth Gospel's account of the feeding (John 6). After the second feeding in Mark, when Jesus is once again in the boat with his disciples, we are given the following curious statement: "Now the disciples had forgotten to bring any bread; and they had only one loaf with them in the boat" (8:14). What does this one loaf refer to? After warning them against both the leaven of the Pharisees and the leaven of Herod (8:16), the disciples misunderstand what Jesus is talking about. They

6. LaVerdiere, *Eucharist in the New Testament,* 54.

think he is referring to their having forgotten to bring bread. Jesus becomes exasperated once again and calls them to remember how much was left over from the two feedings, after he had broken the loaves. Finally he asks "Do you *still* not understand?" More than mere fragments are at hand at this moment in the boat. The disciples had "one loaf" with them, the only one that mattered: Jesus.[7] Not only did Jesus and those who followed him feed the hungry and, after the resurrection, nourish his followers with the Eucharist. People were also fed with the words of Jesus. For the full development of this idea we turn to the Gospel of John.

John's telling of Jesus' giving bread to the crowd (6:1-15) finds its closest parallel in Mark,[8] but John broadens his reflection on this event in his presentation of Jesus' discourse to the crowd (6:22-59). John moves the focus from the act of multiplying food to the person of Jesus himself. It is not the disciples but Jesus who distributes the bread in the Johannine account, which Jesus himself underlines in his discourse the next day: "Do not labor for the food that perishes, but for the food that endures to eternal life, that the Son of Man will give to you . . . ." (6:27). This discourse emphasizes two proclamations: Jesus is the true bread from heaven (6:25-50) and the bread Jesus gives is his flesh for the life of the world (6:51-59). While the latter reinforces the Synoptic emphasis on the bread of the Eucharist, the former points in another direction.

After being told to work for the bread that does not perish, the crowd asks what they must do to devote themselves to the works of God. Jesus responds: "Believe in him whom he has sent" (6:29). Jesus moves his listeners beyond physical hunger and calls them to faith, to belief in the one that feeds their deepest hunger: "it is my Father who gives you the true bread from heaven. For the bread is he who comes down from heaven and gives life to the world" (6:32-33). The emphasis on Jesus as the true bread proclaims him as the One sent from the Father, the Word of God, the Wisdom of God, the Revelation of God. "For this is the will of my Father, that all who see the Son and believe in him may have eternal life; and I will raise them up on the last day" (6:40). Biblical scholar Francis Moloney, S.D.B., notes that in both the wisdom and Jewish midrashic traditions, nourishment from God was identified with the gift of the Law, the life-giving presence of Torah.

---

7. LaVerdiere, *Beginning of the Gospel*, 215.
8. LaVerdiere, *The Eucharist in the New Testament and the Early Church*, 119.

But Jesus is now saying this bread, Torah, has been replaced by the *true* bread, himself, that will give life to the whole world, not just to Israel.[9] Nourishment for eternal life is to be found in Jesus who replaces Moses, manna, and the Torah. Jesus is life-giving food precisely *as* God's revelation, as the Word and Wisdom of God. This bread is found in the Scriptures and offered to those hungering for life. It is distributing this bread that is the work of all who preach the gospel of Jesus Christ.

The stories of the miraculous feedings, as Nathan Mitchell argues, "challenge Christians to remember that eucharistic origins lie not in Jesus' *last* meal but in *all* those events wherein Jesus (as guest or host) satisfied hunger, announced unbridled joy of God's arrival in the present moment (= "God's reign"), and offered healing and hope to the poor and needy."[10] The first three Gospels suggest this when they precede this action of feeding with Jesus either teaching the crowd (Mark) or healing those in need (Matthew) or doing both (Luke). And the act of celebrating Eucharist is often an event that teaches, heals, and nourishes. It nourishes as it instructs, and heals as it nourishes.

The accounts of the feeding of the multitude, then, can speak to all in the ministry of preaching. The experience of feeling there is "nothing much available," or even "nothing—period!" to draw on can occur when the needs of the community threaten to overwhelm us. An exhaustion can set in that makes us want to resist the command: "*You* feed them." In our day, this can particularly be true for preachers who are asked to preach both well and often. So many different occasions might occur within any one week: Sunday liturgies (with different groups as the focus—family liturgy, young adult liturgy, older adult liturgy), daily liturgies, baptisms, weddings, funerals, anointing of the sick, reconciliation, holy days, holidays, and yet other special occasions set within a liturgy. And then there is the diversity in today's "crowd"— so many whose life experiences are vastly different from the preacher's and even from one another's: the elderly, the baby boomers, Generation X, and so on. And then there are the cultural differences. But we have been told, "*You* feed them." And so we must. We turn to the table that offers a nourishing meal, the table of the Word of God. At times it might seem very little, but with Jesus taking, blessing, and giving it back to us to distribute, many can be fed, with some left over.

9. Francis J. Moloney, S.D.B., *The Gospel of John* (Collegeville: The Liturgical Press, 1998) 212.

10. Mitchell, *Real Presence*, 73.

## "Take and Eat": The Primary Role of the Scriptures

Visiting the Holy Land always includes a trip up north to the Galilee region. One of the most popular sites for tour buses is Tabgha, the peaceful setting of the Chapel of the Multiplication of the Loaves, only a few hundred feet from the Sea of Galilee. Going into the chapel and up towards the sanctuary, you will find on the floor beneath the altar a mosaic of a basket containing two fish and four loaves of bread. "The fifth loaf is on the altar," the guide will tell you, thereby linking today's liturgy and yesterday's miracle. But the guide might even go further. When the liturgical reform inaugurated by the Second Vatican Council is taken into account, this same mosaic could be placed in front of the lectern.

The Constitution on the Sacred Liturgy (*Sacrosanctum Concilium*), after affirming that Christ "speaks when the holy scriptures are read in church" (7), extends the table imagery of the Eucharist to the liturgy of the readings: "the treasures of the Bible are to be opened up more lavishly so that a richer fare may be provided for the faithful at the table of God's word" (51).[11] In a similar vein, the 1970 General Instruction of the Roman Missal (*Cenam Paschalem*) affirming that the two parts of the Mass, the Liturgy of the Word and the Liturgy of the Eucharist "are so closely connected with each other that together they constitute but one single act of worship," reinforces this same awareness by stating "both the table of God's word and the table of Christ's body are prepared, so that from them the faithful may be instructed and nourished" (8) and that "in the readings, the table of God's word is laid before the people and the treasures of the Bible are opened to them" (34). And, finally, in the Introduction to the Lectionary for Mass, first published in 1969 and revised in 1981, this nourishing impact of the two tables is given further emphasis: "The Church is nourished spiritually at the table of God's word and at the table of the Eucharist: from the one it grows in wisdom and from the other in holiness. In the word of God the divine covenant is announced; in the Eucharist, the new and everlasting covenant is renewed. The spoken word of God brings to mind the history of salvation; the Eucharist embodies it in the sacramental signs of the liturgy" (10). God's word, therefore, is recognized

---

11. All quotations from the documents of the Second Vatican Council are taken from *Vatican Council II, The Basic Sixteen Documents*, ed. Austin Flannery, O.P. (Northport, N.Y.: Costello Publishing Co., 1996).

as "the sustenance of the Christian life and the source of the prayer of the entire Church" (47).

This wonderful image of God's people gathering around the table of the word which sustains them has great implications for those who "lay the table" each week, bringing forth the word and "distributing" it by reading and preaching. For models in living out this metaphor, we can turn to the Bible itself which offers us Jeremiah, Ezekiel, and John, the Seer of the book of Revelation. The story of Jeremiah's initial calling to serve as a speaker of God's word relates how the divine hand touched his mouth, saying, "See, I place my words in your mouth" (1:9). Jeremiah later says, "Your words were found, and I ate them, and your words became to me a joy and the delight of my heart" (15:16). Some translations have Jeremiah "devouring" God's words.[12] To Ezekiel, the prophet of the exile, a voice says, "Open your mouth and eat what I give you." A hand with a written scroll is given to the prophet, and on it are words of "lamentation and mourning and woe." And the prophet is told again, "Eat this scroll and go, speak to the house of Israel." And when the prophet eats it, it is sweet in his mouth (Ezek 2:8–3:3).

Whereas Ezekiel is sent to "the house of Israel," a broader audience is the recipient of the words of the prophet of Revelation. A voice tells John to go and take a scroll from the angel's hand, and then says, "Take it and eat." The prophet finds it sweet in the mouth but sour in the stomach. Then the prophet is told, "You must prophesy about many peoples and nations and languages and kings" (Rev 10:8-10). These three prophets were called to speak at times of great upheaval: Babylon's destruction of Jerusalem, the carrying of the people into exile, and the Roman Empire's persecution of the early Church. But before taking God's word to others, the prophets were called to consume it, so that it entered their being completely.

Eugene Peterson, former pastor and retired professor of spirituality, finds inspiration in this image, noting that John "is not instructed to pass on information about God, he is commanded to assimilate the word of God so that when he does speak it will express itself artlessly in his syntax just as the food we eat, when we are healthy, is unconsciously assimilated into our nerves and muscles and put to work in speech and action."[13] In this way John becomes a model for all Chris-

---

12. See *New American Bible* and *Revised English Bible*.

13. Eugene H. Peterson, "Eat this Book: The Holy Community at Table with Holy Scripture," *Theology Today* (April 1999) 6.

tians who will find spiritual sustenance by feeding on the Scripture; for this to happen, there is a need for "pulling the Christian scriptures from the margins back to the center as the text for living the Christian life deeply."[14] Such was the goal of the Second Vatican Council when it mandated a richer sharing of God's word by means of a new lectionary for liturgical celebration.

But a new lectionary alone will not do it. A three-year cycle of readings for Sundays and a two-year cycle for weekdays alone will not do it. Assimilation demands a personal response from all involved. One way to begin is a return to the monastic discipline of *lectio divina* (that is, holy reading). This process of reading works that nourish the life of the spirit, particularly the Scriptures, finds it roots in the thought of the early Church Fathers. Figures like Cyprian, Ambrose, and Augustine each wrote that while we speak to God in prayer, God speaks to us in our reading. But it was Jerome, ever straightforward and forceful, who compared reading the Scriptures with eating the Eucharist: "In reading the Bible the Fathers did not read the texts, but the living Christ, and Christ spoke to them. They consumed the Word like the Eucharistic bread and wine, and the Word offered itself to them with the profundity of Christ" and "I believe that the Gospel is the body of Christ . . . and the Scriptures, the divine doctrine, are truly the body and blood of Christ."[15]

I am convinced that *lectio divina* is *essential* for both preachers and readers called to distribute the word to the people of God. Not merely helpful, but essential. This practice engages us at the deepest level of our being. That is why so many turn to the vocabulary of gastronomy to convey the activity involved. Words like "savor," "taste," "consume," "digest," and even "ruminate," and "belch" are used. St. Anthony, the desert father, advised that we should be like camels rather than horses, slowly chewing the cud until the food is gradually broken down and absorbed.[16] Not a pretty picture, but it does convey an important point. *Lectio divina* is an unhurried, gradual, openhearted, and open-minded approach to the word of God. Couching this process in such gustatory language provides a visceral way to imagine what we are about when we open the book to the upcoming readings. You have to slow down to taste, chew, swallow, and savor. Only then are we likely to respond,

14. Ibid., 5.
15. See Ernest J. Fiedler, "Lectio Divina: Devouring God's Word." *Liturgical Ministry* (spring 1996) 65–67.
16. Ibid., 67.

"How sweet are your words to my taste, sweeter than honey to my mouth." Only then are we likely to become part of and help form a very different kind of "consumer society."

The art of oral interpretation has offered a similar appreciation of what it means to engage a text and bring it to a full spoken expression. In her many editions of the textbook *Oral Interpretation*, Charlotte Lee never departed from her first definition of this task as the "art of communicating to an audience a work of literary art in its intellectual, emotional, and aesthetic entirety."[17] This emphasis on bringing across the full experience of a text to others is rooted in a full encounter between reader and text. Similarly, Wallace Bacon called on oral interpreters to come to terms with that "sense of the other" characteristic of every text, approaching it as "thou," rather than as "it."[18] When the text is recognized as having its own inner life, then the goal of the interpreter is to enter into the text in such a way that there is a "coalescence" between the text and reader, between the inner life of the text—its thoughts, feelings, the way that it moves, all that makes up its unique way of being—and the inner life of the reader, his or her thoughts, feelings, physical and psychological responses. The reader offers himself or herself as a vehicle for the text's coming to life. Inner life of text meets and coalesces with inner life of reader and then is given outer expression through an active, thoughtful, "feeling-ful," and kinesthetic engagement of the reader in performance.[19] It is much more than "saying the words clearly." Years ago, I remember reading about Jerzy Grotowski, the director of an experimental Polish theatre group, who said that the one performing a text is called to be "a holy interpreter" who lays down his/her life for the text. For the print to rise from its inert condition on the page to new life, it needs a living body, heart, mind, and soul as its medium. More will be said on this in the final chapter of the book.

"Take and eat." The process begins with the texts that are given to us for liturgical celebration. The achievement of the liturgical Lectionary

17. Charlotte Lee, *Oral Interpretation* (Boston: Houghton Mifflin, 1971) 2.

18. Wallace A. Bacon, *The Art of Interpretation* (New York: Holt, Rinehart, and Winston, 1972) 32–39.

19. I use the coined word *feelingful* instead of *emotional* since the latter can evoke the fear of doing too much with a text, expressing emotion in an overwrought manner, which seems to be one of the great fears of readers but more often results in readings devoid of all feeling. The text will often cue readers as to appropriate feeling. Bacon distinguishes between kinesics, which has to do with overt gestures and bodily movement, and kinesthesis which is "the sensation of body movement, position and tension"; see Bacon, 11.

should not be underestimated. For over thirty years now the worshiping community has been exposed to a wider selection of the books of the Bible than ever before. Gerard Sloyan contends that "these selections from the Bible, if consistently read well and just as consistently commented on, cannot but have the hoped-for effect."[20] For Sloyan, this is the goal of making Catholics once again a people of the Bible. At the same time, the Lectionary's shortcomings, especially on Sundays, have also been duly noted: the fact of having three readings, complicated by a second reading that is unrelated to the other two during Ordinary Time; the brevity of the first two readings; the impression that the Gospel of John has been "worked in" (at the expense of Mark in Cycle B) rather than given its own year; the "devaluation" of the Old Testament due to its selection on the basis of the principle of harmony with the gospel lesson; the exclusion of major biblical themes and principal biblical characters, especially the exclusion of biblical women.[21]

From the above listing, I would like to highlight especially the challenge of having the first two readings register in the minds of the community. People are still settling in when the first reading is read and, unless it is a narrative that immediately engages interest, the reading is over and done with so quickly that any impact is highly questionable. In terms of the table of the word, such snippets are more hors d'oeuvres than substantial portions. The second reading is seldom better in impressing itself on the listeners' consciousness, in addition to turning our attention in a completely different direction during most of the Liturgical Year. After observing communities during the Liturgy of the Word over the last thirty years, I have often wondered if two-thirds of the Sunday readings either stimulate or satisfy any hunger for God's word.

Of course, the mandate to "eat the scroll" is not restricted to those engaged in the public proclamation of the word of God. If *lectio divina* is absolutely necessary for those entrusted with laying the table of the word, it is certainly recommended for the community that gathers to consume this word. Time spent with the readings before the liturgy would help assure a more active listening and assimilation at the time

20. Gerard S. Sloyan, "Overview of the Lectionary for Mass: Introduction," *The Liturgy Documents: A Parish Resource*, 3rd ed. (Chicago: Liturgical Training Publications, 1991) 123.

21. See Robert P. Waznak, s.s., *An Introduction to the Homily* (Collegeville: The Liturgical Press, 1998) 78–87; also, see Sloyan, "Overview," 122–23.

of the celebration. This is more likely to happen when the listeners have had the experience of a lively proclamation, engaging the attention of preoccupied minds and awaking interest in a word that at first hearing may seem totally unrelated to the concerns of daily life. We believe that the Holy Spirit is at the heart of this endeavor, drawing us through the word more deeply into the mystery of Christ. Inspired readers who allow themselves to be involved fully in their interpretive art are the necessary collaborators with both the Spirit and the community. What is to be hoped is that what happens at the table of the word in the liturgical setting might be continued at home with the Bible. If the readings have touched minds and hearts, listeners might be drawn to their own reading of the Bible. Then the lectionary has truly become a vehicle for the work of the Spirit. "Because of the Holy Spirit's inspiration and support, the word of God becomes the foundation of the liturgical celebration and the rule and support of all our life," and it is this same Holy Spirit who "brings home to each person individually everything that in the proclamation of the word of God is spoken for the good of the whole assembly of the faithful."[22]

Eating. Devouring. Consuming. Assimilation. Coalescence. All are ways to think about our engagement with the word of God. A final image comes from François Truffaut's 1966 movie, *Fahrenheit 451*, based on Ray Bradbury's science fiction novel. The title refers to the temperature at which books will burn. The movie created a world in which books were forbidden; anyone possessing them would be arrested, the books seized and burnt. Some people sit anaesthetized before their television sets; others rebel against the book-burning authorities, hiding books away and risking arrest and imprisonment. But the rebellion also takes another form. In the final scene, we are shown the rebels in their camp somewhere in a secluded woods. People are walking by themselves and reciting passages from the classics of literature. As the two main characters enter this camp, people come up and introduce themselves: "I am *Pride and Prejudice*." "I am *A Tale of Two Cities*." People are spending their days becoming a particular book of literature.

Our task is both more modest and more grand. We do not have to memorize any one book within the Bible. Rather, we allow the word of God to make its home in us and become part of our being, and, in the process, the community and each individual becomes word of God for

22. "Lectionary for Mass: Introduction," *Liturgy Documents*, no. 9, 129–30.

the world. It is then that we will be able to respond with a resounding affirmation to the challenge Paul VI issues in his apostolic exhortation, On Evangelization in the Modern World: "Does the Church or does she not find herself better equipped to proclaim the Gospel and to put it into people's hearts with conviction, freedom of spirit, and effectiveness?" For all the Church to be involved in this endeavor, God's people must hear, accept, and assimilate the gospel into all areas of their lives. It is the task of the homily to further facilitate the realization of this end.

## "A Necessary Source of Nourishment": The Role of the Homily

There was a time in Roman Catholic liturgical life when preaching was considered an interruption within the Mass, something unnecessary, even to be cancelled when weather conditions were not favorable. "It's too hot to preach today," I remember our parish priest announcing during the dog days of August, when I was a boy. This was quite a contrast to the role of preaching the Word in the Protestant tradition. "Whoever has the office of preaching imposed on him has the highest office in Christendom imposed on him," wrote Martin Luther.[23] For him there was "real presence" in the preached word; when the preacher spoke, God spoke. The great Reformer John Calvin understood preaching as "the audible Sacrament" through which the listener "actively hears and takes into himself the Word of God."[24]

The Second Vatican Council was the pivotal event for changing the Roman Catholic perception of the importance of preaching by reintroducing the word "homily" into our liturgical vocabulary and asserting in its Constitution on the Sacred Liturgy that it was to be "highly esteemed as part of the liturgy itself" (52). When the General Instruction of the Roman Missal stated that the homily was to be considered "a necessary source of nourishment for the Christian life" (41), the Roman Catholic tradition returned to the high regard for preaching characteristic of the postapostolic and patristic periods when such noted preachers as Justin, Irenaeus, Origen, Cyprian, the Cappadocians, John Chrysostom, Jerome, Ambrose, and Augustine inaugurated

23. Quoted by Eric W. Gritsch, "Luther, Martin," *Concise Encyclopedia of Preaching*, ed William H. Willimon and Richard Lischer (Louisville: Westminster/John Knox Press, 1995) 313.

24. Calvinist scholar T.L.H. Parker as quoted in Beverly Zink-Sawyer, "'The Word Purely Preached and Heard': The Listeners and the Homiletical Endeavor," *Interpretation* (October 1997) 345.

what is nostalgically called the golden age of preaching. Whether it was always so golden can be argued, but what did characterize the preaching was being strongly rooted in the word of God.

The Second Vatican Council, in turn, called preachers to recognize that for the homily to nurture the contemporary community of believers gathered to worship God, it must flow from the sacred Scriptures. "All the preaching of the Church . . . should be nourished and ruled by sacred Scripture," insists the Constitution on Divine Revelation (21); and "sacred Scripture is of the greatest importance in the celebration of the liturgy. For it is from it that lessons are read and explained in the homily," instructs the Constitution on the Sacred Liturgy (24). This latter document also notes that the homily's sources should be both "scriptural and liturgical, for it is the proclamation of God's wonderful works in the history of salvation, which is the mystery of Christ ever made present and active in us, especially in the celebration of the liturgy" and that the homily can serve as a vehicle for expounding on the sacred texts in order to offer listeners "the mysteries of the faith and the guiding principles of the Christian life in the course of the liturgical year" (35.2 and 52). This document thereby brings together two of the preacher's roles: herald and teacher. Both find their origin in the preaching of Jesus who came proclaiming the kingdom of God and teaching the people in stories and parables.

Since the closing of the council, there has been further reflection on the role of the homily. Pope Paul VI and Pope John Paul II have offered different but complementary emphases in their writings that address the role of the liturgical homily in the life of the world community. Paul VI in an apostolic exhortation, Evangelization in the Modern World, emphasized that the homily can be an "important and very adaptable instrument of evangelization . . . to the extent that it expresses the profound faith of the sacred minister and is impregnated with love" (43). Paul VI brought out the importance of the homilist as a personal witness.

John Paul II's thought marked a return to an emphasis on the catechetical role of the homily when he said in his apostolic exhortation Catechesis in Our Time that the homily's purpose was "to familiarize the faithful with the whole of the mysteries of the Faith and the norms on Christian living" (48). He has also stressed the importance of "inculturation," calling preachers to "bring the power of the Gospel into the very heart of culture and cultures." For this reason, the Pope concludes, "catechesis will seek to know these cultures and their essential components; it will learn their most significant expressions; it will respect their particular values and riches" (53). John Paul's hope was that a successful inculturation of the gospel would produce "original expressions of Christian life, celebration, and riches."

This move toward interrelating culture and faith in the preaching task receives one of its strongest statements in the U.S. Bishops' *Fulfilled In Your Hearing: The Homily in the Sunday Assembly* which gave to preaching the task of offering "a scriptural interpretation of human existence" (29) and called on the preacher to be "a mediator of meaning" (7), enabling a community to give God thanks and praise in the Liturgy of the Eucharist. In this document the preacher is an interpreter of life in the world, dwelling with the Scriptures, then using them as a lens to look out onto our world and the life of the community, in order to name how God is acting in the human situation. This document located revelation as ongoing within the life and activity of the world today; it is the preacher's task to offer an interpretation of where God is moving in our midst, comforting and challenging, calling us to walk the way of faith.

When we consider these statements of the council, the Popes, and the document of the U.S. Bishops' Committee, we see that there has been a rich and varied amount of reflection on the role of preaching within the liturgical assembly. This has not abated. Robert P. Waznak, S.S., has cogently summarized the nuances of understanding the homily in his discussion of its nature and the strengths and weaknesses of four images of the homilist that have emerged with new vitality since the Second Vatican Council: the herald, the teacher, the interpreter, and the witness.[25] Waznak concludes his study of these four types by reminding us that "ultimately it is the preacher with the pastoral heart in dialogue with a particular assembly who must decide which image is appropriate for particular liturgical celebrations, seasons, biblical texts, local and national contexts, and pastoral needs."[26]

No matter what role or combination of roles the preacher decides to take on a particular occasion, there are four gifts articulated in *Fulfilled In Your Hearing (FIYH)* that all preachers should be able to offer to the community to help make the table of the word a welcoming and nourishing experience:

---

25. For a thorough treatment of these four images, see Waznak, *An Introduction to the Homily*, 31–67.
26. Ibid., 66.

(a) *the gift of words.* "One of the principal tasks of the preacher is to provide the congregation of the faithful with words to express their faith, and with words to express the human realities to which this faith responds."[27] This injunction reminds us that the first legacy of preachers to their people is language. We live in a world of words our whole lives, and spend innumerable hours learning many different "languages": the languages of various national and ethnic groups, those of the academic disciplines, the idiomatic expressions and buzz words that serve for rapid exchange, the specialized codes that function as a shorthand and make interaction possible in the social, political, economic, and recreational groups to which we belong, and the newest language of the technological-computer world that increasingly envelops us. We can forget what it is like to be deprived of words, or how deftly we maneuver among our linguistic worlds, moving from one language to another.

In her insightful memoir, *Lost in Translation*, Eva Hoffmann has written about the struggle to enter into a new culture and the trials of learning a new language. She reflects on what she calls "linguistic dispossession," a condition where an inability to express oneself and one's inner being can be "a sufficient motive for violence, for it is close to the dispossession of one's self. Blind rage, helpless rage is rage that has no words—rage that overwhelms one with darkness. And if one is perpetually without words, if one exists in the entropy of inarticulateness, that condition is bound to be an enraging frustration."[28] The linguistic dispossession Hoffman refers to here is the condition she met later in life when she lived in New York City and witnessed the frustration of the poor in finding adequate expression for their struggles, compounded by the inner city realities of poverty, desperation, and little hope of escape.

Sociologist James D. Davidson has written of another kind of linguistic dispossession when he notes how many Roman Catholics born since the Second Vatican Council feel handicapped by their lack of a vocabulary "to help them form a Catholic identity and interpret their Catholic experiences."[29] Earlier generations inherited from their Catholic education a distinctive vocabulary that gave them access to

27. Ibid., 6.
28. Eva Hoffmann, *Lost in Translation: A Life in a New Language* (London: Minerva, 1992) 124.
29. William V. D'Antonio, James D. Davidson, Dean R. Hoge, and Ruth A. Wallace, *Laity: American and Catholic, Transforming the Church* (Kansas City: Sheed and Ward, 1996) 88.

the world of Catholic belief and practices. But this has been lost in recent decades for various reasons. A recent document, *The Priest and the Third Christian Millennium*, from the Congregation of the Clergy observed that

> some of the traditional ideas and vocabulary of evangelization have become unintelligible to the greater part of contemporary culture. Certain contexts are impervious to the positive Christian sense of terms such as original sin and its consequences, redemption, the cross, the need for prayer, voluntary sacrifice, chastity, sobriety, obedience, humility, penance, poverty, etc.[30]

Davidson concludes that the lack of a "Catholic word bank upon which to draw" leaves many of those born after the council indistinguishable from the members of any mainline Protestant denomination. This is not to argue for the restoration of some sort of hermetic Catholic dictionary, providing members with their own secret code, but that we need to find a way of helping the contemporary world to "rediscover the profound meaning of these Christian and human terms"[31] in addition to offering a vocabulary commensurate with human experience as the place where God is alive and active, albeit elusively so. How preaching might contribute to this task flows into the next three gifts a homilist might offer in preaching a word that nourishes.

(b) *the gift of insight*. The preacher offers words that help the community to see with eyes of faith. "Through words drawn from the Scriptures, from the church's theological tradition, and from the personal appropriation of that tradition through study and prayer, the preacher joins himself and the congregation in a common vision" (*FIYH*, 6). Thus, the preacher takes on the role of mediating between God and the community through the words offered in the homily. Preachers are called to take on a double perspective by representing both God and the community in their words. "The preacher represents this community by voicing its concerns, by naming its demons, and thus enabling it to gain some understanding and control of the evil which afflicts. He represents the Lord by offering the community another word, a word of healing and pardon, of acceptance and love" (*FIYH*, 7).

---

30. Congregation for the Clergy, *The Priest and the Third Christian Millennium: Teacher of the Word, Minister of the Sacraments, and Leader of the Community* (Vatican City, 1999) 9.

31. D'Antonio, *Laity: American and Catholic*, 88.

In this light, Mary Catherine Hilkert has written eloquently of the preacher's call to "name grace." Preaching is more than bridging the gap between the sacred and the profane by "searching for clues as to where the revealed word of God might touch a chord in 'secular' human experience"; rather, "preachers listen with attentiveness to human experience because they are convinced that revelation is located in human history, in the depths of human experience. . . ."[32] We do more than apply the word of God that has been spoken in the past; we struggle to find how that very word is being spoken to us *now* in the present, calling, challenging, and empowering us to full maturity as members of the body of Christ. Hilkert qualifies this effort to "name grace" by listing three requirements:

> (1) the experience to be named is human experience in its depth dimension; (2) in the contemporary world situation, most people's experience of God is in the face of, and in spite of, human suffering; and (3) the interpretative keys to identifying grace in human experience are located in the biblical story and the basic symbols of the Christian tradition.[33]

The gift of insight then comes from the correlation of human experience in its depths with the biblical word of God proclaimed in the readings, and the liturgical texts and actions.

*FIYH* emphasizes the role of the Scriptures in offering insight when it states that these are "texts which have nourished the church's life throughout all its history, sustaining it in times of trial, calling it back to fidelity in times of weakness and opening up new possibilities when it seemed immobilized by the weight of human traditions" (12). It later notes that "the homily is not so much *on* the Scriptures as *from* and *through* them" and that "the preacher does not so much attempt to explain the Scriptures as to interpret the human situation through the Scriptures" (20). In this way the biblical word becomes a lens to look at life as it is being lived and experienced so that a powerful and interpretive word may emerge.

There has been some recent discussion about moving "beyond scripture"[34] and rethinking the sources for preaching. Edward Foley argues for a greater awareness of the "liturgical bible," that is, "all of the

32. Mary Catherine Hilkert, *Naming Grace: Preaching and the Sacramental Imagination* (New York: Continuum, 1997) 48–49.

33. Ibid., 49.

34. See Edward Foley, "The Homily Beyond Scripture: *Fulfilled In Your Hearing* Revisited," *Worship* (July 1999) 351–58.

'sacred texts' which constitute the liturgy for a given day," including the Eucharistic Prayer, collects, the unchanging and optional texts of the liturgy, the words of the songs, acclamations, hymns, and even taking into account the ritual actions and the feasts and seasons of the Liturgical Year.[35] Such thinking is in line with the 1970 General Instruction of the Roman Missal which delineated the homily's content as "an exposition of the scripture readings or of some particular aspect of them, or of some other text taken from the Order or the Proper of the Mass for the day . . ." (41).

Is making use of such liturgical resources a move "beyond scripture"? Gerard Sloyan notes "the prayers of all the rites, including the eucharistic prayer or canon, are either tissues of biblical phrasing or are inspired by the Bible,"[36] and Nathan Mitchell comments that "for Catholics, Bible and liturgy are not static, compartmentalized entities but lively interactive sources of faith that continue, throughout history, to define one another, comment upon one another, and (sometimes) conflict with one another."[37] What is most important, however, as William Skudlarek observes, is that the text, whether biblical or liturgical, "becomes a key which the preacher uses to unlock the meaning of human life in Christ."

(c) *the gift of motivation.* Preaching is nourishing when it moves the community towards the banquet of the Eucharist or more deeply into full, conscious, and active participation in the celebration of the other sacraments. The definition of the homily in *FIYH* offers an understanding of what the homily is, "a scriptural interpretation of human existence," and then goes on to say what it *does*: "which enables a community to recognize God's active presence, to respond to that presence in faith through liturgical word and gesture, and beyond the liturgical assembly, through a life lived in conformity with the Gospel." The end of the homily is to move the community into worship and into life.

The biblical scholar Walter Brueggemann has written of Scripture's power to offer an "alternative script."[38] We can picture our Sunday

---

35. Ibid., 355. Foley also calls on the preacher to include other "conversation partners," such as World Events, the Arts, and the Human Story, in the process of preaching preparation; see Ibid., 356–57, and his *Preaching Basics: A Model and a Method* (Chicago: Liturgy Training Publications, 1998) 14–20.

36. Sloyan, "Overview," 118.

37. Mitchell, *Real Presence*, 45.

38. Walter Brueggemann, "Preaching as Reimagination," *Theology Today* (July 1994) 320.

gathering as a place where people come, clutching the various scripts that govern their lives, influencing how they think and act. Scripts can serve as prisms or prisons, allowing us to focus or constricting our perspective. There are rationalist scripts, feminist scripts, radical activist scripts, fundamentalist scripts, postmodern scripts, and countless others, prevalent in our day. Brueggemann speaks of the "Enlightenment script" that has been dominant for so long and has only recently begun to release its hold on American society, characterized by an emphasis on individual autonomy, the superiority of reason, the supreme value of objective knowledge. This script has played itself out in various ways that afflict our culture: a consumerism whose major tenet is to accumulate and acquire as much as possible, a political philosophy whose policy of colonialism in third-world countries continues to measure their actions in terms of our own well-being and enrichment, and a barely disguised religious intolerance for any but the Western way of belief and praxis. Through preaching, an alternative way of imagining our world is offered, a way rooted in the vision of the God of Israel, whose full revelation came in the life, death, and resurrection of Jesus of Nazareth. Like any vision, it calls for a response of action.

The gift of motivation is the power of the word of God to move us more deeply into the mystery of God as we celebrate the Eucharist. Preaching serves as the bridge between the Liturgy of the Word and the Liturgy of the Eucharist. After listening to God speak to us in the scriptural texts, the homily motivates our response to God by giving thanks and praise, providing "the motive for celebrating the Eucharist in this time and place" (*FIYH*, 23). Equally, it motivates us to take to heart the final words of the Eucharistic celebration, "The Mass is ended. Go in peace to love God and serve one another." Effective preaching sends the community back to the world of everyday concerns and commitments refreshed, renewed, recommitted, and restored. In this way, our preaching links the Liturgy of the Eucharist with the liturgy of the world.[39] Preaching, then, produces praise and praxis.

Perhaps this expectation of preaching sounds more grandiose than experience warrants. How often does our preaching evoke a world-

---

39. The expression "Liturgy of the World" was used by Karl Rahner to refer to the primary liturgy that the Church celebrates, since the world has been grasped by God's self-communication of grace. For a thorough treatment of this insight see Michael Skelley, s.j., *The Liturgy of the World: Karl Rahner's Theology of Worship* (Collegeville: The Liturgical Press, 1991).

shaking response? But conversion of the heart is a gradual process. I am reminded of one of Marcello Mastroianni's last movies, *Leo the Last*. The title character was the last in a line of Italian aristocrats whose only sign of past glory was a decayed family mansion in a black London neighborhood. Leo decides to blow the mansion up as a sign of repudiating the oppression it symbolized. With bits and pieces of the house scattered all over, one of the neighborhood residents says to Leo, "So what! You've done nothing to save the world!" "No," Leo replies, "but we've changed our street." Living a life "in conformity with the gospel" can result in changing a few streets.

(d) *the gift of inspiration.* The fourth gift the homily offers to the community is that nebulous reality we call "inspiration." In their study of parishes in the early '90s, Forster and Sweetser said that in the typical parish, the 75 percent who come with some regularity ask that the preaching be "current, positive, *inspiring*, and less than ten minutes."[40] The desire to be inspired deserves some attention. The Latin roots of the word are helpful: to *in-spirare*—to breathe into. Inspiration brings a breath of fresh air to our spirits. New breath enters the body of the faithful, bringing new life. The Holy Spirit's work is to inspire, breathe upon us, to get us up and going, whether it is to give thanks in the Eucharist or to give ourselves in generous service for the common good. *FIYH* says that praise and thanks are more likely to flow from language that is "specific, graphic, and imaginative . . . the picture language of the poet and the storyteller" (25).

In an essay that anticipated more recent homiletic writings, Karl Rahner reflected on the relationship between the poet and the priest; (where Rahner refers to "priest," we may hear "preacher.") After noting that the poet is "entrusted with the word" and that "whenever a great word is really spoken . . . there is a poet at work,"[41] Rahner challenged preachers by saying that we are capable of having words on our lips without their coming from our hearts. What the poet teaches us is that the word of God must break forth from the center of our hearts in great words of longing and praise, of truth and beauty, of illumination and transformation.

> Where the word of God says what is most sublime and plunges this most deeply into human hearts, there is to be found a pregnant word of

40. Patricia M. Forster, O.S.F., and Thomas P. Sweetser, S.J., *Transforming the Parish: Models for the Future* (Kansas City: Sheed and Ward, 1993) 18.

41. Karl Rahner, "Priest and Poet," *The Word: Readings in Theology*, Compiled at The Canisium, Innsbruck. (New York: P. J. Kennedy & Sons, 1964) 9–10.

human poetry. The priest calls to the poet so that the poet's great words may become the consecrated vessels of the divine word—with which the priest may effectively proclaim the word of God.[42]

These four gifts of the homilist can make the table of the Word a welcoming place for the community that comes hungry to the table. Like all gifts, these find their source in the Holy Spirit, giver of understanding and wisdom, mover of wills, source of new life. "Everybody's got a hungry heart," sings contemporary troubadour Bruce Springsteen. Let us now turn our attention to the people coming to the table in our own day and consider some of their hungers and how preaching might respond to them.

### "Everybody's Got a Hungry Heart": The Hungers Preaching Feeds

First of all, let us consider some facts about the people today's Roman Catholic preachers are called to feed before naming their hungers. While not every preacher may have to deal with the "huge" or "great" crowd that Jesus did, still it is instructive to remember that from the close of the Second Vatican Council until approximately 1996, while the number of Catholics in the United States has grown from forty million to over sixty million, the number of parishes has only increased from 17,000 to 20,000. Though the number of Catholics who attend Mass weekly has fallen off, historian Charles Morris claims that "like no other generation in our history, active American Catholics are educated, literate, informed, and interested in their religion. And they are participants in it."[43]

This is no monolithic "crowd." Differences in ethnic backgrounds, religious upbringing, and experiences of church communities are only a few of the factors. Sociologist James D. Davidson has looked at the pluralism in today's Church as represented by three groups, the Pre-Vatican II Catholics, the Vatican II Catholics, and the Post-Vatican II Catholics, with varying levels of commitment to the institutional Church, expressed by their attendance at Mass, their financial support of the Church, and degree of allegiance to the doctrinal and moral teachings of the Church. Among the Post-Vatican II group, some

---

42. Ibid., 24.
43. Charles Morris, *American Catholic: The Saints and Sinners Who Built America's Most Powerful Church* (New York: Times, 1997) 430.

would identify themselves primarily as Christians rather than Catholics, would distinguish God's law from the Church's law, and often are more selective about what they believe, yet also less informed about what the Church teaches.[44] Davidson's most recent study sees today's young Catholics as being "least inclined to maintain traditional faith and morals."[45] The commingling of these three "generations" makes for much diversity, pluralism, and division within the Catholic community, leading Charles Morris to conclude that while the more than three decades since the Kennedy assassination have been hard on many institutions, "few have suffered so wrenching a reversal as the American Catholic Church, not only in its public image, but even more corrosively, in its own self-perception."[46]

In addition to the upheaval within the Church, its members belong to the culture and the age that has come to be called "postmodern." In a recent article on preaching to a "postmodern people," Lee Wyatt tells preachers that the postmodern situation confronts them with three rejections: the rejection of Story—there is no story large enough to encompass us the way the Christian story once did; the rejection of identity formation—we live in a world where we are continually reconstructing ourselves, thus there is no stable sense of identity; and the rejection of community—if there is nothing more than fragmented or "in process" selves, how can there be such a thing as community?[47] In response to this analysis, I would propose that these three rejections which characterize postmodernity correspond to what others have recently experienced in the Catholic Church as hungers on the part of people.

In August 1996, a few months before his death, Joseph Cardinal Bernardin called a news conference to introduce the Catholic Common Ground Project and presented an accompanying document entitled *Called to Be Catholic: The Church in a Time of Peril.*[48] After characterizing the situation at that time as one of "polarization that inhibits discussion and cripples leadership," the document stated that the desire of this initiative was to create "a common ground centered on faith in

44. D'Antonio, et al., *Laity: American and Catholic*, 84–89.

45. James D. Davidson and others, *The Search for Common Ground: What Unites and Divides Catholic Americans* (Huntingdon, Ind.: Our Sunday Visitor, 1997) 137.

46. Morris, *American Catholic*, 292.

47. Lee A. Wyatt, "Preaching to Postmodern People," *Confident Witness—Changing World* (Grand Rapids, Mich.: Eerdmans, 1999), 155–70.

48. See *Origins* 26:11 (August 29, 1996).

Jesus, marked by accountability to the living Catholic tradition, and ruled by a renewed spirit of civility, dialogue, generosity, and broad and serious consultation." Of particular interest was the recognition that, even in this situation of "bickering, stalemate, and disparagement," there was *"an undiminished hunger for authentic faith, spiritual experience, and moral guidance."*[49]

The hungers Cardinal Bernardin spoke of are perennial and deep: authentic faith, spiritual experience, and moral guidance. They link up with the rejections of the postmodern age. If there has been a loss of contact with the story of God's revelation in Christ, this can help to explain the hunger for authentic faith. If there has been a loss of any sense of identity formation, this can contribute to the sense of isolation from spiritual experience. And if there is a rejection of community, this could certainly connect to a hunger for moral guidance. Preaching is one way to respond to these three hungers; and the various contexts of the liturgical homily provide many such opportunities.

In a similar vein, when sociologists William V. D'Antonio, Andrea S. Williams, and their colleagues recommend that "clergy and lay persons wanting to foster commitment and perpetuate a Catholic community ought to explore new ways of *cultivating a Catholic identity, a specifically Catholic language,* and *a greater understanding of the Catholic tradition,*"[50] this is a challenge to contemporary preachers. Preaching works through language to form identity and community through the use of Scripture and tradition. Davidson's observation that much recent preaching seldom makes "connections among scripture readings, conciliar documents, and recent encyclicals—all of which communicate God's love and interpret his presence in the modern world"[51] also serves to challenge today's preachers to find ways to set forth words that nourish spiritual hunger. Finally, we can hear a similar call in historian Morris's conclusion of his history of the American Catholic Church, that "the truly hard problems facing the church are in the realm of vision, theology, and purpose. . . . Good leaders should be able to solve them, offering coherent vision and purpose."[52]

The hungers of the human heart can be named in different ways. This book will consider three of them that our preaching can respond

49. Ibid., 1–2.
50. D'Antonio et al., *Laity: American and Catholic,* 99.
51. Davidson, *Search for Common Ground,* 218.
52. Morris, *American Catholic,* 294.

to: the hunger for wholeness, the hunger for meaning, and the hunger for belonging. Liturgical preachers can approach the homiletic task as invitations to address these three hungers: (1) the hunger for wholeness is met on those great feasts of the Lord celebrated as solemnities, those celebrations that focus primarily on the central moments in the story of Jesus, calling us to authentic faith in the living Triune God, reconnecting our age with *the* story that brings human life into contact with divinity; (2) the hunger for meaning can be satisfied within our experiences of the various sacramental rites, since these liturgical events address the most profound human experiences and call the faithful to find in them the redeeming and healing presence of the risen Lord; and (3) the hunger for belonging, for companionship and friendship, for connectedness, is fed by the celebrations of the saints, with special attention to the many feasts of Mary, Mother of Jesus, allowing the preacher to bring together the community of today with men and women who have faithfully walked the way of discipleship in their own time and place, and who now accompany us in communion as we walk in faith.

Preaching is a call to feed the people of God. It is a privileged calling, seldom an easy one, but people have come from a great distance and they need to be fed, else "they will faint on the way, and some of them have a long way to go" (Mark 8:3). "You feed them."

Chapter 2

# Preaching the Feasts of the Lord and the Hunger for Wholeness

*"May the God of peace make you perfect in holiness.*
*May you be preserved whole and entire, spirit, soul and body,*
*irreproachable at the coming of our Lord Jesus Christ."*

(1 Thess 5:23)

*"Lord, free us from our sins and make us whole . . ."*

(Opening Prayer, Monday, Second Week of Advent)

*"What an interesting sculpture. I bet that has a story behind it."*

(Response of a young girl on seeing for the first time
a rendering of Christ's crucifixion)

## The Feasts of the Lord: Access to the Story That Completes Us

Poet and essayist Kathleen Norris has written that Jesus' call, "Be perfect, therefore, as your heavenly father is perfect" (Matt 5:48), contains good news despite that scary word *perfect*. She comments that what we have here is not so much the presence of a scary word—"perfect"—but a scary translation. "The word that has been translated as 'perfect' does not mean to set forth an impossible goal, or the perfectionism that would have us strive for it at any cost. It is taken from a Latin word meaning complete, entire, full grown."[1] "Be perfect" better translates as "Be whole, complete." Thus, the injunction should not be

1. Kathleen Norris, *Amazing Grace: A Vocabulary of Faith* (New York: Riverhead, 1998) 55–56.

heard as urging followers toward that elusive and unattainable self-ful-fillment so many pursue, but to "make room for growth, for the changes that bring us to maturity, to ripeness."[2] The call to wholeness, completion, is seen as the will of God for all. Be complete, fully grown, as the God who lovingly called you into being empowers you to be.

Such growth occurs, paradoxically, in the process of dying to self, of taking up the Cross, of opening ourselves to the gradual changes God works on us from within and without when we respond to those mo-ments of grace that come our way. Such "perfection" or wholeness is, fi-nally, the gift of God, modeled most fully in Christ. We recognize Jesus' own awareness that such perfection is a gift in the words that begin his famous discourse in Matthew's Gospel, "Blessed are the poor in spirit . . . the sorrowing . . . the lowly . . . those who hunger and thirst for holiness . . ." (Matt 5:1-8), or, in Luke's starker version, "blessed are you poor, you who hunger, you who are weeping . . ." (Luke 6:20-21). To these incomplete, not fully satisfied, "imperfect" people belong the kingdom of heaven. They are blessed in their very possession of a char-acteristic that speaks of a lack, an emptiness, a condition of incomplete-ness, and causes them to look to the only One who can complete and make them whole. I propose in this chapter that it is this hunger that the great feasts of the Lord, particularly those liturgically defined as solemnities, can stimulate, address, and offer some degree of satisfaction even now, along with the hope of ultimate fulfillment.

These feasts respond to an appetite we have to connect our life with something that speaks to the deepest level of our being. A little over twenty years ago, Charles Rice wrote that most people try to connect their smaller stories to a larger one. "It is the same in the church. At our baptism, we enter into a story, a very large one; call it The Story. . . . Our stories merge with The Story."[3] While the postmodern age is said either to reject meta-narratives, those overarching stories that speak across time and space, or increasingly to find any meta-narrative inade-quate and lacking, people continue to be drawn to the Jesus story and to enter into some kind of engagement with it. Why? What does it offer us, now into its third millennium of being retold and reinterpreted?

The story of Jesus brings us first of all into an awareness and knowledge of the One who can fulfill this hunger for completeness. On

---

2. Ibid.

3. Edmund Steimle, Charles Rice, and Morris Niedenthal, *Preaching the Story* (Philadelphia: Fortress, 1980) 34.

the solemn feasts we remember and make present the salvation brought into being through particular events in human history, most notably the birth, death, resurrection and ascension of Jesus Christ, and the giving of the Holy Spirit. The story of Jesus also needs to be understood as the culmination of a much longer story that begins with Yahweh's creation of the world and eventual formation of a people, Israel. This larger story charts Israel's history from exodus to exile and return, and includes the voices of patriarchs and matriarchs, prophets, sages, and poets. Finally, this story tells of the creation of a new people of God, the new Israel, composed of Jews and Gentiles, slaves and free, men and women, founded in the person of Jesus, the Messiah, and Son of God.

This story of Jesus as risen Lord and Savior of the World continues to be experienced not only as an historical narrative, but as a power, "the power of God for salvation to everyone who has faith, to the Jew first and also to the Greek" (Rom 1:16). We continue to experience it as such in our own time and to make it known to a new generation in a new millennium. This experience begins with an initial response to the proclamation of the gospel as kerygma and continues and deepens through the many ritual celebrations in the liturgical life of the community. Most formative among these celebrations are those great feasts of the Lord celebrated annually within the liturgical calendar. These special days, designated as solemnities in the liturgical calendar, provide contact with the key moments in the history of salvation, most notably those of the paschal mystery of the suffering, death and resurrection of Jesus and those of his incarnation and manifestation to the world.

The great feasts of the Lord can be daunting. Consider the challenge facing preachers during the liturgical celebrations of the Easter Triduum (the "three days," beginning with the Evening Mass of the Lord's Supper on Holy Thursday, reaching its high point in the Easter Vigil, and concluding with evening prayer on Easter Sunday) and Christmas, the two pivotal solemnities of the year, then add on Epiphany, Ascension, Pentecost, Trinity Sunday, Corpus Christi, the Sacred Heart of Jesus, and Christ the King. These days appear on the liturgical landscape like a range of mountain peaks, monumental in stature and intimidating to those called to act as guides into their terrain. Perhaps it is more helpful to think of them not as peaks to be scaled but as pools whose fathomless depths await our immersion.

These are the days that provide access into the central events in the story of Jesus, those defining moments that provide both identity and agenda for the Christian community, and into those mysteries that encapsulate Christianity's articulation of the nature of God. On these days we are called to recognize Jesus of Nazareth as Emmanuel, Incarnate Word, Risen Lord, Savior of the World, Intercessor with the Father, Giver (with the Father) of the Spirit, Second Person of the Blessed Trinity, the Bread of Life, loving and merciful Sacred Heart, and King of creation. These feasts draw us closer to the mystery of the God of creation and redemption whose most perfect image is enfleshed in Jesus Christ. They also respond to one of the most basic human hungers: the hunger for a story that completes and makes us whole, offering a sense of being at peace in relation to oneself, others, the world and God.

Contemporary social analysts speak of the individual as a "fragmented self" or as having "an unstable sense of self." An endless quest for a sense of identity plagues both individuals and institutions. Robert Bellah has written of both "incomplete persons" engaged in an ongoing quest for fulfillment, and the "porous institutions" that can no longer hold members of society, citing marriage as a primary example with its more than 50 percent rate of failure.[4] In the face of so many experiences of brokenness and fragility, it is no wonder that many either turn to self-help programs that promise easy transformation, look for comfort in various forms of addiction, or sink more deeply into a state of ennui and hopelessness. The gospel continues to speak to the hearts of men and women, offering an encounter with One who came to set us free, who came that we might have life and have it more abundantly, and calling us to conversion, individual and communal. This story needs to be proclaimed anew to each generation and continually reappropriated within the community of believers. The feasts are one means of doing this and offer a way of feeding the most basic human hunger.

Liturgical scholar Robert Taft, s.j., asks, "what are we doing when we celebrate a Christian feast?" What is the relationship between a past unrepeatable act, like the birth of Jesus, or his death and resurrection, and the present celebration that takes place at a particular time in a particular place during the liturgical calendar? Taft proposes that the liturgical celebration allows us to overcome the separation in time and space from the actual saving event, so that "the salvation manifested in the past lives on now as an active force in our lives, if we encounter it anew and respond to it in faith. . . ."[5] For this to happen, we gather

4. Robert N. Bellah, "Religion and the Shape of National Culture," *America* (July 31–August 7, 1999) 12–13.

5. Robert Taft, s.j., "Toward a Theology of the Christian Feast" *Beyond East and West: Problems in Liturgical Understanding* (Washington, D.C.: Pastoral Press, 1984) 2.

to take part in a cultic celebration that is grounded in the act of *anamnesis*, remembering. The events themselves are past, but the reality they initiated and manifested *then* is present *now*, that quality of existence we call salvation, fullness of life. Through celebrating these feasts, then, we enter into the *plerôma*, the fullness of time, in which it is not the past nor the future that becomes present to us, but the *end*, the *eschaton*, understood as the *completion*.

Even more accurately, as Patrick Regan has written, "the eschaton is really not a thing (eschaton) but a person (eschatos). It is the Lord Jesus himself. . . ."[6] The liturgy, then, is the place where we do with Christ what the New Testament itself did with him: "it applied him and what he was and is to the present."[7] At the heart of the celebration of the solemnities is the person of Jesus, living Lord and Redeemer, in his saving life, death, and resurrection. All of this is present and serves as the pattern that must be taken up and repeated individually and communally. This pattern of the recapitulation of all things in Christ is applied to the community through the ministry of word and sacrament. "A liturgy is successful . . . because it builds up the Body of Christ into a spiritual temple and priesthood by forwarding the aim of Christian life: the love and service of God and neighbor; death to self in order to live for others as did Christ."[8]

The feasts then speak to and encourage a deeper penetration of the community into the life of the risen Christ, and through Christ, into the life of the trinitarian God. They are both transformative and informative. Paul VI emphasized this when he wrote that the Church

> needs to listen unceasingly to what she must believe, to her reasons for hoping, to the new commandment of love. She is the People of God immersed in the world, and often tempted by idols, and she always needs to hear the proclamation of the "mighty works of God" which converted her to the Lord; she always needs to be called together afresh by him and reunited.[9]

More recently Cardinal Danneels observed that "we sometimes lack a sense of content. Christian faith is not (ethereal) like the atmosphere. It is the Father, Jesus, the Incarnation, the Passion, the Resurrection, the

6. Quoted by Taft, ibid., 3.

7. Ibid., 6.

8. Ibid., 11.

9. Paul VI, *On Evangelization in the Modern World* (Washington, D.C.: USCC, 1975) no. 15.

Holy Spirit, the Church, the sacraments, eternal life, the resurrection of the body. It has content. It is not a deep sentimental life; it's more than that."[10] It is not that the feasts are primarily educative experiences, with the preaching that occurs taking on the function of a lecture; but, at a time when the ability to articulate what we believe as Roman Catholic Christians is a concern voiced by many, the capacity of the homily to respond to this "lack" is not to be ignored. Whether making use of the evocative language of the poet or storyteller or the purposive rhetoric of the orator, the issue of *what* is being said, in relation to what *can* and *needs* to be said, calls for ongoing examination.

The feasts occur within time and allow us to cross the divide between past and present, present and future. The nature of the feast calls us to reflect on the way we experience time and how the feasts call us to honor it and reflect on how we live within it and whether we take advantage of the opportunities it offers. One of the tendencies that might be at work when we approach the feasts is to see them as isolated celebrations, atomizing their significance into discrete moments, each with its own weight, but relatively unconnected to what has gone before and what will come after. For this reason, before considering the feast itself as the subject of preaching, let us consider the feast in its broader temporal context.

## The Liturgical Year As Formative:
## Of Calendars, Cycles, and Seasons

Calendars work on us in different ways, separating work time from time for other pursuits. The civil calendar provides us with a number of occasions for celebration and relaxation: New Year's, St. Valentine's, St. Patrick's, the Fourth of July, Thanksgiving; some have been turned into longer weekends, like Martin Luther King Holiday, President's Day, Memorial Day, Labor Day, and Columbus Day. But the civil calendar tends to make us think in terms of "days off." For those who live according to a school calendar, the experience of time can be lengthened into longer periods: spring and fall semesters, the Christmas holidays, spring break, and summer. For most people, however, the only extended time they experience is the time of vacation.

The liturgical calendar works differently from the civil calendar, inviting us to live conscious of more extended periods, each with its

---

10. "Interview with Cardinal Danneels," *Church* (fall 1999) 18.

own theological significance. It aims to shape us into a people who move through these periods in a very deliberate way, allowing them to draw us into the mystery of Christ through an annual recognition of particular seasons and feasts. We call this period of time the Liturgical Year. I find it helpful to think of it as divided into three cycles, two of which are further divided into the seasons of Advent and Christmas, and Lent and Easter. Within the three cycles, the great feasts are located and shed their light over what precedes and follows their celebration. Let us briefly review the three major cycles, with their seasons and feasts.

The Liturgical Year begins with the Advent-Christmas-Epiphany Cycle, which includes the great feasts of Christmas, the Holy Family, Mary, Mother of God, the Epiphany, and the Baptism of Christ. The Lent-Easter-Pentecost Cycle centers on the celebration of the Easter Triduum, lasting from Holy Thursday until the vespers of Easter Sunday, and also includes the solemnities of the Ascension and Pentecost. The third cycle is that of Ordinary Time, with the first section beginning after Epiphany and lasting until Ash Wednesday, and the longer section following Pentecost, which begins with the solemnities of Trinity Sunday and The Body and Blood of Christ, and concludes with Christ the King.

The liturgical calendar draws the community into an ongoing celebration of Christ's saving work in the paschal mystery. "By means of the yearly cycle, the Church celebrates the whole mystery of Christ, from his incarnation until the day of Pentecost and the expectation of his coming again."[11] The great feasts of the Lord provide points of contact with the central moments in the Jesus story, most importantly the celebrations that draw us into the mystery of the incarnation and the paschal mystery. The other feasts and seasons of the year can be placed in relation to these two primary events. What can be especially helpful for preachers is to keep in mind the centrality of the two major solemnities of Christmas and Easter in relation to the other feasts and seasons of the year. For instance, in the Easter season, the celebration of the Ascension and Pentecost are not to be disconnected from the Easter event: it is the risen Lord who now intercedes for us with the Father, and continues with the Father to send the Holy Spirit upon his people. It is all one movement, not three isolated events. And during

---

11. Sacred Congregation of Rites, *The General Norms for the Liturgical Year and the Calendar* (21 March 1969) no.17. Printed at the beginning of the Sacramentary.

the Christmas season, the other major celebrations can be seen as extensions of the mystery of the incarnation. Furthermore, this also can be helpful when preparing to preach on the Sundays of Lent, Easter, and Advent. We will discuss this with greater detail in a later section. For now let us turn to the solemnities themselves.

## Preaching on the Feast: Primary and Secondary Resources

The richness of the solemnities of the Lord calls preachers to take into account a number of resources when preparing to preach:

*Attend to the name of the feast.* While it is true that a rose by any other name would smell as sweet, the name given to each great feast and season can make a difference in guiding the preacher. Does Christmas help as a name? We know it is a contraction of Christ's Mass. So? How about Easter? Both are shorthand forms for naming these days. More helpful can be naming the mystery being celebrated. Doing this can provide an immediate focus. For instance, we can name Christmas as the celebration of the birth of Jesus, the Savior of the world, the Son of God, or Christmas as the Incarnation of the Word of God, the Word become flesh. The former is more appropriate to the texts selected for the Midnight Mass, the latter for those of Christmas Day. Again, Trinity Sunday can be approached as the celebration that calls us to ponder the ineffable mystery of the Triune God, a mystery which is for most Christians a very abstract dogma removed from life, or, more dynamically, as the celebration of the living God which proclaims that "everything comes from the Father and returns to him through the Son, in the Spirit."[12]

It can be helpful to name the feast in as many ways as possible. A helpful exercise might be to respond to an invitation to rename Easter. For instance, Easter might be called the resurrection of the Lord, the raising of Jesus by the Father in the power of the Spirit, the celebration of the paschal mystery of Christ's suffering, death, and resurrection, the inauguration of the new covenant. In workshops I have invited participants to rename a particular feast from three different perspectives: as a theologian, as a pastor, and as a poet. The first perspective makes us attentive to our tradition, the contribution of theology, and how we ourselves as responsible teachers of the faith have come to understand the feast; the second calls us to focus on the people to whom we will

12. *Days of the Lord,* vol. 7 (Collegeville: The Liturgical Press, 1994) 5.

be preaching, and how we can draw them into a deeper understanding of the feast's meaning; and the last invites us to be imaginative, appeal to the senses, offer insight, evoke an affective response, and help bring about a stronger appropriation of this feast into one's life. All of this naming can sharpen awareness of what lies at the heart of the feast and then challenge the preacher to convey this meaning to others. Furthermore, this threefold naming can be done more than once; consider it after each of the following steps.

*Immerse yourself in the biblical texts.* Take time with all three texts. Remember that "the scriptures, above all in their liturgical proclamation, are the source of life and power."[13] On the solemnities the three biblical texts are related according to the principle of harmony. One might think of the three Scripture readings selected for a feast as offering three related roads of access into the mystery being celebrated. Or consider them as three concentric circles, with the Old Testament being the outermost circle, the epistle reading within that, and the gospel the innermost circle in relation to what lies at the heart of this celebration. Or, as three intersecting circles that can mutually influence each other, depending upon which is chosen as a "controlling text" for the message of the homily. We have already discussed the kind of close reading, study, and prayer that enables you to assimilate the word and eventually help others to do the same. There are also a number of ways that a text, particularly the gospel reading, can help to shape the day's homily. Consider the following.

Attend to the movement of *thought*. For instance, the gospel for Christmas morning is John's prologue. For years I wished that Luke's version of the birth of Christ would be used in the morning. But the majesty of this prologue has finally had its impact on me. What helped was locating the movements of thought in the text itself: "In the beginning was the Word. . . . The Word became flesh and made his dwelling among us, and we have seen his glory. . . . Of his fullness we have all had a share—love following upon love." Such a structure can be used in the homily (see the homily at the conclusion of this chapter), beginning with an emphasis on the transcendent, creative Word of God, then moving to the historical enfleshment of the Word in Jesus, and finally to the present communion that exists between the faithful and the Word that has come to birth in us through baptism.

Or attend to the movement of *action*. Both gospels for Christmas Midnight Mass and for Epiphany provide us with narrative movement.

13. *Lectionary for Mass: Introduction,* no. 47.

Christmas first brings us the Lukan version of the birth of Jesus (Luke 2:1-14) with its movement from a bird's eye view of the political world of the Roman Empire, its leadership, and the edict of Caesar Augustus for a census, to the small world of a couple journeying from Galilee in the north to Bethlehem in the south, to the moment of the birth of a firstborn who was wrapped in swaddling clothes and laid in a manger, then out to the world of the lowly, represented by the shepherds who receive a message from the world of heavenly host. Worlds colliding and connecting, the different faces of power, contrasts of powerful emperor and a homeless couple, proclaiming angels and trembling shepherds, and a newborn child who binds all together. While the Christmas gospel easily shifts from one scene to another, the Epiphany gospel (Matt 2:1-12) moves sequentially. A homily was also developed from this text (see end of chapter) that made use of the various important narrative images within the story: the wise men, the star, the guiding words of the prophetic text, the gifts of the Magi, and the message of the dream. At the center of all: the child, the gift of the Father. In both instances narrative movement can guide homiletic development.

Or attend to the movement of *characters*. The Johannine gospel for Easter Sunday morning (John 20:1-9) provides three of the Easter people this gospel features in its telling the Good News of Jesus' resurrection. The text begins with Mary Magdalene, then moves to Peter, and ends with the beloved disciple. Each character provides us with a ground for reflection in terms of our own acceptance of the Easter mystery. Magdalene interprets the empty tomb as indication that the body has been taken; Peter, arriving at the tomb, merely observes the wrappings and the cloth; the beloved disciple, however, sees and believes. A movement from darkness to light, from death to life, from sadness to joy, from unbelief to belief.

Sometimes the texts offer a gestalt of *images*, as on Pentecost. The crowning feast of the Easter season provides a series of images capturing various experiences the early Church had of the presence of the Holy Spirit: as fire and wind (Acts 2:1-11); as giver of gifts for the common good (1 Cor 12:3-7, 12-13); and as breath of the risen Christ that forgives and reconciles (John 20:19-23). Any one could be the basis for the homily, or one might work with them in a sequence. Using the words of three contemporary poets, my Pentecost homily several years ago reflected on the Holy Spirit as the Spirit that burns (Acts), blesses (1 Cor), and binds (John) the body of Christ. The biblical texts for the Triduum and the other solemnities of the Lord offer a rich imaginal selection to touch the minds, hearts, wills, and imaginations of the community and move its members to a greater awareness of the fullness of life offered in the Christ event.

What is important in working with the biblical texts is to remember the mystery being celebrated and focus on some particular aspect of a text that will provide access to its Good News of what God has done for us in Christ. The most common failure in preaching on the feasts is *not* to decide on precisely what it is you want to say, becoming paralyzed by the fact that "so much *can* be said." Bishop Ken Untener suggests that preachers offer "just one pearl . . . but of great price." A pearl implies something well worth listening to, its beauty due to a certain compression, and recognized as a gift from and to the heart. "If a homily revolves around a pearl, it goes vertically into the depth of one thought."[14] While Bishop Untener stresses the value of the *core thought* offering depth over the broad theme that stays on the surface linking many thoughts, yet another way to bring focus and unity is to settle on a *controlling image*. Patricia Wilson-Kastner writes about it in this way:

> Normally we will want to make one particular image central; other images will either clarify or support it. Sometimes another major image will appear along with or support the primary image in a sermon. Sometimes these other images find their places as deliberate contrasts to the primary image. . . . The key to the integrity of the sermon is the underlying cognitive and affective unity of its imagery.[15]

Such attention to the scriptural texts and the multiple understandings they offer might send a preacher back to the naming of the feasts. Is there a fresh metaphor that can be employed for naming a particular feast? Are there further additions or modifications that might be made to your first naming? Playing in a fresh metaphorical field can unearth new treasures, located just below the surface.

*Attend to the other liturgical texts.* The biblical texts do not exist in solitary splendor. While preaching certainly looks to the Scriptures as its primary resource, the liturgy itself is a rich resource. Liturgical scholar Edward Foley has written about "the liturgical bible" which includes "all of the liturgical elements that are not already included in the

14. Ken Untener, *Preaching Better: Practical Suggestions for Homilists* (New York: Paulist Press, 1999) 43. This is a practical book for preachers; a good examination of consciousness regarding the good and bad habits we pick up over the years.

15. Patricia Wilson-Kastner, *Imagery for Preaching* (Philadelphia: Fortress, 1989) 49.

'lectionary' element."[16] This extends to the Eucharistic Prayers, the prayers from the ordinary and proper parts of the Mass, (especially take note of the collects and the particular preface composed for a feast), the hymns, acclamations, actions, objects, and gestures, and whatever pertains to the particular season of the Church year.

Consider, for instance, the two opening prayers on Easter Sunday, each giving emphasis to different, though related, sets of imagery. The first prayer speaks of this day as the one when the Father conquered death and opened for us the way to life, then goes on to ask for renewal of our lives in the Spirit that has been placed within us. The second prayer highlights the day as being one of joy, speaks of the risen Christ appearing to those who had begun to lose hope and opening their eyes to the truth foretold in the Scriptures: that Jesus would die, rise, and ascend to the Father. (Notice the connection made here with the Ascension as part of the one movement of Jesus' returning to God.) The prayer then focuses on the present celebration, asking the Lord to "breathe on our minds and open our eyes that we may know him in the breaking of bread and follow him in his risen life." In the first prayer, the emphasis is on the Father's conquest of death in the raising of his Son; in the second, we conclude by asking that "the risen Lord breathe on our minds and open our eyes that we may know him in the breaking of bread . . ." The latter is especially appropriate for the Easter Sunday evening liturgy when we can read the story of the two disciples who meet Christ on the road to Emmaus and come to recognize him in the breaking of the bread (Luke 24:13-35).

The prefaces for Pentecost, Trinity Sunday, Sacred Heart, and Christ the King can also help to reinforce a particular focus, and might provide a phrase useful in preaching. Actions such as the washing of feet on Holy Thursday, the veneration of the cross on Good Friday, and the blessing of the Easter fire and baptismal water at the Easter Vigil, offer controlling images that can integrate biblical texts, liturgical gesture, and communal identity. Being attentive to the hymns of the season can also bring a homily to life, with the homilist singing a verse or even inviting the congregation to sing a refrain.

*Attend to Other "Conversation Partners."*[17] In addition to the world of the liturgical texts, gestures, and actions, there are other worlds the

---

16. Edward Foley, *Preaching Basics* (Chicago: Liturgy Training Publications, 1998) 13.
17. Ibid., 14–20.

listeners move in and bring with them to worship: the world of current global and local events, the world of the arts and sciences, the world unique to each family with its own joys and sorrows. I will not forget the Christmas of '89, a few days after the Pan Am flight had exploded over Locherbie, Scotland, nor the celebration of the Epiphany the day after New Year's, 2000. People do not come to church out of a vacuum; recent events can hang heavy on our hearts or make us more than ready to offer thanks to God. This does not mean, of course, that every liturgy has to have a news insert, more that the preacher might need to build a bridge from where the community is coming over to that place where they are ready to lift up their hearts. Making connections is one of the tasks of the homily. If no connection is ever made between these great days of celebration and the events of our lives, then the former will *seem* to have no relevance to life as it is being lived. As Meister Eckhart wrote, paraphrasing Augustine, "The birth (of Christ) is always happening. And yet, if it does not occur in me, how could it help me? Everything depends on that." Preachers are to help people see how Christ is being born in them, in the events of our world, and enable them to respond to the challenge to believe in God when our experience witnesses only to God's absence. This is not an invitation to be glib or overly facile in making connections, but to wrestle honestly with the difficulty and the possibility of believing Jesus truly is Emmanuel, Risen Lord, Christ the King, when so many events signal the opposite. Just as the study of the Scriptures and the other liturgical texts can send you back to reconsider how you named the feast, so too can your exegesis of the world of your listeners and the events that impact all our lives.

The world of the arts is another rich resource for bringing feast, texts and life together. Sometimes a painting may give us a new way of looking at some aspect of the mystery being celebrated. Caravaggio's *The Taking of Christ* captures the horror of Judas' betrayal in striking contrast to the humility of Jesus, the light of heaven meeting the darkness of hell. William Tanner's *Annunciation* presents Mary suddenly faced with a form of light forceful and vibrant yet awaiting her response, a wonderful depiction of the glory of the Lord that waits on human freedom. Artist Michael McGrath, O.M.I., has painted a nativity scene with Mary and Joseph in a shed, surrounded by implements for cutting and pruning, evoking the seed that must fall into the ground and die in order to bring forth a hundredfold. Jim Crace's poetic novel, *Quarantine*, takes us into the desert with Jesus in a story unexpectedly epiphanic in impact. His Jesus is one of a group out in the barren wilderness—the strangest one, and the one person that undergoes a true conversion is the one least expected or hoped for by the reader. The result is a moving reimagining of a story whose annual reading on the first Sunday of Lent may have lost its impact.

Movies and television shows, commercials and song lyrics, all can provide insights into the human experience of living, loving, losing, and dying. All can serve as resources for keeping our focus on the feast and bringing the Christ proclaimed closer to the lives of the people present. But the feast day must not be approached merely as a singular event, a "one day only" affair. This often makes preachers feel they have to come up with a "great sermon" for every great feast. And in this instance, "great" more often has to do with length (as in interminable) or weight (as in "heavy") or size (as in ponderous), than with evoking awe and wonder. Bishop Ken Untener has suggested that "the bigger the event, the shorter the homily," reasoning that "the rituals and components of the event do their own share of preaching, and all we need to do is help the flow."[18] While that is true, there are other factors that assist the homilist. Preachers can look beyond the day itself to the seasons that surround it so that the entire cycle can assist the celebration of a solemnity. To this consideration we will now turn.

### Preaching on the Feast: Making Use of the Larger Context

The celebration of the passion and resurrection of the Lord during the Easter Triduum is recognized as "the summit of the whole Liturgical Year," with the solemnity of Easter having the same kind of preeminence in the Liturgical Year that Sunday has for the week.[19] In *The Three Days*, Gabe Huck urged that in preparing to celebrate the paschal mystery as the passing of the Lord from this world to the Father, the entire Triduum should be looked upon as "one moment that lasts three days, one rite with its private and its public moments."[20] The fact that Holy Thursday has no dismissal rite, Good Friday has no opening or closing rites, and the Vigil has no opening rite, reinforces the unity of the three days. This should prevent our approaching them simply as three distinct historical remembrances, as a series of individ-

---

18. Untener, *Preaching Better*, 82.
19. *General Norms for the Liturgical Year*, no. 18.
20. Gabe Huck, *The Three Days: Parish Prayer in the Paschal Triduum* (Chicago: Liturgy Training Publications, 1992) 10.

ual moments in the final days of Jesus. Rather than focus on the three days as events of the past, keep in mind that these celebrations of the saving power of God embrace us in the present. Then the entire Triduum can be a celebration of the one paschal mystery, the passing of the Lord from this world to the Father.

It is not only these three days that call for this sense of wholeness and unity. The *General Norms for the Liturgical Year and the Calendar* states, "The fifty days from Easter Sunday to Pentecost are celebrated in joyful exultation as one feast day, or better as one 'great Sunday.'"[21] A similar approach is appropriate for the seasons of Lent, Advent, and Christmas. Each has its own mood and emphases, but each is intrinsically oriented to the great feast that lies at its heart. And by taking into account the relation of the other feasts that might fall within the particular season, for instance, the feast of the Holy Family in the Christmas season or the Ascension of the Lord within the Easter season, we help our communities come to a stronger sense of the integrity of the mystery of Christ that we are commemorating liturgically over a period of time.

This awareness of the feasts in relation to their seasons helps preachers realize that preaching the mystery of the incarnation and the paschal mystery does not take place only on the one day, but extends outwards in both directions, before and after. Thus, throughout the Advent and Christmas seasons, we are preaching the incarnation—the salvific event of Jesus Christ who continues to come and to be born among us, in us, through us; throughout Lent and Easter, one is preaching the paschal mystery—the dying and rising of Christ for our sakes and our ongoing immersion into this pattern of divine life; and throughout ordinary time, one is preaching the mystery of the gift of the Holy Spirit and our ongoing life in the same Spirit. The feasts that fall within these various cycles are also not seen as separate celebrations but part of a whole: Ascension and Pentecost as further extensions into what the dying and rising of Christ mean for us; Epiphany and Baptism of Jesus in terms of what the birth of Jesus, son of God, means for us; and Trinity Sunday, The Body and Blood of Christ, and Christ the King in terms of our ongoing life in the risen Lord.

The mysteries of the two great cycles of Advent-Christmas-Epiphany and Lent-Easter-Pentecost have been shown to complement each other. Kenneth Hannon has set out how these two cycles share similar clusters of images and three common motifs: illumination,

21. *General Norms for the Liturgical Year*, no. 22.

restoration-divinization, and the Eschatological New Day.[22] This assertion can be confirmed by comparing the opening prayers and prefaces of the two cycles to see how they support each other. Hannon concludes, "Easter keeps Nativity from becoming a meta-historical commemoration of the hypostatic union, and Nativity/Epiphany locates the depth of the transcendent significance of what happened historically to Jesus."[23] Furthermore, the preparatory seasons of Lent and Advent are not only catechetical and baptismal in character, but both offer conversion and transformation imagery. In summary, the seasons work together to bring us into the paschal mystery of Jesus, the incarnate Word, risen Lord, Son of God. Preachers can help make the liturgical celebrations throughout the year more cohesive with the seasons that precede and follow them. Connections can be made by first considering the various Sunday gospel readings for a particular season in light of the central feast they lead towards or away from. We will take a brief look at the various liturgical seasons in relation to the great feasts that give them meaning.

*The Lenten Season.* Lent leads the community to the celebration of the paschal mystery at the Triduum. It has a double character: to prepare catechumens to celebrate the sacraments of Christian initiation and the faithful to renew their baptismal promises; and to instill within the community a penitential spirit leading to deeper conversion. The period of Lent is a time of grace that leads us either toward making an initial commitment or deepening our present commitment to the risen Lord Jesus Christ. The Sundays of Lent are days when preachers can invite the community to a more conscious encounter with this risen Lord who calls us to deeper intimacy, and can raise the issue of what it means for a community to renew its baptismal promises at the Easter celebration. In this way, Lent can truly become a season of purification, enlightenment, and ongoing conversion intrinsically linked to the celebration of the paschal mystery.

Consider how the Gospels for Lent provide the preacher with a series of images communicating who Jesus is and, by implication, who we are called to be as a community of conversion and deepening commitment. For instance, the Sunday Gospels for the A Cycle were chosen especially for their connection with Christian initiation. Over the

22. Kenneth Hannon, "Great Seasons in Dialogue," *Liturgical Ministry* (fall 1996) 145–50.

23. Ibid., 150.

six weeks, Jesus is presented as: the One Who Withstands Temptation (first Sunday of Lent), the Transfigured One (second Sunday of Lent), the Living Water (third Sunday of Lent), the Light of the World (fourth Sunday of Lent), the Resurrection and the Life (fifth Sunday of Lent), and, finally, the Jesus of Matthew's passion, the just and innocent one who dies for our salvation (Palm/Passion Sunday). All of these present very specific images of the Christ whose paschal mystery we will celebrate at the end of the forty days; and all of these present ways of self-understanding for the community who follows in his steps: a people empowered to withstand temptation, called to life in the hope of glory to come, who continue to need and are called to be living water, to be light for the world, to know in their own lives the raising up from death to life, and to be a people of the palm and of the passion, proclaiming Jesus and willingly entering his dying and rising. The Gospels of these weeks proclaim what we are called to grow into as the household of faith, the temple being built on the cornerstone, Jesus. They can be employed to encourage the community to make the renewal of baptismal promises on Easter a very deliberate and thoughtful recommitment to the Jesus they have come to know more fully through certain specific gospel passages during the Lenten season.

The readings for Lent, Cycle B, reveal the many faces of the God of Israel who again and again called the people to covenant, speaking to Noah, Abraham, Moses, and the exiles, both through events and words (Jer 31:31). And the Gospels, after presenting Jesus tempted and transfigured, emphasize the paschal mystery as the hour of glory, with Jesus presented as the temple raised after three days, as One lifted up like the serpent in the desert, as the seed dying to bring forth fruit, and finally in Mark's passion, as the One who died in complete abandonment, even by God. Images are here both for the community to know Jesus and to recognize its own call to be part of this new temple and to bring new life through dying to self. The readings of this cycle of Lent prepare us to meet now the risen Christ of the paschal mystery. The Sundays can be considered portions of a mosaic, each one surrounding and leading toward the central figure of the risen crucified Lord.

Finally, the Sunday readings of C cycle with their emphasis on conversion and repentance offer us a different series of images. Who is the Jesus who calls us to ongoing conversion and what characterizes the community that answers this call? As on every first Sunday of Lent, we have the gospel of Jesus being tempted in the desert and withstanding it, Luke's version. This account is accompanied by two readings particularly helpful for preparing the community to renew their baptismal promises: Deuteronomy 26:4-10 and Romans 10:8-13 feature confessions of faith. I found the presence of these can shift the usual emphasis on presenting Christ as one tempted like us to Christ as one who confesses his faith in the God of Israel when facing temptation. Jesus responds to each of the temptations with a biblical text that professes faith in the God who delivered Israel from Egypt and called them to covenant. This first Sunday with its three voices professing faith allows preachers to alert the community to the destination of Lent: making our own profession of faith with a renewed heart at the Easter celebration.

The second Sunday, as always, presents the Jesus of the Transfiguration, imaging the destiny of all those who turn to the Lord and walk the way of discipleship. The following three Sundays offer two parables from Luke and one narrative from John, each emphasizing conversion. On the third Sunday, after speaking of two events of the day that brought sudden death to groups of Israelites, Jesus rejects any suggestion that these victims were greater sinners than those listening to him; he then tells the parable of the tree that gives no fruit and the gardener who pleads for another year, corresponding to the community's call to a conversion that bears fruit. On the fourth Sunday, Jesus tells the story of the prodigal son featuring a father who wants both of his sons *inside* the house for the celebration, signaling our call to be "insiders," with the second reading giving a complementary emphasis on the community as called, in turn, to be ambassadors of reconciliation in the world. Then on the fifth Sunday we hear the story of the woman caught in adultery, with Jesus confronting both the Pharisees and the woman, and calling the community to repentance and compassion. The passion of Luke gives emphasis to a compassionate suffering Christ, whether speaking to the women of Jerusalem, or about those who crucified him ("Father, forgive them . . ."), or to the thief at his right.

The Gospels of the C cycle, then, present images of Jesus that reflect what a converted community looks like: a community that professes its faith, and lives in hope of transfiguration, that bears fruit, and both reconciles and is reconciled, a people who "sins no more," and one who is marked with the compassion of its Lord, which it brings to today's world. Preachers can direct the community to ponder this powerful set of images and evoke the response of a converted heart, to be given specific expression at the season's end when all renew the baptismal promises on Easter.

*The Easter Season.* As the Sundays of Lent call us to a renewal of our baptismal commitment to the crucified Lord, the Sundays after Easter call us to celebrate the resurrection life that flows from this commitment. What does the risen Christ bring to the community? What does it mean to live in the risen Christ? According to the C cycle of Easter Gospels, it means: being empowered like the beloved disciple to see and believe (Easter Sunday); receiving Easter peace and joy and the commission to forgive, like the Twelve, and the invitation to believe "without seeing," without any conditions that would restrict our access to the risen Lord (second Sunday); being fed by Jesus like the disciples and commissioned like Peter to show our love for Jesus by feeding others (third Sunday); being tended by the Good Shepherd who gives eternal life and suffers no sheep to be lost (fourth Sunday); being empowered to keep the new commandment of loving as the risen Lord has loved us (fifth Sunday); being visited by the Father and Son who will dwell in us, and gifted with the Paraclete who will instruct us in everything (sixth Sunday); and being strengthened and supported in our mission by Jesus' ongoing prayer for those who believe because of us (seventh Sunday). Within this arc, the feast of the Ascension sends us into the world as evangelizers while the risen Lord intercedes for us, and Pentecost proclaims the gift of that Spirit who blows us forth like a mighty wind, enflamed, gifted, and purveyors of Christ's own peace. Living in communion with the Easter Lord involves the move from commitment to commission, and from Lenten penance to Easter peace, joy, and trust in the abiding presence of the Spirit.

*Advent.* This season prepares and anticipates the Christmas season in proclaiming that God continues to come. All three cycles of Sunday readings have gospels that follow the same pattern: Christ will come again (first Sunday), Christ does come today (second and third Sundays), and Christ has come (fourth Sunday). As Christmas has its choir, Advent has its chorus: main soloists include Jesus (first Sunday), John the Baptist (second and third Sundays), and either Joseph or Mary, in the company of Gabriel, or Elizabeth; back-up singers include Isaiah, Paul, and an occasional appearance by Jeremiah, Baruch, Zephaniah, Micah, the authors of Hebrews and 2 Peter, and James. As Lent is a season of sensory deprivation, silence and sorrow for sins, Advent is a season of the senses and songs. We are called to "Wake up," "Listen," and "Behold." We are told to "Watch for the day," "Prepare the way of the Lord," and "Rejoice, again I say, rejoice!" We hear the songs of Isaiah and the canticles of Mary and Zechariah. Advent is a season of exclamation and excitement. Something wonderful came but something wonderful still comes and, most wondrous, will come in glory. When Advent is preached in relationship to Christmas, this season evokes a readiness for the recognition of incarnation, filling people with a sensitivity and sensibility for the God who came and will come, but, most of all, who draws us to our celebration of "Christ's Mass" this year.

*Christmas.* The Christmas season is characterized by a centrifugal flow. The day itself moves from an angelic proclamation to shepherds of a savior born at Bethlehem to the great prologue heralding the incarnate Word of God, from whose "fullness we have all received, grace upon grace . . . God the only Son, who is close to the Father's heart, who has made him known." The following Sundays and feasts flow outward from this celebration, extending its embrace to the family (Holy Family Sunday), the Church (Mary, Mother of the Lord as image of the Church), and the world (Epiphany). The season concludes with the baptism of Jesus, reminding us again of our baptismal empowerment to share in his ministry and work to bring the fruits of the incarnation into our world.

*Ordinary Time.* The cycles of ordinary time flow both from the Christmas and Easter seasons. In the former, from the final seasonal image of Jesus acknowledged as beloved son at the baptism, we move into his ministry, and begin the first part of the ordinary time cycle that calls us to participate in that ministry as sons and daughters in whom God has staked a claim. After the Easter season concludes with the celebration of Pentecost and the sending out of the apostles on mission, the major part of Ordinary Time begins with two feasts that remind us of our participation through baptism in the saving work of the Trinity (Trinity Sunday) and of our growth into both identity and maturity as the body of Christ through our renewal of the new covenant in the celebration of Eucharist (The Body and Blood of Christ). The solemnity of the Sacred Heart, also at the beginning of this part of the Ordinary Time cycle, turns us toward the loving, compassionate heart of Christ for support and challenge, reminding us that faith seeks not only understanding but affective expression. These feasts send us into the longest period of reflection and celebration of what it means for the community to live week after week in the Spirit of Christ. It concludes by bringing us to celebrate the Christ who is Lord of all creation and who will return on the last day (Christ the King).

The major liturgical seasons and the Ordinary Time cycle of the year need to be appreciated as closely related to the major feasts, whose meaning flows outward both to the weeks that precede and follow these major celebrations. Thus, these days of celebration do not stand in solitary splendor but beckon the community to deeper conversion and commitment and enable ongoing celebration and appropriation of the divine life that the salvific work of Christ continues to offer those who live in the community of faith. Any self-imposed and unrealistic expectation on the part of preachers for oratorical sublimity on a feast can be greatly lessened when one's preaching takes the central mystery into account for several weeks prior or subsequent to the day itself. Preachers can see their task as one of gradually leading the community to the feast as a fulfillment of the seasons of Advent and Lent, and then celebrate the great days themselves as a first dawning of a mystery to be slowly unfolded in the subsequent weeks, as is the case with the Christmas and Easter seasons. Looking over the Sunday Gospels to be read during a particular season *before* that season begins can provide a sense of the inexhaustible riches that a particular major feast signals, either in anticipation or fulfillment. To begin to pray over them early on can lead to a more productive engagement when the hour of preaching finally arrives.

## Homilies on the Solemnities of the Lord

I offer these homilies as the fruits of my own struggles to proclaim the mysteries of the great feasts. The homilies included in this and the following chapters were given either at Holy Trinity parish, Georgetown, Washington, D.C., or at Holy Redeemer College, the residence of the Redemptorist community, Washington, D.C. In addition to homilies given on some of the solemnities of the Liturgical Year, I have included one Sunday homily during Lent as an example of explicitly linking the Lenten season with the approaching celebration of Easter.

### A. Homily for Holy Thursday

"People of the Table, People of the Towel"
(Texts: Exod 12:1-8, 11-14; 1 Cor 11:23-26; John 13:1-15)

The memory of the past provides guidance for the present.
These three days that we call the Triduum are days of memory.
Now, there are different ways to remember.
We can take a memory trip—going back to a happy time—a birthday, an anniversary.

A nostalgia trip, easy to take, without any of the inconveniences of
modern travel.
We visit the past and come back unharmed and refreshed.
That is not what we do tonight.

A second way of remembering is to bring a saving event initiated in the
past into the present as an event of ongoing power inviting our participation.
A friend who lost her husband years ago once told me that she brings
him into the present moment, and she talks to him about what is
happening in her life.
In this way what was past becomes present, influences the present, even
reshapes it, and helps us to move into the future.
That is how we remember tonight.

Tonight we remember that long ago a people gathered around a table
to eat, nervous, anxious, standing up, filled with dreams of freedom.
They were a people excited, frightened, not quite able to believe what
they had heard: that God, their God, the God of Abraham and Sarah,
of Isaac and Rebecca, and of Jacob and Rachel, had heard their cry.
They were told to eat, clothed for a journey, packed and ready to flee,
to eat hurriedly the unleavened bread,
("hurried bread" that did not have time to rise).
They needed to be ready to escape at a moment's notice,
leaving behind a kingdom of death for a new land of divine promise.
Tonight we remember this people that gathered to feast on a lamb,
whose blood covered their lintels and doorframes,
alerting the destroying angel to pass over,
blood that protected all their firstborn,
protected them by the blood of the lamb.

And tonight we remember another meal—of particular importance to
us—more than a millennium after that first meal.
Some say it was another Passover meal, others that it was the night be-
fore Passover.
Whichever it was, the shadow of that first Passover hung over this one.
A dinner with Jesus and his friends.
Tonight we remember that meal which took place the night before the
angel of death came again, this time to claim only one firstborn—
God's.
Tonight we remember that Jesus gathered his friends, and what he said
and did: taking and blessing bread, "Take and eat—my body."

Then, lifting a blessing cup of wine, he said, "Take and drink—my blood."

And from the earliest days, whenever believers remember this second meal, they gather around the table to eat and drink and proclaim his death until his return.

Tonight we again remember that meal and this memory is a mirror for us.
It reflects who we are.
We are a People of the Table.
We continue to gather around the table—to eat bread and drink wine, the bread changed into his body and the wine transformed into his blood.
Sometimes we come in joy, and sometimes in sorrow,
    perhaps even in fear, carrying our pain or our sickness,
    weighed down with heartbreak, or a sadness too deep for words.
Sometimes we come confused, sometimes hurting,
    sometimes ready to give it all up or to take it all on.
Sometimes we come with new plans and new dreams, full of hope.
And sometimes we come with dreams deferred, plans defeated, expectations crushed.
We might come enraged, excited, exhausted, or expectant.
But we come.
We come because we are a people of the table and here we know that we are part of something bigger than *me* or *us* or *them*.
We are the People of the Table of the Lord.
Here we can eat and be nourished, and celebrate
    and remember the sacrifice of a new covenant.
Here we know the presence of the Lord, crucified and risen,
    present to us as food for us, his body.
We, the people of his table.

But that's not all.
We also are something else.
We are People of the Towel.
Peter knew something was going on when he saw Jesus reach for the pitcher and basin.
He probably thought Jesus was going to give it to him—to wash the feet of the others—another little lesson in humility and the importance of being like a child.
But he was appalled when Jesus picked up the towel and wrapped it around his own waist.

That was the task of a slave.

And so, as impetuously certain as ever, he rejected the offer: "Never, never, never!"

For Peter, Jesus was master—and the way of master and slave was set.

Each knows his place.

There is a comfortable inequality to this arrangement.

One knows where one stands.

And one hopes in time to be master in one's own right.

Perhaps for this reason, the superior-inferior relationship remains as popular as ever.

Of course, there is one alternative that inverts this relationship completely.

One can "master" things—and people—*as* a servant.

One can work it to be quite "in control" as a servant.

Somewhere along the line we meet these powerful "servants," pretenders to servanthood.

"After all I've done for you . . . ," as you feel the leash being pulled tight.

"I can do that for you—it's no bother, no bother at all,"—but wait until the bill arrives.

Parents can bind their children to themselves and children, their parents.

As can spouses, friends, and even acquaintances.

Not the bond that endures but the bond that suffocates.

Jesus had something else in mind—a true alternative.

Neither a serving master nor a mastering servant will ultimately do.

The relationship is to be one of equals.

At the heart of washing feet is the gift of friendship.

And among friends any act of service is permissible.

So Jesus is very firm in responding to Simon:

"I don't do this and you don't have to do with me."

And you got to love Peter, in for a penny, in for a pound.

"Not only my feet then, but everything!"

You can see Peter stripping down.

And I can see Jesus laughing, perhaps his last laugh.

But he goes on to make his point.

Kneeling before them, he washes their feet—all twelve of them at this point, (which means Judas was included—merit was not a criterion) and says:

"What I have done, *you* also must do. . . ."
In a short time, they would come for him with clubs and weapons,
    and he was arming them—and all future disciples—with a towel.
Let us build a kingdom; our arsenal includes a basin with water,
    and a never-ending supply of towels.

Brothers and Sisters,
We are the people of the table and of the towel.
And the two are deeply connected.
The table leads to the towel and the towel back to the table.
This meal nourishes us for lives of self-giving love.
The table turns us towards our brothers and sisters in the world and
    sends us out to "wash feet."
It fuels us for friendship.
To be friend first of all to one another;
    the first foot washing was among the community of disciples
    and these can be the most difficult feet to wash.
But, in the end, our mission is to the world; it is a redemptive mission
    to whomever needs a friend, crossing all boundaries.
And while a towel might look light, it can grow heavy over time.
It's a strain to be a foot washer—all that bending down,
    all that vulnerability.
And all that resistance.
Some do not want their feet washed.
    Too embarrassing, or even too intimate.
To accept this as Jesus meant it, is to accept equality.
    And equality carries demands.
On the other hand, some do not want to see the feet of others washed.
It is almost as if the recognition of God's gifts so freely given to others
    takes away from their own dignity or sense of self-worth.
And so, the more one serves with the towel, the more one needs the table,
    and the strength it gives to keep on giving.

This night proclaims how we find the balance in living our lives in Christ:
We are people of the table and people of the towel.
In being faithful to both, we are truly a priestly people, a holy people,
    God's chosen people, bearers of life and love into a world starving
    for both.

*B. Homily for Good Friday*

"Behold the wood of the Cross. Come, let us adore"

(Texts: Isa 52:13-53:12; Heb 4:14-16; 5:7-9; John 18:1–19:42)

Like many young boys growing up in the '50s,
  I belonged to that elite organization known as "The Altar Boys."
As I was working my way up the chain of command,
  I was appointed first acolyte for the Good Friday service.
In those days, back in the '50s, it was the crucifix that was venerated in
  my parish, rather than a bare cross.
And, as acolyte, I was one of those who held it up during this time.
In my memory, I can still see the people coming forward:
  schoolmates, our parents and their generation, our grandparents and
  their friends, the single and married, the preschool children and the
  aged.
As they came up to the crucifix, some would bow, others genuflect,
  but then all would kneel before the crucifix
  and there was the lovely gesture of devotion when people would
  kiss the figure of Jesus crucified.
Some would kiss the feet, others would kiss one or both of the hands,
  and some would kiss the wounded side at the mark of the lance.
I remember especially how the elderly struggled to get back up again.
What I carried away from the Good Fridays of my childhood was that
  I belonged to a community that worshiped Jesus crucified for our
  sakes.
In recent years, with the reform of the liturgy,
  we no longer venerate the figure of the crucified Lord on the cross.
We venerate the cross, without any figure on it.
And I must say when the change came I found myself resistant to it.
  But as the years have gone on I have concluded that only the cross
  will do, for it is the cross that proclaims the mystery of this day with
  the greatest eloquence.

I say this first of all in light of the passion we just heard.
John's passion is the same in many respects as the other three evangelists:
  telling the story of Jesus' arrest, his trials before the religious and
  civil authorities, his carrying the cross, his being crucified upon it,
  and, finally, his dying and being laid in the tomb.
But there is a particular difference between the Jesus of John's Gospel
  and the Jesus of the other Gospels:

John's Jesus is marked by great calm and control.
John's gospel gives us no agony in the garden.
The meeting with Annas shows a Jesus who is singularly dispassionate,
   with his response after being struck, "If I said anything wrong, produce
   the evidence."
This Jesus carries his cross by himself, no help needed from Simon of
   Cyrene, nor sympathy accepted from the women of Jerusalem.
Even from the cross, John's Jesus has the composure to attend to his
   mother's future, entrusting her to the care of the Beloved Disciple.
And then to utter one statement, "I thirst," to fulfill the Scriptures,
   and a final one to announce, "It is complete."
Then, we hear, "he delivered over his spirit."
No heartrending cry of abandonment, no sense of total desertion found
   in the Synoptics.
This Jesus fulfills the words uttered earlier in this gospel:
   "No one takes my life from me; I lay it down of my own will."

Now, you might find this Jesus particularly attractive,
   especially if you are into control.
It could be quite comforting to find this very quality in the Son of God,
   and could even justify all our efforts to impose more control on life,
   and on the people in our lives.
On the other hand, perhaps you might find this Jesus a bit chilly, aloof,
   very much the divine, but rather less the human Jesus so dear to our
   age.
Well, neither estimation is on the mark.
It is important to attend to that conversation between Jesus and Pilate.
"My kingdom is not of this world," Jesus says.
"So then," Pilate retorts, "you are a king?"
Jesus' response to this question is the heart of this brief dialogue.
"You say I am a king. For this I was born and for this I came into the
   world, to testify to the truth. Everyone who belongs to the truth lis-
   tens to my voice."
And we know Pilate's famous response, "Truth! What's that?"

For the community of John, after years of reflection,
   truth was not a *what*—truth was a *who*.
This Jesus was the Way, the Truth, and the Life.
He was the Word of the Living God,
   the Word of Truth sent by the Father.
And what is that truth?

That God so loved the world that God sent the only Son.
That this Son came into the world to reveal the Father.
From the beginning of his mission Jesus was focused on "the hour"
    when this revelation of God would happen.
And in John's Gospel, this "hour," the hour of glory, was the hour of the
    cross,
when the Son in being lifted up would draw all things to himself.
The passion of John draws all believers to the cross.
And so does this second day of the Triduum,
which is, literally, the *crucial* day.
Last night in our celebration of Holy Thursday
    we remembered and celebrated that we are a people of the towel and
    the table, a people of service and celebration—
And tomorrow we shall celebrate that we are a people of fire and water,
    a people meant to be light and life-giving for a dark and thirsting
    world.
But it is this middle day that holds the other two together.
And it is this image of the cross, the life-giving tree,
    which roots us in the saving death of Jesus.
The power of the cross transforms towel and table
    just as it re-creates fire and water.
And so we come to venerate the cross.

When we come to venerate the cross, we are reminded that we cannot
    stay with the past.
The crucifix can restrict us to what happened almost 2,000 years ago.
True, we continue to meditate and reflect on the fact that this Jesus suf-
    fered, truly suffered an agonizing dying, and experienced a brutal
    death.
But the cross reminds us that he was taken down, laid in a tomb,
    and was raised on the third day.
We celebrate this death as a saving death and we live in the awareness
    that death did not conquer, that death itself died in this dying.
We come to venerate the cross as the instrument of our salvation
    and the sign of God's great commitment to us and our world.
And this is where our veneration turns round on us.
When we venerate the cross, we are called to make a commitment.
To venerate this cross is to signal the acceptance of the cross in our lives
    as the community of the Crucified Risen Lord.
To venerate the cross is to sign ourselves as a people who are committed
    to dying and rising with Jesus for the life of the world.

What exactly does that mean for our lives?

Perhaps, in the past, the Church, or at least some of its spokespersons,
have been too willing to identify what cross God had given to various
members of the community.

People have been told to make peace with intolerable situations
in the name of accepting the cross.

Or individuals have been told with too much ease that "this" was God's
invitation to share in the cross of Christ and that to refuse was to
reject God's offer.

And so we might find ourselves resistant to any talk about the cross.

But the lesson of Good Friday is that the cross can be the way of self-
giving, so that others might live.

It can evoke from within us a genuine willingness to bear the cross in
our lives, both individually and communally, for the sake of others.

That truth is found repeated again and again through all the Gospels
and in all the works of the New Testament.

"If you wish to follow me, take up your Cross daily."

And so again and again we must ponder what Cross is the way of
salvation.

What Cross are we to take up to win life for others?

What form of self-sacrifice is to be borne?

I do not think anyone can definitively tell you that,
nor can anyone with certitude assign you a particular Cross.

While another may help you discern, to recognize a particular situation,
as the Cross in your life,
only you can make that decision as to whether it truly is,
and decide on how you are called to bear it.

The Cross can come in so many different ways.

Perhaps it is the Cross of continuing to love when the returns are negli-
gible, when our love is not appreciated, even thrown back in our faces.

Or perhaps it is the Cross of humbly accepting that an old dream must
be allowed to die,
so that life can go on,
that to continue down a certain path is destructive for oneself
or for those for whom one is responsible.

There is the Cross of accepting myself, whether gay or straight, as flawed
and sinful, but as part of God's good creation, to accept what God
has made and be grateful.

There is the Cross of continuing to work for justice in a world, and
even in a Church, where racism, sexism, homophobia, and indiffer-
ence to the poor continues, and where it may seem there is little
chance of anything changing.

And there is the Cross of living with what can not be changed and
clinging in trust to a God whose face I cannot see and whose voice
I cannot hear.

There is the Cross of sickness that debilitates both body and spirit,
yet within which God is present, working out with us our salvation.

And, ultimately, there is the Cross of struggling to look into the face of
death with faith and greet it as a brother believer did centuries ago
as "Sister Death."

To discern what is one's own Cross is an Easter grace,
to define what is another's is everyday foolishness.

At the heart of the Triduum is the celebration of the passion and death
of Jesus.

It is not to be cut off from the other two days, but to shed its light on
them.

Only one symbol is given us for this day—the cross—
on which Jesus of Nazareth died,
and from which he was proclaimed as king.

Come, let us adore the Crucified One.

Come, let us die with him that we might rise with him.

Come, let us venerate the cross as the life-giving event
which continues, through us, to bring redemption and salvation to
the world.

### C. Homily for the Fourth Sunday of Lent (C Cycle)

#### "We Are All Called to Be Insiders"

#### (Texts: Josh 5:9, 10-12; 2 Cor 5:17-21; Luke 15:1-3, 11-32)

Lent is an Old English word that means spring,
reminding us that this season of the Church year is a season of the
heart.

Forty days are given over to awakening our hearts, heeding the call to
"*rend* our hearts" (a word related to "rind"—the tough skin that
needs to be peeled away.)

Spring is a time for lovers and Lent is a time for becoming caught up
in God's love.

Lent builds to our renewing the promises made at the time of our
  baptism, our vows of covenant with our God.
We do this either at the Easter Vigil or during the Easter morning liturgy.
Today's readings put a particular face on what this means for us:
  We are called to be ambassadors for Christ, ambassadors of recon-
  ciliation.
The challenge is whether we are up to being ambassadors.

In the movie *Wag the Dog*, Dustin Hoffman is a Hollywood producer
  who suddenly finds the representatives of the president of the
  United States standing in his home one day.
They have come to ask him to produce a false war
  to be shown on television as the real thing,
    to distract the attention of the American people from an indiscretion
    of the president.
The election is only a week away.
To entice the producer to do this, one of the representatives says that
  "there might be something special in this for you,"
then after a dramatic pause, "maybe an ambassadorship . . ."
The producer responds immediately:
"An ambassadorship—what do I want with that. I don't even go to
  Brentwood."
The producer had no desire to go to the next town.
And to be an ambassador definitely means leaving home, security, comfort.
And to be an ambassador for Christ means going out to others in Christ's
  name.
Lent gives us time to prepare ourselves for the job, even to make some
  practice runs.

Paul's words today speak of our work as ambassadors for Christ:
  "So whoever is in Christ is a new creation: the old things have
  passed away; behold, new things have come. And all this is from
  God, who has reconciled us to himself through Christ and given us
  the ministry of reconciliation, namely God was reconciling the
  world to himself in Christ, not counting their trespasses against
  them and entrusting to us the message of reconciliation. So we are
  ambassadors for Christ, as if God were appealing through us."

We are called by baptism to be ambassadors of reconciliation,
  entrusted with the message of reconciliation, drawing all in the new
  creation.

And this work of reconciliation involves leaving home,
   going out to others in love and bringing others into our community.

The parable we heard this morning images this work of reconciliation.
It presents a father who will not rest with his sons on the "outs,"
   geographically or relationally.
The father of the parable is one who wants his sons to be inside their
   home, better yet, to be at home with him.
Twice he leaves his house to bring a son inside.
But he always allows them their freedom.
The younger son can only see the freedom of living outside his Father's
   embrace.
When Jesus told this story, his listeners would have gasped.
By asking for his share of the estate now, and by selling it off,
   the younger son broke up the family inheritance.
To ask for this while the father lived was to say, "Father, drop dead."
The older brother would have been furious because usually brothers
   worked the family estate together, but now half of it was gone, sold off.
The extended family would also be furious; the boy had jeopardized
   their future, too.
The village would be appalled, seeing the boy as both ungrateful and
   disrespectful.
It is important to realize this to get the impact of what happens next.

The young man has a great time for a while.
Then fame, fair weather, and friends fade.
The funds run out and famine follows.
The boy is sitting there with the pigs.
(There is no worse humiliation for a Jew of the covenant).
And, the story says, "He comes to himself."
Better supping with his father's servants than pining for the pig's food.
So off he goes with a touching little speech.
Is it genuine? We really don't know.
But it is designed to press the right buttons in Dad.
The focus then moves to the father, the ambassador of reconciliation in
   this story.
While the boy is still far off, the father sees him.
The father had to have been on the lookout.
The father knew that if his son came home, and if the others found
   him first, his brother might kill him, and the neighbors would throw
   stones at him, chasing him off.

He had disgraced his father, no worse sin in the Middle East.

So the Father is on the watch, and probably has been for some time,
leaving home again and again to climb the hill and look out over the
countryside.

Finally, after weeks and even months had passed,
his father caught sight of him and was deeply moved.

He runs to his son.

A key moment! Old men do not run in the Middle East.

Such an act would cause him to lose his dignity;
even more, he would make a fool of himself.

To run, he would have to pick up his long garment and his underwear
would show.

The father does this and more.

He runs the gauntlet for his son, heading off any possibility of others
getting to him first. Thus, he goes out and brings him in—*inside*.

The boy's speech he doesn't pay any attention to, nor does he give one
of his own.

Just a series of joyful commands: "A robe! A ring! Sandals! And kill the
calf!"

He is caught up in joy at this son who was outside for so long, lost,
dead, but is now back inside his father's home, found, living.

So we have the tale of a father who offers reconciliation.

But once told is not enough.

The story is retold, in a different key.

When the neighbors would come into the banquet,
they would see the father beaming, arm around the boy, and this
would silence them.

But then they would notice the older son, whose obligation it was to
stand with his father, was *not* next to him, not in the same room, not
even in the house.

Once, again, an action that said, "Drop dead, Dad."

Now the father could have sent out the servants to bring this eldest son
in, and take him to his quarters to be dealt with later.

But instead, once again, the father himself leaves his home and goes out.

Again, he has to move through the neighbors,
Hearing their "tsk"-ing, snickering, sneering,
shaking their heads at the total breakdown of custom, this violation
of respect.

Again the father runs the gauntlet for his son.

Again the father turns aside his son's words with his generous invitation.

"Come in, come in. All that I have is yours. Everything. Come inside."

Jesus told this story when they asked him why he ate with sinners and
    tax collectors.
He told the story of a father with two sons.
The message? The children of the father's house belong inside, cele-
    brating, feasting.
The Father wants everyone in. But someone has to get them.
Jesus was the one sent by the Father to reconcile all to the Father,
    to bring everyone back inside, no one lost, no one alienated, no one
    excluded.

That was then. What about now?
Now we who are God's children are invited to take on this work.
God doesn't want anyone at a distance.
God sends us outside, to bring others in.
This work began when Abraham was invited to enter into a covenant
    with God.
It continued with Moses, and then the prophets.
But it came to its fulfillment in Jesus.
And we who have been baptized into Christ are called to continue it.
So if anyone is an outsider, whether in our family, our society, or our
    Church, our work as ambassadors is to bring them in.
Sometimes it is done in simple ways; sometimes in more dramatic and
    costly ones.

When I was in Israel, I heard the story of Hassan Dehqani-Tafti,
    President-Bishop of the Episcopal Church in Jerusalem and the
    Middle East and bishop of Iran.[24]
The fundamentalists hated him, and tried to kill him a number of times.
They did not succeed in that, but they did succeed in killing his only
    son, Bahram.
The bishop, outside the country, was warned not to attend the funeral.
After praying about this, he said he would send a prayer to be read.
This prayer is the work of an ambassador of reconciliation:

---

24. I am indebted to Dr. Kenneth Bailey who shared this prayer during a series of
lectures on the Gospel of Luke in the spring of 1995 at the Tantur Institute, outside of
Jerusalem. The prayer was written by Bishop Dehqani-Tafti on Cyprus on May 6, 1980.

## A Father's Prayer Upon the Murder of His Son

"O God, we remember not only Bahram, but also his murderers.
Not because they killed him in the prime of his youth
    and made our hearts bleed and our tears flow;
Not because with this savage act they have brought further disgrace on
    the name of our country among the civilized nations of the world;
But because through their crime we now follow Thy footsteps more
    closely in the way of sacrifice.
The terrible fire of this calamity burns up all selfishness and possessive-
ness in us.
Its flame reveals the depth of depravity and meanness and suspicion,
    the dimension of hatred and measure of sinfulness in human nature;
It makes obvious as never before our need to trust in God's love as
    shown in the cross of Jesus and his resurrection.
Love which makes us free from hate toward our persecutors;
Love which brings patience, forbearance, courage, loyalty, humility,
    generosity, greatness of heart;
Love which more than ever deepens our trust in God's final victory
    and his eternal designs for the Church and for the world;
Love which teaches us how to prepare ourselves to face our own day of
    death.

O God,
Bahram's blood has multiplied the fruit of the Spirit in the soil of our
    hearts; so when the murderers stand before Thee on the Day of
    Judgment, remember the fruit of the Spirit by which they have en-
    riched our lives, and forgive."

This prayer does not spring from any human spirit alone;
it comes from the power of the Spirit of reconciliation.
This prayer echoes the very heart of God:
    that even those who sin against us are to be reconciled,
    that all are to be forgiven, even the murderers of an only son.
We are called to this work of reconciling all in and through Christ.
On Easter, when we renew our baptism promises, we accept again this
    commission: to be ambassadors of reconciliation, ambassadors of
    Christ.

*D. Homily for the Feast of the Epiphany*

The following homily was given at Holy Trinity Church in George-town with the director of liturgy, Margaret Costello (MC).

"Recipe for an Epiphany"
(Texts: Isa 60:1-6; Eph 3:2-3, 5-6; Matt 2:1-12)

JW: As a child, on this feast of the Epiphany,
   I always looked forward to the statues in front of church.
There was one Asian, one African, and one Caucasian.
The combination communicated that Jesus had come for everyone.
MC: As a child I loved the name *Magi* and the word *Epiphany*.
They were strange, exotic words speaking of an ancient world and long-ago peoples.
JW: But in our aging in wisdom and grace,
   we've come to see this gospel less as an account of a past wonder
   and more as a story of a future promise
   —because Epiphanies continue to happen.
MC: And one way to think about this story is that it contains a recipe
   for an Epiphany. And if the right ingredients manage to come to-gether, you too might have an epiphany.
JW: To begin with, you need some wise men . . .
MC: Some wise *people*.
There can be no epiphany without wise people, people looking up, being attentive.
For God to manifest Godself, people have to be looking.
The Magi were astrologers, searchers of the heavens, looking beyond their own world.
They were people willing to travel, to journey, to move.
People capable of wonder.
That's why I still like the word *Magi*.

JW: Secondly, you need a star.
In the story, the star signals all those forces of nature that spoke to the Gentiles, that spoke to all those "others," the people who did not know the God of Israel.
And God continues to send stars across our horizons.
It can be *something* that suddenly snatches our attention, illumines our night, getting us to look up and away from the ordinary things that occupy and preoccupy us.

Or it can be *someone*—a Dalai Lama, or Thich Nhat Hanh or a complete
    stranger.
For many people in the past year, I think it was Cardinal Bernardin.
Both for believers and nonbelievers he was a star that shot across the sky.
He called on us to work to find "common ground," to find a space where
    all could meet and talk, and listen, and move to a deeper awareness
    of what binds us in Christ.
He also reminded us that death is a passing-over and that it is possible
    to die with dignity.
So, in addition to wise people, you need a star to get things moving.

MC: We also need to have wise words.
The words of the long departed prophet Micah pointed the Magi in
    the right direction.
And the words of Scripture continue to point us in the right direction.
These remain among our wisest words.
As we learn to pray with Scripture, we find that these words speak pro-
    foundly to the reality of our lives in the present.
The popularity of Bill Moyers' series on Genesis shows how people
    continue to find life, meaning, challenge, and even excitement in the
    old stories.
Of course, there were other words in the story, too.
Like the words of Herod: "You all come back when you find the child."
Both prophet and prince spoke words with authority.
We need to distinguish between words that lead to life and those that
    would crush it.
You need wise words for an epiphany.

JW: And, very importantly, you need to have a gift, at least one gift in
    particular.
It's instructive to consider the gifts the Magi brought.
At first glance two of them seem very practical.
Mary and Joseph could certainly have used a little gold, what with an-
    other mouth to feed, and incense would certainly come in handy in
    a stable.
But the gift of myrrh is puzzling, being something used for burial, to
    anoint a corpse.
And it's this gift that tips us off to the deeper level of all three gifts.
Giving myrrh to this child signals that he was to suffer,
    indeed it signals to future generations that he was the Suffering Son
    of Man.

And this causes us to look again at the other two gifts.
Gold was for kings, in this case the King of kings.
Frankincense speaks of divinity, for this child was bringing God to us
    as no one ever had.
Still as meaningful as these gifts were in themselves,
together they symbolized a more fundamental gift:
    the gift of adoration.
The Magi came to adore Jesus, born of Mary, Emmanuel, God-with-us.
The poet Jessica Powers opens one of her poems with these words:
    We walk along a road
    at the day's end, a little child and I,
    and she points out a bird, a tree, a toad,
    a stretch of colored sky.

    She knows no single word
    But "Ah" (with which all poems must commence,
    at least in the heart's heart), and I am stirred
    by her glad eloquence.[25]
"Ah"—the first syllable of adoration.
"Come, let us *a*-dore him."
It's not just a carol's refrain, but a habit of the heart for believers.
We are primed for praise, our souls aching to adore.
Epiphany happens when we realize we are being wooed into worship.
We come here every week, Magi-like, to give the gift of an adoring
    heart to the Father through the Son in the power of the Spirit.
We come here to adore, to bend the knee, to fall prostrate.

MC: And as we leave here, we can not forget the final ingredient in
    this story:
    a dream that bids us return to our world differently.
For the Magi it meant a different way back home.
For us it might mean:
    a reexamination of where we are headed in our personal or professional
    lives,
    or a call to some new and deeper commitment,
    or even a change in how we view the prospect of a serious illness or
    death.
What is it we are going home to at the end of this Christmas season?

---

25. "At Evening with a Child," *Selected Poetry of Jessica Powers*, ed. Regina
Siegfried, ASC, and Robert F. Morneau (New York: Sheed and Ward, 1994) 140.

Is it the "same old same old"?

Or might we be called to go home to someplace quite different,
   someplace that mirrors tonight's first reading, a place that shimmers
   with radiance:

"Upon you the Lord shines, and over you appears God's glory . . .

Raise your eyes and look about . . .

You shall be radiant at what you see, your heart shall throb and overflow . . ."

In the end we are all beckoned home to this shining and radiant city.

This week a friend gave me a wall hanging which said,

"Just to be is a blessing. Just to live is holy."

At the end of our lives, whenever that may be,
   may this feast of Epiphany call us home,
      perhaps by a route that we would not have chosen, but, nevertheless,
      confident that we are destined for that shimmering city, the new and
      eternal Jerusalem.

JW: So it's more than a tale of three exotically dressed travelers and
   several camels.

MC: It's a call to move out into the unknown, guided by the light that
   is Christ.

JW: It's a promise that God, revealed in this child, is and continues to
   be a God of all peoples, and for all peoples.

MC: It's a declaration that our destiny is to be caught up in wonder,
   worship and wisdom,

JW: so that we all become wise men,

MC: wise women,

Together: Wise people. Happy Epiphany!

## Summary

The preaching that occurs on the great feasts of the Lord and during the seasons related to these feasts can be envisioned as feeding
people hungry for wholeness, offering a sense of self-identity and mission rooted in Christ to both the individual and the community. Over
the course of this chapter, several suggestions have been made:

1. To begin to reflect on any great feast, jot down various ways in which
the solemnity can be named. Consider names which are theological, pastoral, and poetic. Eventually you will decide which title or phrase best
captures the emphasis of the homily for this particular celebration.

2. To develop a homily that offers substance and sustenance, ask: "How do the scriptural and liturgical texts contribute to our understanding of the feast?" Are there any words or phrases in the texts that could help the community to appreciate the proclamation of the great feast and would be useful in the homily?

3. To speak to the community you serve, consider how the feast through its texts helps the community understand its identity as individuals and as people in Christ. How does the feast engage with any world or local events? What kind of response does this feast evoke from the community in terms of action, attitude, or value?

4. To allow the feast to be celebrated in its fullness, how do the seasons leading up and away from it provide ways to prepare for the celebration of the feast? Look first to the Sunday Gospels for images of Christ and the implications for the community as both recipient of the grace he offers and follower along the way he leads.

5. For further reading:

- *Liturgical Ministry* "Liturgical Year," 5 (fall 1996).
- David J. Schlafer, *What Makes This Day Different?: Preaching Grace on Special Occasions* (Boston, Mass.: Cowley Publications, 1998).
- James A. Wilde, ed., *At That Time: Cycles and Seasons in the Life of a Christian* (Chicago: Liturgy Training Publications, 1989).

# Chapter 3

# Preaching within the Sacramental Rites and the Hunger for Meaning

*"We had the experience but missed the meaning."*[1]
*(T. S. Eliot, "The Dry Salvages")*

"Without ultimate meaning, we are ultimately unsatisfied." (*FIYH*, 7)

## Our Search for Meaning and the Experience of Ritual

In an interview in 1996,[2] Holocaust survivor and author Elie Wiesel was reflecting on the importance of the great writer Franz Kafka. He noted that Kafka's importance was linked to his attitude towards absurdity. "Everywhere Kafka is asking, What is the meaning of all this? All his characters ask this question again and again." Wiesel immediately made a connection with his own experience during World War II, saying that during that horror-filled time he was always asking himself about the meaning of events, "What is happening here? The flames, what is the meaning of the flames?" He then related this personal experience with the Rabbinic tradition exemplified in the Talmud. "That is actually a Talmudic question. In the Talmud, it is called *mai ka mashma lan*: 'What does it mean?' You hear a text, you read a text and you must ask, What does it mean to us? From my childhood on, I was asking this question."[3] Another Holocaust survivor, Viktor Frankl, came to the same conclusion that the great human quest is this search for meaning. In his most famous work, *Man's Search for Meaning*, Frankl the psychiatrist quotes Nietzsche the philosopher: "He who

---

1. T. S. Eliot, *Four Quartets* (New York: Harcourt Brace Jovanovich, 1971) 39.
2. "A Conversation with Elie Wiesel," *Image* (fall 1996) 43–58.
3. Ibid., 48.

has a *why* to live for can bear almost any *how*."[4] Frankl stressed in his writing that the human person has a capacity rooted in freedom to transcend suffering and find a meaning in life no matter how terrible and tragic the circumstances.

The hunger for meaning is a basic human hunger. But this hunger can be lost sight of, as the poet T. S. Eliot recognized when he wrote that we can have the experience but miss the meaning. We can move from experience to experience, allowing little time to reflect on what each one means in our lives. Do we recognize ourselves as "seekers of meaning?" Where do we turn to meet this need? How do we satisfy this hunger, albeit temporarily? *Fulfilled In Your Hearing (FIYH)* affirms that effective preaching springs from an awareness of the experiences that touch the lives of the community.[5] The preacher must be conscious of the daily experiences of the community that can lead to its recognizing the presence of the living God, or, perhaps more common in our age, to questioning whether God is really active and present at all in our world today. Only then is it possible to mediate meaning by bringing together the Christian revelation, especially as it is articulated in the biblical texts read during the liturgy, and the events of the world we live in. Meaning can come to us in different ways: through solitary reflection, that quiet pondering that stills our soul and allows us to penetrate beyond the surface of life; through heart-to-heart conversations with discerning friends; and through those communal ritual celebrations that have served to bond communities of believers through the ages. This powerful area of ritual concerns us in this chapter.

A few years ago during a sabbatical in Israel I heard the following story from Professor Yehezkau Landau, a professor of Judaism at the Tantur Ecumenical Institute. During the Second World War in a city in eastern Europe occupied by the Nazis, the Gestapo were sent out early one morning to round up all the Jews from the ghetto area where they had been confined and bring them to the train station. They were told to take nothing but the clothes on their backs because there would not be room on the trains for luggage. Jewish men, women, and children were marched down to the station and crammed into cattle cars for the trip to Auschwitz. Inside the cars there was almost total darkness. People were barely able to move, not even to relieve themselves. In one of the cars near the back was an elderly woman who had taken

---

4. Viktor E. Frankl, *Man's Search for Meaning* (New York: Touchstone, 1984) 109.
5. *FIYH*, 7–8.

with her a single bag, hidden under a long, heavy coat. After several hours of riding on the train, the woman sensed that evening was near. It was Friday and the Sabbath would begin at sunset. She leaned down with great difficulty, opened the bag she had dropped at her feet, and brought out two small loaves of bread and two small candlesticks. She had no matches, but as word spread through the car, someone found a pack in a coat pocket and passed it along. The candles were lit and held by two people, their faces momentarily warmed by the light. Then someone began to sing in Hebrew the words of the great sixteenth-century hymn, *"Lecha dodi likrat kalah, P'ney shabbat nekablah,"* that is, "Come, my beloved, to meet the Bride; let us greet the face of the Sabbath." Every man, woman, and child joined in, and the sound of voices filled that train moving ever deeper into the darkness of night. Professor Landau paused at this point, then said to us, "The rabbis say that while it is true that the Jews have kept the Sabbath, it is equally true that the Sabbath has kept the Jews."

Meaning comes through rituals lovingly handed on from generation to generation. In the Roman Catholic tradition, we employ them at the most important moments of our lives: when life itself begins or ends, when we desire to commit ourselves to another, when we fall seriously ill or fail in our moral responsibilities. Rituals provide an access to something deeper, to the Mystery that surrounds and underlies all of life. Sometimes ritual brings light into the darkness, as it did on that train ride to Auschwitz, lifting those present above the fear of the moment and the horror of the coming days and allowing them to touch the transcendent. On such occasions, ritual offers meaning that can counter what our senses and reason tell us. At other times, ritual deepens what we already know, confirming it, but also opening our eyes to see more fully into the depths of life, intuiting what lies beyond in the realm of promise. Ritual enables us to have an experience *and* to grasp its meaning—or, at least, *a* meaning. And, at its best, ritual gives a glimpse into ultimate meaning which is to be found in the plan of God.

When Professor Landau concluded by saying that "it is equally true that the Sabbath has kept the Jews," I found myself reflecting on the rituals of the Roman Catholic tradition, asking myself, "Can't we say the same thing about the celebration of the sacraments? Isn't it true to say that not only have we kept these sacramental rites, but that these rites have kept us over the centuries?" How else to explain that impulse that brings people back to church to be married, to have their children baptized, to bury their loved ones after a church service. It is not just that we have kept the sacramental rites, but they have kept us, joining us with the larger community across time and space. Andrew Greeley has written, "To the extent that people remain Catholic, it is because they are caught up in the beauty of sacramental Catholicism and the stories it tells, no matter how shoddy the presentation of beauty nor how inept the telling of stories."[6] Through the beauty of these rites we can come to meaning, even to that ultimate meaning—namely, that our lives are enveloped in the mystery of the God who calls, woos, liberates, saves, and is both the source and destiny of all creation.

Over thirty years ago, the Constitution on the Sacred Liturgy reminded us that "the purpose of the sacraments is to sanctify people, to build up the body of Christ, and finally, to give worship to God" (no. 59). Out of this understanding, Cardinal Godfried Danneels of Belgium recently said, "When you touch the symbols and fundamental rites of religion, you touch the heart of religion and faith."[7] The U.S. Bishops' Committee on the Liturgy was not engaging in hyperbole when it stated in its 1972 document *Music in Catholic Worship*: "Faith grows when it is well expressed in celebration. Good celebrations foster and nourish faith. Poor celebrations may weaken and destroy it" (6). The effect of these celebrations depends a great deal on the ability of those responsible for their enactment to draw the gathered community into full, conscious, and active participation. Preaching has an important role to play here, contributing to a community's understanding and evoking its full participation in the rite, or helping to effect a ritual experience that is ill-prepared, poorly performed, and indifferently received. What preaching attempts to do flows from an understanding of sacramentality. Before addressing the homily within the sacramental rite, let us look briefly at the nature of a sacrament.

## The Sacramental Rites: Events of Meaning and Empowerment

In considering the sacramental rites, I would like to highlight four aspects central to our present experience of the sacraments, which, in turn, can influence how we approach preaching within the rites:

1. "*A sacrament is physical, and within it is God's love . . . ,*" wrote Andre Dubus, in his last book, *Meditations from a Movable Chair*.[8] In

---

6. Andrew Greeley, "Authority as Charm," *America* (Nov. 20, 1999) 12.

7. "Real Reform: An Interview with Cardinal Godfried Danneels," *Church* (fall 1999) 17.

8. Andre Dubus, *Meditations from a Movable Chair* (New York: Knopf, 1998) 85.

1986, Dubus was helping to change a tire when he was hit by a car; he lost one of his legs and was confined to a wheelchair until his death in 1999. In one of his final essays, he wrote with great eloquence on his need for sacraments: "I need sacraments I can receive through my senses. I need God manifested as Christ, who ate and drank and shat and suffered and laughed. So I can dance with Him as the leaf dances in the breeze under the sun."[9] Dubus grasped the sacramental principle; he knew that the human person needed God's compassionate touch expressed in a physical form: "A sacrament is physical and within it is God's love."

The sacramental rites bring us into contact with this physical aspect in several ways. There is the physical contact with creation that is part of every sacrament, whether it is the water, oil, bread and wine, bands of gold, the paschal candle, the funeral pall, or the significant gestures of blessing, laying on of hands, bowing of heads, signing another's body with the cross, anointing various parts of the body with oil, eating and drinking, or assuming various bodily positions such as prostrating, kneeling, sitting, or standing. The sacraments involve bodies, both our own and the "stuff" of creation. Through this materiality, through our physical contact with certain things and each other, God touches our minds, hearts, and spirits in a loving manner, reaching out to embrace, comfort, heal, soothe, nurture, and nourish. The operative word here is *touch* and the motive is *love*. Sacraments are experienced when the God revealed in Christ again touches the bodies of those brought to him with healing and redeeming love and calls forth the bodily response of all those present through movement, recitation, stillness, and song.

Sacramental rituals, then, demand embodiment. And such embodiment must be marked by a worthy and appropriate physical expression. Sacramental theologian Peter E. Fink, S.J., writes that whereas the scholastic tradition articulated at the Council of Trent was insistent that sacraments *effect* what they signify, the contribution of the Second Vatican Council was its demand that "sacraments *signify* what they effect, because it is by *signifying* that sacraments are effective for those who enact them."[10] The quality of the sign, of the material, the concrete expression of the sacrament, is what works on the human

9. Ibid.
10. Peter E. Fink, S.J., "Sacramental Theology after Vatican II," *New Dictionary of Sacramental Theology* (Collegeville: The Liturgical Press, 1990) 1110.

person. It is the matter that matters. Through the physical nature and qualities of objects, actions, and people, meaning is communicated in a deeply human way. Again, the Constitution on the Sacred Liturgy says: "It is therefore of the greatest importance that the faithful easily understand the symbolism of the sacraments, and should eagerly frequent those sacraments which were instituted to nourish the Christian life" (no. 59), and "There is scarcely any proper use of material things which cannot thus be directed toward people's sanctification and the praise of God" (no. 61). Thus, let preachers keep in mind first of all that "sacraments are physical." For the words we choose to speak must facilitate the community's engagement with these various expressions of physical reality.

2. *A sacrament is a transformative encounter of the Church with its Lord and Savior Jesus Christ.* In celebrating the sacramental rites, the community of faith comes into contact with the salvific presence of the risen Lord: "By his power he is present in the sacraments . . ." (SC 7). These occasions carry with them a transformative power: "for well-disposed members of the faithful, the liturgy of the sacraments . . . sanctifies almost every event of their lives with the divine grace which flows from the paschal mystery of the passion, death, and resurrection of Christ. From this source all sacraments . . . draw their power" (SC 61). In writing on the sacraments, theologian Bernard Cooke expresses this transformation in terms of divine friendship and grace:

> Because of God's saving presence in the risen Christ and their Spirit, people are transformed as people beyond what would otherwise be possible; divine friendship realizes a potential for existing personally that would not otherwise be ever known. This transformation of persons under the impact of divine presence, of God being for them, is what traditionally has been called "sanctifying grace"; and because this occurs through the changed sacramentality of human experience, the term "sacramental grace" points to the effect of sacraments on people's lives. So, as the Council of Trent insisted, the sacraments through which God is made present to believing Christians do "contain and give" grace; for the entirety of human life is—if its *meaning* is deepened by the *meaning* revealed in Jesus' death and resurrection—filled with the transforming presence of God.[11]

While being aware of the transforming nature of the sacramental celebrations, we want to remember that the sacraments are not reducible

---

11. Bernard Cooke, "Sacraments," *New Dictionary of Sacramental Worship*, 1123.

to their rites. The rite addresses a particular human experience, such as responding to the grace of conversion, making the commitment of marriage, begetting new life, sinning, falling seriously ill, suffering the death of a loved one. Then, in its ritual expression, it serves as the vehicle by which the paschal mystery is made present to the community through the whole of this particular experience. Again, Cooke observes, "Rituals do not function apart from that which they ritualize."[12] The sacrament includes the entire human experience and its ritual expression. And for the transforming power of the sacrament to be effective and to flow over into life, those taking part must enter the rites with understanding and awareness of what is being addressed and what that implies for life beyond liturgy.

Liturgical scholar Kathleen Hughes makes this dynamic the goal of her latest work which looks to deepen the quality of experience participants have of the rites when "understanding (of the sacramental liturgies) leads to loving, loving to participation, participation to commitment and commitment to a transformed way of living."[13] The transformative encounter of a sacrament, then, begins with human experience, comes to ritual expression, and leads back to life. What makes a rite transformative has to do with the revelatory capacity of language. Part of the labor of language, particularly in preaching the homily, is to offer words that enable an encounter with Christ to take place by making the participants conscious of and responsive to the presence of the risen Lord who joins and empowers the community through this moment of grace.

3. *A sacrament is a "language event."* Liturgical scholars have reflected a great deal recently on liturgy as an act of communication, attending particularly to the role of liturgical language within this act. Language here is not limited to words alone but also includes "all human media of encounter and exchange, bodily and ritual, as well as verbal."[14] Thus, words spoken as well as found as directives for action, gestures, objects, and actions fall within the sphere of liturgical language. Furthermore, the approach to sacramental celebration as a language event is not confined to the use of language as a vehicle for didactic purposes. Mary Collins writes that

12. Ibid., 1119.

13. Kathleen Hughes, *Saying Amen, A Mystagogy of Sacrament* (Chicago: Liturgy Training Publications, 1999) 1.

14. David N. Power, *Sacrament, The Language of God's Giving* (New York: Crossroad, 1999) 59.

liturgical scholars agree that what liturgical language aims to disclose is something more profound than information about doctrines. Its purpose is to reveal the essentially unfathomable mystery of salvation at work in the world of human history. Liturgical speech and non-verbal ritual elements cumulate and coalesce in liturgical action to serve the divine mystery.[15]

The recent work of liturgical theologian David N. Power has done much to give emphasis to the nature of the celebration of the sacraments as a "language event" whose foundation is the Word of God:

> While the sacramental event is that of the language addressed to a particular community in Christ's name and that of the language spoken by the community in Christ's name, it is always the same Word which finds speech in many forms. The language event of Christian sacrament is the event of the Word of God, through the creative testimony of the Spirit, taking root again, in rich diversity, in time and place. It forms anew and it builds up a body which in its celebration and action testifies to the gift of God at work in the world and inviting into the divine communion of Father, Word and Spirit.[16]

The sacramental rites, then, are events of divine-human communication which effect transformation by offering meaning rooted in the life, death, and resurrection of Jesus Christ, the Word of God. Ritual formally states this meaning and relates human life to the significance of Jesus' saving action. The complexity, though, of the human aspect of language is rooted in what Power calls the "verbal polyphony"[17] characteristic of the rites and its interaction with the other nonverbal ritual aspects. This "verbal polyphony" includes the various genres of all the texts, both biblical and liturgical. The interaction of such biblical genres as narrative, prophecy, wisdom texts, psalms, and canticles, with the liturgical forms of blessings, prayers of exorcism and offering, declarative formulas, and petitions, come together to form a unique experience in relation to the other ritual components such as liturgical objects, gestures, actions and the environmental setting. Also not to be forgotten are the unique cultural adaptations that are integral to the liturgical life of a particular community.

---

15. Mary Collins, O.S.B., "Language, Liturgical," *New Dictionary of Sacramental Worship*, 655.

16. Power, *Sacrament*, 87.

17. Ibid., see especially chapter 5, 149–77.

The biblical texts are central to "keeping memorial of the Christ event," i.e., *anamnesis,* and relating the present to both the past and the future. The community remembers through these texts and then expresses this memory both in its liturgical prayers and actions, and finally, in the ethical commitment a particular rite evokes. Memory leads the community to its self-awareness as the body of Christ, formed by the Spirit, and to participation in the mystery here and now, i.e., *mimesis,* deepening its communion with the life of the Trinity and with all creation. The words of preaching play a central role in linking *anamnesis* with *mimesis,* and providing motivation for living out of the mystery as it flows from this particular event in the days ahead.

4. *A sacrament is an act of worship.* When the Constitution on the Sacred Liturgy refers to the threefold purpose of the liturgy, it appropriately names giving worship to God as one of these ends. The celebration of these rites provides a communal expression of praise and adoration for what God continues to do for us in Christ. This act of worship brings us into contact with the realm of the transcendent: "In the earthly liturgy we take part in a foretaste of that heavenly liturgy which is celebrated in the holy city of Jerusalem toward which we journey as pilgrims, and in which Christ is sitting at the right hand of God, minister of the sanctuary and of the true tabernacle (see Apoc 21:2; Col 3:1; Heb 8:2)" (SC 8). Such worship extends beyond the liturgical action so that we offer to God our bodies as living sacrifices of praise in all that we do. Thus, worship embraces the transformation of our entire selves in an ongoing process through the presence and power of the paschal mystery encountered in symbol. "The liturgy in its turn inspires the faithful to become 'of one heart in love' when they have tasted to the full of the paschal mysteries; it prays that 'they may grasp by deed what they hold by creed'" (SC 10). The celebration of the sacraments should send us forth afire with the compelling love of Christ, worship flowing into daily life; and the words of the preacher should evoke this disposition and desire to praise God within God's holy dwelling, both in church and in the world.

Bearing these four aspects of the sacraments in mind can help influence what the preacher does. The nature of the sacrament as physical reminds us that our words should not ignore the physical realities at the heart of these events. The sacraments are rooted in human experiences of the body and its joys and sorrows. They are grounded in the material of creation. May our words also keep us in contact with these experiences and the elements of creation brought to bear within each sacrament. The sacraments are encounters with the risen Lord; a primary function of our words is to make the presence of Christ palpable, to facilitate this meeting with Jesus. As language event, the preaching is one of the integral components of the rite, crucial in bridging the gap between the Liturgy of the Word and the Liturgy of the Sacrament, between *anamnesis* and *mimesis*, between remembering what God has done in the paschal mystery of Christ and what we are presently engaged in doing as an act of realizing the presence of salvation in our midst.

Preaching offers a word that interprets past and present, joining them, and leading those involved to give praise and adoration. It does this by speaking in a way that deepens the community's appropriation of the meaning of the event that has brought the community together. While preaching need not say all that can be said, it should assure that an effort has been made to draw meaning from the experience and evoke from those present their "full, conscious and active participation" in what is to follow and motivate their ongoing committed response to "a life lived in conformity with the gospel." Thus understood, the preaching task is essential in the formation of a worshiping people by offering words that mediate meaning at events of profound human significance.

## Preaching within the Sacramental Rites: Liturgical Guidelines

Each rite provides an understanding of the task of the homilist. Note the similarities and differences in what the rite itself asks of the homilist:

*The Rite of Baptism for Children*: "After the reading, the celebrant gives a short homily, explaining to those present the significance of what has been read. His purpose will be to lead them to a deeper understanding of the mystery of baptism and to encourage the parents and godparents to a ready acceptance of the responsibilities which arise from the sacrament" (no. 45).

*The Rite of Marriage*: "After the gospel, the priest gives a homily drawn from the sacred text. He speaks about the mystery of Christian marriage, the dignity of married love, the grace of the sacrament, and the responsibilities of married people, keeping in mind the circumstances of this particular marriage" (no. 22).

*The Rite of Penance*: "The homily is based on the texts of the readings and should lead penitents to examine their consciences and renew their lives" (no. 52).

*The Rite of Anointing Outside Mass*: "The priest may then give a brief explanation of the reading, applying it to the needs of the sick person and those who are looking after him or her" (no. 120).

*The Rite of Anointing Within Mass*: "In the homily the celebrant should show how the sacred text speaks of the meaning of illness in the history of salvation and of the grace given by the sacrament of anointing" (no. 137).

*Order of Christian Funerals*: "A brief homily based on the readings is always given after the gospel reading at the funeral liturgy and may also be given after the readings at the vigil service; but there is never to be a eulogy. Attentive to the grief of those present, the homilist should dwell on God's compassionate love and on the paschal mystery of the Lord, as proclaimed in the Scripture readings. The homilist should also help the members of the assembly to understand that the mystery of God's love and the mystery of Jesus' victorious death and resurrection were present in the life and death of the deceased and that these mysteries are active in their own lives as well. Through the homily members of the family and community should receive consolation and strength to face the death of one of their members with a hope nourished by the saving word of God. Laypersons who preside at the funeral rites give an instruction on the readings" (no. 27).

In light of these statements, I would like to make several observations. First, the understanding of the role of the homily within the rites has grown more nuanced over time. Note the difference between the description found in the earliest rite to be published, the Rite of Marriage (1969) and the latest one, the Order of Christian Funerals (1989). The former is worthy of a description for a marriage preparation course, being both broad in scope and primarily didactic in intent. The latter bears the thoughtful nuances of a longer period of reflection, with a strong emphasis on proclamation of the paschal mystery of Christ and a pastoral sensitivity towards those suffering the loss of a loved one.

Secondly, look for directives on the homily both in the Introduction to the particular rite and within the rite itself. In the Order of Christian Funerals, for instance, an understanding of the homily is only found in the General Introduction; within the rite of the Funeral Mass, it is succinctly noted: "A brief homily is given after the gospel reading" (no. 166). However, in the Rite of Penance, there is both a statement within the rite (see above), and then a more detailed and helpful statement in the Introduction to the rite with suggestions for the content of the homily (no. 25). The Introduction to the Rite of Baptism for Children states: "the liturgy of the word is directed toward stirring up the faith of the parents, godparents, and congregation, and praying in common for the fruits of baptism before the sacrament itself" (no. 17); this is complemented by the description of the homily within the rite which gives emphasis to the homily's laying out the meaning of the texts to deepen the community's understanding of the sacrament and to motivate the willing acceptance of parental and godparental responsibilities.

Certain emphases are consistent in the guidelines of the rites: (1) employing the Scripture texts that have been read as the basis for the homily; (2) deepening the community's understanding of the particular sacrament; and (3) motivating the community, especially the principal participants, to carry out their responsibilities arising from this sacrament. At the same time, there is a decidedly instructional emphasis on the understanding of the homily as presented in the various rites, in keeping with a more catechetical approach to preaching. This is where the contribution of *FIYH* comes into play.

This document, concerned as it is with preaching in the Sunday assembly, emphasizes the homily as offering a word of meaning to "a people hungry, sometimes desperately so, for meaning in their lives" (7). The vision of *FIYH* offers the homilist as a "mediator of meaning" (7), working in that space between God and the community, religious tradition and contemporary experience, revelation past and present. The preacher's work has to do with "making connections between the real lives of people who believe in Jesus Christ, but are not always sure what difference faith can make in their lives, and the God who calls us into ever deeper communion with himself and with one another" (8).

While *FIYH* is concerned with the Sunday homily and calls preachers to offer a scriptural interpretation of the community's life week in and week out, enabling the community to celebrate Eucharist on this particular Sunday, it also indicates that this same goal extends to the other rites when it says that the preacher's purpose is "to turn to these Scriptures to interpret peoples' lives in such a way that they will be able to celebrate Eucharist—*or be reconciled with God and one another, or be baptized into the Body of Christ, depending on the particular liturgy being celebrated*" (20–21). Thus, the preacher is not primarily concerned with evangelizing, catechizing, exhorting to a particular course of social action, but to offer the faithful a way of seeing this event that makes it meaningful and enables them to participate in the sacrament.

The preacher offers a word that interprets such events as the birth of a child, the taking of marriage vows, the death of a loved one, falling seriously ill, and recognizing and repenting of one's sinfulness as an event "in Christ." Such events allow for various understandings, depending on what "lens" is being employed. Marriage is often seen as a social event; birth as an occasion of joy, but also of worry if a couple has limited resources, financial or otherwise; sickness as inevitable suffering; and death as a cause of sorrow rather than hope. But the preacher looks at these events in life through the optic of the paschal mystery, inviting others to see them as ways of participating in the dying and rising of Christ. The homily interprets the human experience people bring with them in light of this saving mystery, making use of the selected biblical texts to do so.

When the various rites were first revised, the approach to the homily articulated in *FIYH* was not envisioned. A more didactic approach was at the heart of most of the descriptions of the homily found in them. I do not want to place *FIYH* in opposition to the other guidelines, but I think that approaching these events primarily as occasions for responding to the deep hunger for meaning keeps the moment of preaching pastoral in its deepest sense, joining with the good shepherd who sets a table before those entrusted to his care. Taking the directives and *FIYH* into account, I would like to offer a profile for a homily within the rites that would meet this hunger for meaning.

## Preaching within the Sacramental Rites: A Homilist's Proposal

To feed the hunger for meaning at these transitional events in life, the homily will focus on the human experience the rite addresses, giving priority to the biblical texts for their capacity to name that experience from a faith perspective, and to present Christ at work within the rite to the gathered community in a concrete way that facilitates worship and is both personal and brief. I would therefore propose the following characteristics for a homily within the rites: (a) experiential; (b) biblical; (c) Christocentric; (d) ecclesial; (e) liturgical; (f) personal; and (g) brief. A few words about each.

(a) *Experiential.* Find a way to name and evoke the experience being celebrated and to express the particular feelings and mood of the community that has come together. What is it *like* to celebrate new life, to love another so much that you want to spend the rest of your life growing in that love, to suffer the loss of a loved one, to live with a life-threatening sickness, and to recognize oneself as one who has sinned against others and God. The rites themselves call us to be attentive to the specifics of these occasions, being conscious of "the particular needs of the people." The occupational hazard for presiders and preachers is to allow a sense of routine to settle over these events. An experienced priest told me when I was first ordained, "If you are attentive and kind to people at these times, they will never forget you; if you are not, they will never forgive you."

A preaching student once asked about the preaching at weddings: "Is anyone really listening?" A good question—and not just for weddings when the service can be approached as the necessary ordeal before the reception. The preoccupation with the babies at baptism, the deep sorrow of the bereaved at funerals, the discomfort and anxiety of the sick—such conditions hardly seem ideal for having a preacher's words penetrate the minds and hearts of those present. Even so, I have found that many people really are listening, especially if I am engaged in the message, caught up in expressing what I have prayed over and studied and worked at, and especially if I communicate to the listeners that I have some understanding of what they are feeling at the moment, have entered into the joy of the day, or have empathy for the worry or sorrow or grief gripping their hearts.

Honesty must be the hallmark of naming where people are as the rite begins. *The Washington Post* quoted the words of Bishop Josef Homeyer of Hanover, Germany, at the memorial service for the ninety-six Germans killed in the Concorde flight outside of Paris on July 25, 2000: "God, where were you in Paris? Why have you deserted us? Our hearts are heavy. The brute force of sudden death shocks and confounds us."[18] I am sure everyone was listening to these words; they spoke to the heart of the moment. They addressed people where they were. Sometimes our work is to help people move away from or through whatever grips them as a service begins, at other times to move more deeply into it. In both instances, the goal is to help people recognize God's presence in all of life. The birth of a long-awaited child, the marriage of two people whose love is palpable, the death of parent, spouse, child, or friend, a sickness that is gradually weakening or suddenly ravaging the body and spirit of a friend or of oneself—such events, often accompanied by tears, laughter, contentment, or wonder, sometimes in strange combinations—await to be addressed.

18. William Drozdiak and Charles Trueheart, "God, Where Were You in Paris?" *The Washington Post*, July 27, 2000, A19.

Where do we turn for the words to name these experiences? First of all, look to the people themselves. The good homilist begins as a listener. What has *their* experience been? I often ask couples several questions when I meet with them before marriage: how did they meet, how did the proposal come about, what does each see as the greatest gift he or she brings to their marriage and what is the greatest gift the other brings? At the wake, take some time to talk with some of the family, asking about their loved one, allowing them the opportunity to talk about the deceased, the loved one's qualities, what they will miss most. While some occasions might be too shattering for any words, more often people welcome the chance to reflect on the deceased. Over the years I have become aware of certain common experiences and almost universal reactions: the anger people feel at a sudden death, the depression that settles on people as their bodies fail them, the excitement—and tension—surrounding a wedding day, the wonder evoked when looking at a baby, the physical expression of a couple's love.

At other times, the unique experiences surrounding these events can be reflected on and perhaps even referred to in preaching. Two personal examples come to mind: my cousin proposed by sending his fiancée around the city, leading her from one spot to another by a note with a rose attached left at each place, until she arrived at home to find the final rose and the request to dress for dinner. At dinner he proposed. Another instance occurred when my cousin came to me at my mother's wake and told me of a dream she had a few nights before. In the dream my mother was standing in the middle of a group of people talking and laughing. As my cousin drew near she recognized some of the people, among them our long-deceased grandparents. One young man she did not recognize. But, that day in the funeral parlor, this same cousin was looking at the collage of pictures of my mother taken at various times of her life that my brothers and I had put together. Among the pictures was a wedding picture of my mother and father who had been killed in World War II. My cousin said to me, "That young man in my dream was your father. I had never seen any pictures of him. But it was your father. He was the man in the wedding picture." The night my cousin had that dream was the night my mother went into a coma before dying the next day. I used that dream in the funeral homily, linking it with the words of Jesus, "I am going to prepare a place for you" (John 14:3), a place where those who loved in this life will gather together again.

While we preachers can become used to these events and especially to the rites that celebrate them, for those directly involved and those who gather with them, the ritual can have a powerful impact because of its ability to address these most profound human experiences. We serve by finding the words to name the experience and the feelings surrounding them, and our first resource can be the people themselves. The eloquence that comes from their own hearts can have greater power than the stored up files of poems, anecdotes, and literary quotations we preachers collect.

(b) *Biblical.* There is a stronger awareness today that the Scripture readings and the liturgical texts are our primary resources for naming and deepening the community's understanding of the human experience at the heart of the sacrament and for evoking a faith response of adoration and praise within the rite. Gerard Sloyan has written, however, that over the ages the quality of our sacramental celebrations has varied and this has had much to do with how the biblical word was employed. "The word of the bible that gives them (i.e., the rites) meaning has at times been minimized, even disregarded to the point that the non-verbal symbols have come close to being meaningless to the devotees; worse, the signs have sometimes come to have a meaning other than the biblical one assigned to them."[19]

Liturgist Mark Searle has called attention to the imaginal power of both biblical and liturgical texts, urging that they not be approached merely as "didactic messages wrapped up in some decorative covering which can be thrown away when the content is extracted." Rather, he argues, the images that come to us through the texts and in the rites are "to be toyed with, befriended, rubbed over and over again, until gradually and sporadically, they yield flashes of insight and encounter with the 'Reality' of which they sing."[20] This task falls particularly to the homilist: engaging the images of text and ritual and deciding which will serve as a "controlling image" on this occasion. Approaching these texts as imaginal realities, the preacher tries to offer listeners an entry into the mystery being celebrated. Images found within the text can both name the human aspect of the experience of those gathered and lead them to an awareness of the transcendental and transformative presence of Christ who is active through the sacrament. The texts thereby become opportunities (from the Latin word *porta* meaning gate) for encountering Christ present now.

---

19. Gerard S. Sloyan, "Do Catholics Understand the Sacraments?" *Church* (fall 1995) 12–13.

20. Mark Searle, "Images and Worship," *The Way* 24 (April 1984) 108.

To be more concrete regarding this capacity of the biblical text to name the human experience, let me offer an example. John Conway, a priest of the Archdiocese of Newark, wrote about going to a wedding where the bride and groom did the first reading together from the Song of Songs.[21] As the words of the text echoed through the church, speaking of eyes like doves and lips a scarlet thread, breasts like two fawns and legs like alabaster columns, some listeners began to squirm and others to giggle. Conway waited to see what the preacher was going to do with this reading in the homily. And what did he do? The preacher ignored it. Not a mention.

A couple had chosen the reading from Scripture that captured their experience of desire, of wanting to explore and discover the other, of reveling in the physical beauty of the other, of passionate, bodily love—the stuff of sacramentality. It captured one face of love just as the often-read Pauline text from 1 Corinthians (12:31–13:8) captures another face of mature married love as "patient, kind, not envious or boastful or arrogant or rude . . . (a love that) bears all things, believes all things, hopes all things, endures all things" (vv. 4ff.). The love expressed through our bodies flows into the love expressed in our souls. In different ways, both help to identify that fire of love which "deep waters cannot quench . . . nor floods sweep away" (Song of Songs 8:7).

Biblical texts can often be helpful in naming the feeling of the occasion as a liturgy begins. The joy of a recent wedding was captured succinctly in the lines from the first reading from Sirach 42: "How desirable are all God's works and how sparkling they are to see" (v. 22). The truth of the day was also captured in a later verse: "All things come in pairs. . . . Each supplements the virtues of the other. Who could ever tire of seeing God's glory?" (vv. 24–25). The deep sadness, even anger, that people carry in their hearts when a tragic death occurs is given expression by Martha, sister of Lazarus, who greets Jesus with the words, "Lord, if you had been here, my brother would not have died" (John 11:21). And the weariness and depression of illness can find an echo in the words of Elijah in the desert who cries out, "It is enough; now, O Lord, take away my life" (1 Kgs 19:4). It is a shame that Old Testament texts are rarely heard, apart from the snippets at Sunday Eucharist and certain celebrations like those of the Triduum. The biblical texts from Genesis suggested for the Rite of Penance

21. John W. Conway, "Have Patience—We'll Be in St. Croix Tonight," *Preaching Better*, ed. Frank J. McNulty (New York: Paulist, 1985) 122–30.

bring their mythic power to bear on naming the desires of the human heart to be "like God" (Gen 3:1-19) and to destroy what threatens to diminish us, even when it is our brother or sister (Gen 4:1-15).

Such stories witness to the human condition in a profound and timeless manner, holding up alternatives that demand ongoing choice in our lives: Adam and Eve deciding in favor of the autonomous "I" over the covenanting "Thou"; Cain and Abel reminding us that our relationship with God will only be as good as our relationship with each other. Both texts offer a provocative image of sin, first as a seducing serpent (Gen 3), which Walter Brueggemann describes as "the first to seem knowing and critical about God and to practice theology in place of obedience,"[22] and then as a crouching lion (or demon, depending on the translation) lurking at the door and lusting after Cain, ready to leap and devour him (Gen 4:7).[23] Such images correspond to our experience of sin on levels of both cognition and affect. Furthermore, each text memorably presents the Creator God, from the beginning intensely intimate with these human creatures, calling them to care for creation, seeking out human company in the cool of the evening, and, even after discovering they had turned away, clothing them for life outside the garden, and even putting a protective mark on the fratricidal Cain, as the blood of his brother cries out from the earth for vengeance. This Creator God becomes the redeeming God of the Exodus, wooing Abraham's descendants through his chosen servant Moses, the first, but not the last, unwilling prophet, a God always at work shaping Israel into a people peculiarly God's own, despite persistent infidelity and hard-heartedness—qualities in the human family that evolution, cultural development, and civilization have done little to alter in any substantial way.

The biblical texts mirror not only the human condition past and present and God's ongoing engagement with it, but also the future that comes to us as the gift of a gracious God, as when Isaiah speaks of the nations streaming to the holy mountain, where God will destroy "the veil that veils all peoples, the web that is woven over all nations; he will destroy death forever. The Lord God will wipe away the tears from all faces . . ." (25:6-7). These texts depict the God who promises "though your sins are like scarlet, they shall be like snow; though they are red as crimson, they shall become like wool" (Isa 1:18). The prophets, poets, and storytellers of the Old Testament offer us images and stories that

22. Walter Brueggemann, *Genesis* (Atlanta: John Knox Press, 1982) 48.
23. Ibid., 57–59.

mediate encounter with the merciful, loving God who is fully revealed to us in the story of Jesus, the Christ. While naming the experience conveys the homilist's presence to the community in the event that has brought them to church, and making use of the biblical text to do this brings Scripture and the community together in an immediate way, all this is at the service of bringing Christ and community together. This brings us to the third and most important characteristic of the homily.

(c) *Christocentric*. If the heart of the ritual celebration of the sacraments is an encounter with the saving mystery of Christ, then the heart of the homily is the presentation of this living, risen Lord. Through words, the homilist makes Christ present to the community's consciousness. Through words, an image of Christ can be planted in the communal imagination to bring about a deeper awareness and appropriation of the life of grace freely offered. Such an image often serves as the controlling image of the homily, with all other imagery leading up to and away from it. Thus, at the baptism of a child, the homilist may first read the story of Jesus and the children (Mark 10:13-16), then present Jesus in the homily as one who takes *these* children to be baptized into his arms *this* day, embraces and blesses them, declaring them children of the kingdom of God, and then turns to us and gives them back into our arms, entrusting them to our care. At the baptism of adults, these catechumens enter into the waters as into the tomb with Christ, dead to sin, but rising from the waters, alive to God in Christ Jesus (Rom 6:3-5).

The Christ of the wedding celebration can be the Lord of the banquet table calling and empowering the couple to live in his love (John 15:9-12), or the Christ transforming their human love, as water was changed into wine, into a love interpenetrated by divine love, a love that is to become a sacrament in the world, a love like the richest of wines (John 2:1-11). The Christ of the anointing of the sick is the same one who moved among the sick of his day, calling on them to rise up in faith (Matt 15:29-31); and the Christ of reconciliation is that one who today comes to those of us who have chosen to be "outsiders" as both the younger and older sons did, and bids us to come into the hall of celebration, rejoicing in our return (Luke 15:11ff.). The Christ of the funeral liturgy is the one who promises, "Have trust in God and trust in me. In my Father's house there are many mansions. I am going to prepare a place for you" (John 14:1-6), or the Christ who gently declares to us in our grief, "I am the resurrection and the life; the one who believes in me even though he or she should die, will live." And then, he asks us, "Do you believe this?" (John 11:26-27).

If there is a key question for the homily preached during any sacramental rite, it is this: how are your words making Christ present to the community on this occasion? How will you have Christ speak to *this* community at *this* time? It is not enough to read the story that situates Christ in the past. Nor is it enough to provide an instruction on the nature and effects of the sacrament, or the responsibilities of those receiving the sacrament. For a sacrament to be "something physical" which contains God's love, for it to mediate an encounter with the crucified, risen Jesus, for it to be a language event that speaks of the gift of God in Word and Spirit, and for it to convey that even now we are part of the worship of the eternal kingdom, the community needs to experience and know the presence of Jesus. This Jesus whom the evangelists and other New Testament authors captured long ago in their words, images, and stories continues to manifest himself in the objects, actions, and, particularly, the meanings mediated through the words of the sacramental rites—and most notably, through the homily.

(d) *Ecclesial.* The sacraments are ecclesial actions; they are celebrations *of* the Church, *by* the Church and *for* the Church. As the Constitution on the Sacred Liturgy reminds us, their end is to enable God's people to grow in holiness, becoming more fully the Body of Christ in the world, and to give worship to God the Father through Jesus in the power of the Holy Spirit (59). Liturgical theologian John Allyn Melloh reminds us that

> the rites do not focus singularly on an individual or individuals as objects of special ministrations. The couple to be married, for example, call the assembly together by their desire to proclaim publicly their mutual love and fidelity. The object of the celebration is not solely or even primarily the couple. The wide-lens focus is what is happening to and within the Church *because* of what this couple is doing as members of the ecclesial body.[24]

The homilist takes care to keep the "wide-lens focus" in operation so that the preaching within the rites remains directed toward the growth of the entire people of God, and their full, active, and conscious participation in the rite.

When preaching's focus becomes too narrow, the preacher gives in to the temptation of addressing only the participants at the center of the rite: the parents and godparents of the baptized, the couple to be

24. John Allyn Melloh, "Homily or Eulogy? The Dilemma of Funeral Preaching," *Worship* (November 1993) 504–5.

married, the sick to be anointed, the immediate family at the funeral, losing sight of the larger community. This does not necessarily exclude addressing a homily, or at least part of one, to the couple at a wedding or to the family at a funeral; preaching a homily that the congregation "overhears" has been accepted as a viable rhetorical strategy for some time.[25] Still, the homily functions in the sacramental rites as the transitional moment, enabling the community to move from attentive listening to the word of God to the celebration of the sacrament. It is even foreseen that the Liturgy of the Word might enable those who come as strangers to the occasion to draw closer to the mystery being celebrated. In the introductions to several of the rites, presiders are asked to keep in mind those present who take part in liturgical celebrations or hear the gospel only on such special occasions, either because they are not Catholics or are Catholics who rarely participate in liturgy or have left the practice of their faith.[26] The preaching at these occasions participates in the task of evangelization. Although this is not preaching's primary purpose here, as can be seen from the next characteristic to be considered, it is a reminder that the hearers of the word include all present.

(e) *Liturgical.* The homily has been designated as *integral* to the liturgy (General Instruction of the Roman Missal 41), that is, a necessary part of the whole of a particular liturgical action. It is not an occasion for a lecture on the nature of a particular sacrament or a prolonged exhortation on duties and responsibilities, or even primarily an opportunity to evangelize. As *FIYH* states, "the liturgical gathering is not primarily an educational assembly. . . ." The homily may well include evangelization, catechesis, and exhortation, but its primary purpose is to be part of the liturgy. It serves to bridge the Liturgy of the Word and the Liturgy of the Sacrament, offering a word of meaning that interprets both the wonderful event that has caused the community to come together and the ritual action that immediately follows. The homily prepares the community for what is about to occur, evoking the faith of those gathered so that the prayers and hymns of the rite truly become those of the community and the ritual action expressed in the rite is affirmed by the body of Christ here present. The homily calls on those

25. See Fred Craddock, *Overhearing the Gospel: Preaching and Teaching the Faith to Persons Who Have Heard It All Before* (Nashville: Abingdon, 1978).

26. For instance, see *Rite of Marriage*, Introduction, no.9; also *Order of Christian Funerals*, General Introduction, no. 12.

directly affected to be conscious of the responsibilities flowing from the sacrament, to take them up willingly and joyfully.

Liturgy as the work of the people is first and foremost the worship of God. And the immediate purpose of preaching in the liturgy is to enable this worship by stirring up the faith of the community. But do we ourselves trust the liturgy to do its work, to have any effect either on us or God? Annie Dillard wrote years ago that we tend to be blissfully unaware of ritual's power:

> Why do people in churches seem like cheerful, brainless tourists on a packaged tour of the Absolute?. . . Does anyone have the foggiest idea what sort of power we so blithely invoke? Or, as I suspect, does no one believe a word of it? The churches are children playing on the floor with their chemistry sets, mixing up a batch of TNT to kill a Sunday morning. It is madness to wear ladies' straw hats and velvet hats to church; we should all be wearing crash helmets. Ushers should issue life preservers and signal flares; they should lash us to the pews. For the sleeping god may wake someday and take offense, or the waking god may draw us out to where we can never return.[27]

When we come to recognize liturgy's power and allow it to seep into our beings, it may then overflow into the ongoing mission of the Church in the world, empowering us further for our work there as disciples of Jesus Christ and calling us joyfully to take on the responsibilities flowing from a particular celebration. This can include supporting parents and godparents in the religious formation of their children, caring for the sick, being responsive to the grieving.

The immediate purpose of preaching, then, is to evoke a response of faith leading to worship of God. As preachers, our failure to trust liturgy often reflects itself in an overly didactic approach when presiding and preaching. Kathleen Norris writes that when liturgy is given over to didactic purposes, "it becomes sluggish, like a bad poem, with the weight of ideas, the gravity of political ideology."[28] When we do begin to go with the flow of the liturgical rite, we will find that our words can be more selective, taking on the characteristics of good poetry: suggestive, evocative, allusive. Then we are more likely to effect those good celebrations that foster and nourish faith, instead of those poor celebrations that weaken and destroy faith.

27. Annie Dillard, *Teaching a Stone to Talk* (New York: Harper, 1983) 40.
28. Kathleen Norris, *Amazing Grace, a Vocabulary of Faith* (New York: Riverhead, 1998) 247.

(f) *Personal. Can* every homily be personal? *Should* every homily be personal? It depends on how you understand "personal." If "personal" means that the preacher offers some revealing, intimate aspect of his or her life in the course of preaching, I would say, "Spare us." If "personal" means saying something that touches the hearts of the people involved and that is specific to this occasion, I would give a tentative yes. Most likely preaching at a communal rite of the anointing of the sick or a communal Rite of Penance will not have the same kind of personal touch that can characterize the wedding of a couple you know very well or the baptism of that same couple's first child. But all these occasions can be personal in the way noted by *FIYH*, which refers to a survey taken several years ago in which parishioners were asked what they hoped to experience during a homily. The majority said they wanted simply to hear "a person of faith speaking" (15). This willingness to share one's faith makes a homily profoundly personal. It does not mean one has to share intensely intimate anecdotes or bare one's soul regarding inner demons and ongoing struggles. Certainly there is room on occasion for the personal story that witnesses to the power of the gospel in one's life, but this could hardly be sustained every week. Let's face it, our lives are not that interesting. When in doubt about the appropriateness of a personal story, share it first with someone whose critical sense you respect; if such a person is not at hand, keep it in reserve.

A homily can be personal in other ways. The preacher might refer to something said or done by those, whether living or deceased, for whom the rite is being celebrated. The funeral rite is quite clear on the homily not being a eulogy; at the same time, "the homily may properly include an expression of praise and gratitude to God for God's gifts, particularly the gift of a Christian life, to the deceased person."[29] While the eulogy points to the achievements of a particular life, a homily always places the proclamation of the paschal mystery at the heart of preaching. The primary criterion I use in dealing with personal material at a funeral concerns how it serves the end of preaching: will such material lead the community to pray for the deceased and to celebrate the paschal mystery as an expression of praise and thanksgiving for God's salvation given to us through Christ? Or does it focus attention

---

29. This statement is found as a parenthetical remark in the Introduction to the Rite of Funerals, no. 41, found in *The Rites of the Catholic Church* (New York: Pueblo, 1976) 674. It was not included in any further editions, but I have found it helpful when discussing the difference between a homily and a eulogy.

elsewhere? On other occasions, the homily is not the place for a "roast" or to try out one's comic skills. If I am thinking of including something said in conversation, I will first discuss it with the people involved, asking their permission. Weddings and funerals are the occasions most likely to need extra care in this regard. What might seem amusing at a first reflection might later prove lamentable.

(g) *Brief.* When speaking of the homily, the rites themselves often use the qualifier "brief." What constitutes "brief" is a cultural phenomenon. Certain communities do not expect a brief word, nor want one. In some African-American faith communities, the funeral is a time when many voices are invited to speak about the deceased. In other communities, brevity is always appreciated. With the catechesis provided in preparation for the various sacramental celebrations, the principal participants should have received adequate formation, so there is no need for a prolonged instruction. As for the rest of the community who gathers to participate, trust in the communicative power of the rite itself. We tend towards overkill in our use of words and towards neglect in our use of silence. Barbara Brown Taylor calls on preachers in all situations to practice the virtue of *economy*: "to say only what we know to be true, to say it from the heart, and to sit down."[30]

To feed the hunger for meaning is to be engaged in a never finished project. Perhaps one of the greatest gifts the Church has received recently has been the recovery of the Rite of Christian Initiation of Adults (RCIA), which reminds us that the reality of conversion is an ongoing process. One is never finished walking the road it puts us on. Certainly the catechumens are not "finished" before they are baptized. Kathleen Hughes writes: "The question is not whether the catechumens are finished, perfectly converted products, but whether they give evidence that they have committed themselves to the process: a lifelong journey of faith formation in the context of the community, its worship and its mission."[31] The Church formally recognizes this condition of the catechumens being unfinished. Although the elect are baptized into the body of Christ at the Easter Vigil, the following weeks bring a time of further mystagogy, deepening their understanding of the mysteries they have entered. But, again, neither the catechesis of the yearlong period of the RCIA nor the mystagogy of Easter results in a "finished product." They—and we—remain "unfinished" until we pass

---

30. Barbara Brown Taylor, *When God Is Silent* (Cambridge: Cowley, 1998) 101.
31. Hughes, *Saying Amen*, 46–47.

through death into eternal life. This reminder is something the entire community needs. The celebration of the sacramental rites is a continual invitation to turn more fully to the God who never stops coming to seek and save us.

One final comment concerns the deep impact these rites can have on all preachers. The celebration of the sacramental rites has the potential to expand preachers in two ways, one internal, the other external. First, by developing what has been called the "sacramental imagination," so necessary for engaging in the work of preaching, so that it might be at work in our approach to all of life.[32] This capacity allows preachers to recognize God's presence and the workings of grace in both daily and special events in the human story, and to make insightful and integral connections with the biblical writings, especially the words and deeds of Jesus. For this to happen with greater ease and frequency, preachers need to cultivate the sacramental imagination as they do other faculties. Again, Andre Dubus reminds us, "Sacraments are myriad. . . . It is limiting to believe that sacraments occur only in churches, or when someone comes to us in a hospital or at home and anoints our brows and eyes and ears, our noses and lips, hearts and hands and feet."[33] It is the sacramental imagination that allows us to see that all is holy and that "whatever mirrors the presence of Christ and the power of God in our world can be considered a sacred mystery,"[34] that is, a sacrament.

Secondly, celebrating the sacramental rites can also make us more alert to the need to develop new rituals in response to other human experiences. Herbert Anderson and Edward Foley[35] have reflected on this need in relation to such experiences of loss as miscarriage, stillbirth, newborn death, the withdrawal of life-support systems, as well as divorce, leaving home, retirement, and making a recommitment in a relationship

---

32. See David Tracy, *The Analogical Imagination: Christian Theology and the Culture of Pluralism* (New York: Crossroad, 1981); also see Mary Catherine Hilkert, O.P., *Naming Grace: Preaching and the Sacramental Imagination* (New York: Continuum, 1997); Andrew Greeley, *The Catholic Imagination* (Berkeley: University of California, 2000).

33. Dubus, *Meditations from a Movable Chair*, 86.

34. Dennis C. Smolarski, S.J., *Sacred Mysteries: Sacramental Principles and Liturgical Practice* (New York: Paulist, 1994).

35. Herbert Anderson and Edward Foley, Capuchin, "Experiences in Need of Ritual," *The Christian Century* (Nov. 5, 1997) 1002–8; see also their *Mighty Stories, Dangerous Rituals: Weaving Together the Human and Divine* (San Francisco: Jossey-Bass, 1997).

("promising again"). Such experiences invite ritual with its gifts of silence, word, and symbol, a time to ponder, to speak, and to engage in some symbolic action that allows movement of the spirit—and the Spirit!—by intertwining the human and divine story. Lacking these elements, people might continue to have the experience but miss the meaning.

I would like to conclude this reflection on preaching within the rites with the words of Nelson Mandela, spoken within the ritual of his inauguration as the president of the Republic of South Africa. Mandela's words reveal his own exercise of the sacramental imagination within the powerful ritual event that marked the transition of his country from apartheid to its new future. His words challenge all his hearers, present and future, to join him in a common understanding of the meaning of their lives:

> Our deepest fear is not that we are inadequate. Our deepest fear is that we are powerful beyond measure. It is our Light, not our Darkness that most frightens us. We ask ourselves, who am I to be brilliant, gorgeous, talented, fabulous? Actually, who are you NOT to be? You are a child of God. Your playing small does not serve the world. There is nothing enlightening about shrinking so that other people won't feel unsure around you. We were born to make manifest the glory of God that is within us. It is not just in some of us; it is in everyone. As we let our own light shine, we unconsciously give other people permission to do the same. As we are liberated from our own fear, our presence automatically liberates others.

## Homilies within the Sacramental Rites

*A. Homily for the Rite of Baptism within the Sunday Eucharist:*

*Children will listen . . .*

(Texts for Seventh Sunday, Cycle A:
Lev 19:1-2, 17-18; 1 Cor 3:16-23; Matt 5:38-48)

Near the end of the Stephen Sondheim's fairytale musical,
   *Into the Woods,*
   (a musical about parents and children, in addition to witches and giants)
a witch turns to a baker holding his infant son and sings:
"Careful the things you say, children will listen.
Careful the things you do, children will see and learn."
The song goes on to say that children do not always obey, but they do
   listen.

And they look to us to learn what they should be.
So we, in turn, need be very careful before we say, "Listen to me."

If the silence in the theatre was any indication, people were listening to
    this song.
It strikes a chord of truth.
Children do listen and see and learn—from us!
Frightening, when you think about it.

Today on this ordinary Sunday in Ordinary Time,
    we have come here to witness a wonderful event.
A child will be claimed as an adopted daughter of God.
In bringing Kara to be baptized, Bill and Anne,
    you have agreed to have her immersed into the waters of new life,
    and joined to the living body of Christ.
She has no idea what will be done to her and for her in a few minutes.
If she is to learn about what happened this day, she will learn it from us
—from this community of faith, most likely from her parents and god-
    parents.
More importantly, if she is to learn the meaning behind what hap-
    pened today, she will learn that from us, most especially, from you,
    her parents, and you, John and Claire, her godparents, from what
    you say and do.
Children will listen. And see. And learn.

So, we pause a moment, after listening ourselves to the three readings
    this morning.
We ask, "Do they help us to grasp this mystery of entering into the life
    of the Trinity?"
They are given to us for our own understanding, first of all.
For we must understand what it means to live in the Spirit of adoption
    before we can teach it.

"Be holy," cries the book of Leviticus.
No beating around the bush on that.
"Be holy as the Lord, your God, is holy."
Quite an agenda to lay on an adult, much less on one so young as Kara.
But that is where the word of Leviticus connects with Paul's word to the
    Corinthians, a most contentious community not particularly success-
    ful at being holy.
"You are the temple of God," Paul writes, adding, "with Christ as the
    cornerstone!"

The call to be holy is given today to a people, not just to individuals.
And this people has been empowered by the Spirit of Jesus, the risen Lord,
    and in the process is being shaped into God's own dwelling place.
Kara joins us in this, becoming part of the temple of the living God.
So, "Be holy," urges Leviticus.
And with confidence in the power of the Spirit, we answer, "So be it.
    Amen."

When we sing, "Holy, holy, holy" at every Eucharist,
    this is as much a political and social cry as it is the prayer of church
    people.
We are committing ourselves to the holiness of God,
    which is meant to flow through us and out into the world.
God's holiness is found in our doing justice, God's justice,
    which is not to be confused with human justice.
Jesus' words today image that justice:
"You have heard it said, 'An eye for an eye, and a tooth for a tooth,'
    but I say to you, 'Don't resist the evildoer. Turn the other cheek.'"
"This is wisdom?" we ask, just as the listeners of Jesus' day asked,
    skepticism written on their faces.
And they were right to question, for the old "eye for an eye" approach
    did have a certain logic to it.
It meant that if I took one of your sheep, you could not take my herd.
If I killed one of your kin, you could not attack my whole family.
There was wisdom in all this—the wisdom of proportionate retaliation.

Anyone can understand that.
But this turning the cheek, going the extra mile, giving the cloak in
    addition to your coat—that was just crazy.
"No," Jesus says patiently, "it is God's wisdom."
And that is what *you*—what *we*—are supposed to teach this child.
Careful the things you say . . . careful the things you do . . . children
    will see and learn.

What might happen if Kara listens?
She might turn up outside prison the night they are going to give some
    murderer a lethal injection, protesting it, like that "bleeding-heart
    nun" Sr. Helen Prejean.
She might end up working in a soup kitchen like some of these "naive
    idealists" you find at S.O.M.E. (So Others Might Eat) or the Catho-
    lic Worker, rather than going to a good job at a prestigious law firm.

She even might end up in some hellhole like Sarajevo or Rwanda
  or in a more familiar but no less violent Inner City, U.S.A.

Careful the things you say, and do.
The gospel of Jesus runs counter to the wisdom of our age as it has to
  most ages.
It tells us the way of domination, accumulation, and manipulation is
  not the path to peace.
"Maybe not," the sensible say, "but it is the way to security."
"Be perfect, be complete, be whole," Jesus invites.
"Well, what about being nice? Isn't nice good, or good enough?" we ask.
"Be holy," comes back to us. "Be poor in spirit, hungry for justice, for-
  giving."

How will she ever do this?
And how will we ever teach her? Since we so often avoid it.
This day, Jesus breathes on us once more, and the Spirit moves over us,
  as it will move over this bread and wine.
And just as it will be changed, so too we will be, into the body of Christ,
  Grain by grain, ever so gradually.
And we will eat and drink and we will be holy, as God in heaven is holy,
  as Jesus is holy, and as the Spirit is holy.
And we will be swept up ever more completely into the mystery of God,
  the very holiness of God, enfolded into the body of Christ.
All of us and Kara with us. Amen.

*B. Homily within the Rite of Marriage*

"Just Forty Words"

(Texts: Song of Songs 2:8-10, 14, 16; 8:6-7;
Rom 12:1-2, 9-13; Matt 22:35-40)

When I asked Ann and Brendan how they met, they said, "At a party."
And once they began to talk to each other that evening, something
  happened, clicked, they ended up talking and talking and talking . . .
  long into the night and beyond.
I have heard this a lot from couples—how when they first met, they
  talked and talked.
One couple's meeting was on the New York subway.
When the fellow got on and he saw this lovely woman sitting there,
  reading, he was smitten.
He said he forgot all about his friend with him.

He did all he could to get this totally unknown woman's attention,
  trying to find a way to talk to her.
He knew the odds were against him.
After all, it was a subway, and the next stop could be the end.
So he started soliloquizing about Mark Twain—she was reading
  *Huckleberry Finn.*
He brought up everything he knew about Mark Twain and Huck Finn
  and the Mississippi River, but she kept trying to ignore him—it *was*
  a subway.
At one point he took off one of her shoes,
  so she couldn't walk out if they reached her stop.
(She said that when she was explaining this meeting to her parents
  and said how he took off her shoe, her father reacted: "I don't want
  to hear any more.")
But they began to talk and then got off the subway and went for a drink
  and then for coffee and hours later were still talking.
And he said that at a certain point he found himself thinking,
  "God must really love me."
I have two thoughts to share with all of you today.
First, there are words and there are *words.*
Brendan and Ann, like many other couples, began their relationship with
  words.
Words are very important, as you know, and not only when first coming
  to know another.
Words are crucial for the deeper knowing that comes with the years.
Words share news but more important are the words that share the
  heart—speaking of daily joys, surprises, sorrows, fears, and hurts.
Words bring laughter, and words offer apology and ask forgiveness.
Words are very important for growth in a relationship,
  but the words you will speak in a few moments are among the words
  of a lifetime.

Today we have all come here to hear you say some words—forty to be
  exact:
"I, Brendan, take you, Ann, to be my wife.
I promise to be true to you in good times and in bad, in sickness and
  in health,
I will love you and honor you all the days of my life."
And something wonderful will happen—a transformation—in just
  forty words.

It will no longer be Ann and Brendan in a way that it was up until now.
More like AnnandBrendan or BrendanandAnn—
     That is how you will be thought of together for the rest of your lives.
These words will change the reality of your life together, pledging you
     to a commitment that is breathtaking in its depth and extent—for it
     is a commitment for always.
Today begins the lifelong process of two becoming one as a married
     couple.
In so doing, you are committing yourself to a love that is faithful, fruitful,
     and forever.
In so doing, you are committed to being a force for love in this world.
All this because of the forty words you are about to say to each other.
Just forty words . . .

And that brings me to the second point:
As the young man on the subway realized, God really does love you.
I hope you know this for no other reason than the wonderful fact
     that God has brought you two together and has bound you in mutual
     love.
God has said, "I love you" through the gift God has given in each other.
The three readings today speak of the different faces of love.
There is the passionate love of the couple in the Song of Songs.
This wonderful love poem has been heard by devout Jews and Christians
     as expressing the voice of God's love for the people chosen to be God's
     own.
God is the lover who comes seeking the beloved.
And the passionate love of a man and woman mirrors this divine love,
     indeed, human love is empowered to be a sign of this divine love in
     our world.

The love Paul is speaking about in his letter to the Romans can be
     thought of as a practical love, but one that is a special gift of God,
     the love God has poured into our hearts at baptism with the gift of
     the Spirit.
This love moves us towards God and others, the breath of God breathed
     into us, the wind of the Spirit moving us out into the world, the fire
     of God that transforms our living bodies into a sacrifice to God.
Paul paints a portrait of a people alive in God's Spirit of love:
"Prefer the good to evil.
Love each other with respect; be hopeful when trials come and keep
     praying.

Treat everyone with kindness; make real friends with the poor.
Be hospitable and live at peace with everyone."
While the love in the Song of Songs witnesses to passion's power,
    the love in the letter to the Romans is grounded in everyday effort.

Jesus' words today come from a section of Matthew's Gospel that has
    been called "Jesus' final exam."
Different groups have been coming to question him;
    here we have a lawyer sent in by the Pharisees.
There were 613 laws of Moses—
    the experts were endlessly debating which was most important.
And so the lawyer asks Jesus for his opinion.
Jesus turns to the book of Deuteronomy: "Hear, O Israel, you shall love the
    Lord your God, with all your heart, all your mind, and all your soul."
Then he quotes the book of Leviticus: "And you shall love your neighbor
    as yourself."
For Jesus and his followers, life was to have its priorities.
Jesus knew that God's law was not about the priority of rules,
    it was about the priority of love.
We have heard this so often that perhaps it has lost its power.
Yet we need to be reminded again and again about the priorities of life.
We live in a culture that tells us life is about accumulation and achieve-
    ment, promotions and portfolios.
Tom Wolfe says the American credo is "Acquire, acquire, acquire."
The words of Jesus invite us to think and act otherwise.
When life is drawing to a close, what is going to matter?
Acquisitions? Achievements? Activities listed on our resumes?
Or *whether*—and *how*—we have loved?
The best legacy we can leave to our children, family, and friends is a
    legacy of love.
That is what lodges in the hearts of those whose lives you touch.

It is a wonderful thing to be here today for all of us.
Brendan and Ann, you call us to think about what really matters.
We come here to the place where the Catholic community celebrates
    its most important moments as a community: its baptisms, Eu-
    charists, confirmations, anointings, reconciliation services, and fu-
    nerals—and, happiest of all, its weddings.
All of these occasions celebrate God's love and promises,
    done in the name of Jesus Christ and in the power of the Holy Spirit.
We celebrate something God wants to last forever.

We delight in sharing this moment with you and we promise our prayers
and support.
But now we turn to you.
Come forward and face the community that loves you.
It is time for you to speak—just 40 words.

### C. Homily for the Rite of Anointing of the Sick
### within the Sunday Liturgy

Several times a year Holy Trinity parish celebrates the liturgy of
the anointing of the sick within the Sunday Eucharist. In addition, this
particular Sunday (the fourth Sunday of Easter) had been designated
"Vocation Sunday" and preachers were asked to address this, asking the
community to recommend individuals perceived as potential candi-
dates for the diaconate, religious life, and priesthood for the purpose of
inviting them to a retreat.

### *Shepherds—in this day and age?*

(Texts for the fourth Sunday of Easter,
B Cycle: Acts 4:8-12; 1 John 3:1-2; John 10:11-18)

I once had a New Testament professor who proposed tearing John 10
from the Bible. He thought it had done too much damage throughout
our history to ever redeem itself. The problem was not Jesus as the
Good Shepherd, but the other side of the equation. He thought that
holding up an image of the people of God as sheep had created the ideal
of passive people whose purpose in life was to "pay, pray, and obey."
I suspect he was being facetious, but he made us think about this image
of Jesus and us. Today, however, I would certainly counter his proposal.

God as shepherd is one of the oldest images in Scriptures:
    "The Lord is my shepherd; I shall not want," begins Psalm 23.
"He makes me lie down in green pastures; he leads me beside still waters;
    he restores my soul."
Both Jeremiah and Ezekiel present God raging against the "bad shep-
    herds" who neglect God's people; God then declares, "*I* will shep-
    herd my people."
The image of the shepherd spoke of God's care and love for the people
    of Israel.

And when the leaders of a later generation asked Jesus why he hung
out with sinners and ate and drank with them, he started off with a
story about a shepherd going in search of just one sheep, leaving
ninety-nine behind.

This same Jesus looked with compassion at the crowd who had followed
him out to a deserted place "because they were like sheep without a
shepherd."

And today we hear Jesus say to us: "I am the good shepherd;
the good shepherd lays down his life for the sheep."

For all the problems with the image in our urban setting,

and all the inherited problems that accompany having people see
themselves as sheep, there is still life left in the old image.

It conveys the message that Jesus will not let us stay lost, no matter
what form that takes.

This Jesus continues to search us out and carry us back,
when we can't make it on our own.

The world continues to need shepherds.

We need those who are willing to do it as a lifetime occupation,
by lives of service as priests, religious, and permanent deacons.

The Washington archdiocese has a program entitled "Called By Name."

Today we are asking you to let us know about anyone you think might
have a calling to be a priest, sister, brother, or permanent deacon.

Don't worry; no "Vocation Squad" is going to bang at someone's door
after midnight.

But an invitation will be extended to come to a special diocesan event
where they will have a chance to speak with those who have chosen
this way of life.

I learned in my own life not to underestimate the power of an encouraging word.

I would not be here this morning if Sister Leonardine, S.S.N.D., had not
said one spring morning, "Jimmy, do you think it's possible God
might be calling you to be a priest?"

I was only thirteen at the time, but a seed had been planted—

or, more fitting for today, the voice of the Shepherd had been heard.

You might ask how you would know if a person might have such a calling?

People talk about looking for "leadership qualities," which can be a bit
vague.

I think we might go back to today's gospel for its criteria:

"The good shepherd lays down his life for his sheep."

First criterion: is there a capacity for self-giving, self-sacrifice, living for others?

Second criterion: is there an ability to live simply?

"The good shepherd is not a hireling"—that is, one who works just for the pay.

If you are looking to make a lot of money, this is not for you.

(*The Washington Post Magazine* today published a list of salaries in today's D.C. area;—mine falls between the Domino Pizza delivery person and a fellow who bills himself as "The Human Gorilla.")

Third criterion: "The good shepherd knows his or her people,"
    that is, a person who understands people, takes an interest in them,
    listens to them, recognizes their gifts and abilities,
    and works to empower them further.

Fourth criterion: "The good shepherd has other sheep that do not belong to this fold."

The good shepherd is concerned beyond his own boundaries, aware that God wants a family that includes *all* people, not just the present members, aware that God's will is that there be one flock, one shepherd.

And the last criterion: good shepherds are in communion with the One who sent them; they are men and women intimate with God, pray-ers.

There is a need for shepherds on many occasions.

As the community of the one Good Shepherd, baptized into his dying and rising, we all share in the work of the Shepherd in different ways.

There are many ways to care for the little ones, the lost, and the weak.

Today we will do this in one particular way by calling forth the sick and elderly among us to receive the sacrament of the anointing of the sick.

Sickness can be isolating, and people who find their bodies failing them in different ways can feel cut off from others.

And what begins in the body can affect our soul.

Sickness can make us wonder about God, whether God cares, where is God in all this.

So we gather here this morning as we celebrate the Eucharist to support and pray that the Good Shepherd will raise up our sick from their illnesses, lift their spirits, bless them with the grace of the Holy Spirit.

We hold them in the embrace of our love and the support of our faith.

We place our hands upon them and silently pray for the Spirit to come upon them.

Then we will anoint them with oil on the forehead and hands, the
    soothing oil of healing.
This event also reminds us to reach out in other ways to any sick we
    know whether in our families or among our friends, and especially
    to be on the watch for those among us who have no one.
The Risen Lord, our Good Shepherd, will come at the end of time and
    say to those who heard his voice in their lifetime: "I was hungry and
    you fed me, thirsty and you gave me to drink, sick and you visited
    me . . ."
Is there a need for shepherds today? Without a doubt.
Pray the Good Shepherd to raise up men and women in his image.

### D. Homily for a Funeral Liturgy

My uncle's funeral was a few days before Christmas in 1997. Be-
sides the comfort that the liturgical and biblical texts are capable of
bringing to the grieving, on this occasion the Liturgy of the Hours
contained an eloquent word.

### Death Is a Passing Season

(Texts: Isa 25:6a, 7-9; Phil 3:20-21; John 6:37-40)

George died as the season of winter was beginning,
    and as the season of Advent was ending.
Both seasons speak to us this morning as we gather to pray for him,
    and as we try to find comfort in the hope our faith in Jesus offers.

Winter is the time of darkness, of cold, of the fading of the light.
When someone we love dies,
    we know that winter is not just a season of the year,
    but also a season of the heart.
With George's dying, we know winter.
At this moment, the world seems colder;
    we already miss the warmth he brought us.
George Leo Wallace was a man of faith, a man of family,
    a man devoted to his country which he served for thirty years in the
    Navy.
He was respected as a generous man by his friends and neighbors.
If you needed a favor, or help with the odd job, you could always ask
    George.

But George was more than this: he was fun and funny.

When I asked my aunt what she thought his children would remember
most about him, she replied, "He loved to party!"

And those who saw him do the Hawaiian dance with hula hoop and
coconut shells can testify to the truth of this.

We will miss the laughter he brought us, the kindness, the ease of being
with him.

So it seems fitting that winter was beginning as he was leaving us.

But how equally appropriate that we are in the final days of Advent,
rich in promise for those who believe.

Even though the world around us went into Christmas mode weeks ago
with mall decorations and endless repetitions of Christmas carols,
we gather here as a people of Advent, longing for the One who will
come again.

As Paul's words remind us: "our citizenship is in heaven, and from it
we await a savior, the Lord Jesus Christ."

We wait on the Lord to return because life is not all we would wish.

We know this especially when someone we love dies.

And we cry out, "Come, Lord Jesus. Restore what has been taken.
Wipe every tear away. Gather us all into the fullness of the reign of
God."

George died during the final days of Advent.

Each night during the eight days before Christmas,
as darkness settles, the Church calls on Jesus to come, giving him a
different title.

"O Root of Jesse," "O Ancient Lord of Israel," "O Emmanuel" are some
of these titles.

On the night George died, the Church was praying these words during
its Evening Prayer:

"O Key of David, O Royal Power of Israel, controlling at your will the
gate of heaven:
Come, break down the prison walls of death, and lead us into freedom,
the freedom from sickness and pain, the freedom from loss and
sorrow."

And last night, as we gathered at the wake,
these words were prayed throughout the world:
"O King of all the nations, the joy of every human heart, . . .
come and save the one you fashioned from the dust."

This morning Jesus says to us in our loss that the very reason he came
   was to save all of us "fashioned from the dust":
"Everything that the Father gives me will come to me,
   and I will not reject anyone who comes to me, because I came down
   from heaven not to do my own will but the will of the one who sent
   me.
And *this* is the will of the one who sent me,
   that I should not lose anything of what he gave me,
   but that I should raise it on the last day."

Today Advent speaks to Winter.
Advent speaks to the winter that lodges in our hearts,
   reminding us that the Child whose birth we soon will celebrate
   came to bring us life, to be born in us, to walk with us all our days,
   and that he died for us, and we were baptized into that death.
But today, above all, we remember that this Jesus was raised from the
   dead, and is the pledge of new life for all who believe in him.
Advent challenges winter, proclaiming before its barrenness that Jesus
   is Lord of life.
And in these final days of this season, Advent gives us its own gift:
   a vision that all who have died have crossed over into a new way of
   being in God.
As the Preface of the Eucharistic Prayer reminds us:
   "for those who die in Christ, life is not ended, merely changed."
We trust that George has already passed over into that life,
   joining his son Mike and his daughter Karen who have gone on ahead.

Tears may flow this morning as we take George to his final resting place,
   but we are moving toward that mountain where God will destroy
   death forever, where the Lord God will wipe away the tears from all
   faces and where we will join in joy and laughter with Jesus, the Lord
   of life.
May we walk in the peace and comfort that our faith in Jesus Christ
   brings.

## Summary

   The preaching within the sacramental rituals calls the preacher to
feed the hunger for meaning. We desire to understand the meaning of
both the everyday random events that impinge on our lives and those
special, transitional moments that mark more dramatic changes. While

the liturgy of the Sunday and daily Eucharist can be often approached as offering a word of meaning for the former, it is the other sacramental celebrations that allow preachers to address those more life-altering occasions such as birth, marriage, death, and the need to come to terms with sinfulness and sickness. Preaching within the rites that responds to the hunger for meaning may be helped by the following suggestions:

1. Take time to reflect on the human experience that has brought the community together for a ritual celebration. What are the feelings that surround this event? How does culture and custom influence how they, and we, approach this experience. Allow sufficient time for the crust of habit and familiarity to crack. The occupational hazard of "been there, done that" can be very much at play for the overworked presider-preacher who loses touch with the great importance of these events in the lives of the people.

2. Immerse yourself in the biblical and liturgical texts. The images of the gospel and other texts of the Liturgy of the Word can serve as primary vehicles for naming what is about to happen in the sacrament. Allow time for the images to work on you, to evoke other images that might aid the community's movement into meaning. Allow the readings and prayers to inform your message. Even reading the introduction to the rite can be helpful for rekindling the fire and enthusiasm needed to enlighten minds and warm hearts.

3. Focus on one way to present Jesus Christ as present and at work within the sacramental ritual. Look especially to the gospel reading, choosing a text that is fitting for this particular occasion. Then, feature a specific image of the Lord; consider allowing this Jesus to address the community whether through the exact words of the gospel (the power of direct discourse is great) or through other appropriate words that proclaim the Good News. Help the faithful to see and hear him.

4. The ultimate function of the homily is to lead all present into the celebration of the sacrament as an act of worship. Take care to address the homily to the community of faith, with attention given to those more directly involved in the sacramental rite. All are called to be participants. Neither intense individualism nor canned anonymity serves preaching within the rites.

5. For further reading:

- Kathleen Hughes, *Saying Amen: A Mystagogy of Sacrament* (Chicago: Liturgy Training Publications, 1999).

- James M. Schmitmeyer, *The Words of Worship: Presiding and Preaching at the Rites* (Staten Island, N.Y.: Alba House, 1988).
- William Skudlarek, O.S.B., *The Word in Worship: Preaching in a Liturgical Context* (Nashville: Abingdon, 1981).

# Chapter 4

# Preaching Through the Saints and the Hunger for Belonging: I—The Saints

*"The Saints come,*
*as human as a mouth,*
*with a bag of God in their backs . . ."*[1]

(Anne Sexton, "The Saints Come Marching In")

*It is most fitting, therefore, that we love those friends and co-heirs of*
*Jesus Christ who are also our sisters and brothers and outstanding bene-*
*factors, and that we give due thanks to God for them . . .*

(*Lumen Gentium* 50)

## The Saints and Our Hunger for Belonging

The final hunger of the heart this work will address is the hunger for belonging; it can also be named as our deep desire for connectedness, community, and companionship. Robert Wuthnow uses the metaphor "loose connections" as a title for his book on the breakdown of community in our nation.[2] In a recent study, 75 percent of the public thought this a serious national problem. The term "loose connections" is primarily applied to those tenuous bonds that hold together groups and organizations, but it can also extend to marriage, the family, friendship, and other forms of social contact. Consider the family. Many of today's children live in fear their parents will divorce; parents

1. Anne Sexton, *The Awful Rowing Toward God* (Boston: Houghton Mifflin, 1975) 79.
2. Robert Wuthnow, *Loose Connections: Joining Together in America's Fragmented Communities* (Cambridge: Harvard University Press, 1998).

share in that, in addition to having a fear of losing their jobs; grandparents fear the future, wondering if they will end their days alone and abandoned. One indication of the degree of loneliness and isolation in our society reveals itself in the fact that suicide is the second highest cause of death among teens. The fastest growing category of households is the one-member household, which is presently about 25 percent of all households.[3] Despite the continuous growth of the population, loneliness has not lessened. The craving for community continues.

Preachers address this hunger when they help people to experience a connection with the larger faith community. It is appropriate to think of the homily as "a unifying moment in the celebration of the liturgy, deepening and giving expression to the unity that is already present through the sacrament of baptism" (*FIYH*, 6–7). But the homily not only has the power to deepen the bonds of those present by joining them in a common vision of faith, it can also extend the sense of community beyond the immediate setting to include those who have gone before us. This is particularly true when preaching on the feasts or memorials of the saints. These days allow for a face-to-face encounter with one or several of those who have fought the good fight, finished the race, and kept the faith, and have already received the crown reserved for them in heaven (see 2 Tim 4:7-8). It is with these companions that the feasts allow us to make contact and form connections, enabling us to cross the boundaries of time, space, culture, and whatever else can separate us were it not for Christ who brings all together.

When poet Anne Sexton spoke of the saints as having "a bag of God in their backs," I see them arriving on the human scene bearing the *weight* of God, which is another way of saying the "glory of God": the *kabod Yahweh*. These men and women of all ages and cultures continue to approach us as bearers of the divine glory. They are the enfleshed response over the centuries to the request some Greeks made long ago to the apostle Philip: "We wish to see Jesus" (John 12:21). God is revealed in their lives inasmuch as these men and women have been transformed into the image of Christ, the Constitution on the Church instructs us (no. 50). That mystery of faith traditionally called "the communion of saints" reminds us that we are part of a much larger community. And this community can help meet that hunger we have

3. Robert N. Bellah, "Religion and the Shape of National Culture," *America* (July 31, 1999) 13.

for communion with God and with each other, for belonging to something that deepens our hope in what is often invisible to modern eyes: the working of grace in our own lives and the lives of others. Through the preaching that occurs on the feasts of the saints we are reminded of our connectedness to those who have gone ahead of us, the holy men and women who have handed on the faith from generation to generation. And they come reminding us that we are now both the inheritors of their legacy and the continuation of it; we are today's saints, the holy ones who fulfill both the command of the God of Moses, "Be holy, as I am holy" (Lev 19:2) and the admonition of Paul, "For this is the will of God, your sanctification" (1 Thess 4:3; also Eph 1:4). In our own day, the saints come to us after a period of absence, one might even say a time of exile.

Although the Second Vatican Council spoke positively of the important role of the saints in the life of the Church, past and present, in the Constitution on the Church (nos. 49–51) and the Constitution on the Sacred Liturgy (nos. 108, 111), this did not prevent their fading from the Catholic consciousness, both in our communal liturgical life and in our private devotional lives. In a 1971 essay, theologian Karl Rahner compared the response of Catholics to the council's call to venerate the saints to a young man listening to a mother sing the praises of her daughter, hoping her words will move the young man to consider the daughter as a worthy candidate for marriage. Rahner observed that the young man "hears the message and does not dispute its accuracy, yet no love is aroused in him. The fact that the girl is worthy of love does not mean that there is any corresponding ability to love on the part of the young man."[4] Almost twenty years later, in 1990, liturgical theologian David N. Power showed this attitude to persist when he began an essay by commenting: "In the Catholic Church at present, devotion to the saints seems to be at a point where people are asking what is it all about . . . there seems to be considerable uncertainty about the meaning of devotion to the saints and about the place which their commemoration ought to have on the liturgical calendar."[5] While both Rahner and Power supported the role of the saints in the life of today's Church, only in the last few years does there seem to be a renewal of interest in

---

4. Karl Rahner, S.J., "Why and How Can We Venerate the Saints?", *Theological Investigations* 8, trans. David Bourke (New York: Herder and Herder, 1971) 4.

5. David N. Power, "The Church's Calendar: Are the Saints Neglected or Misrepresented?" *Culture and Theology* (Washington, D.C.: Pastoral Press, 1990) 143.

these ancestors in the faith, and the possibility for a new relationship with them. We preachers can play an important part in fostering this development for the enrichment of our people. To this end, I will discuss the role of the saints in the life of today's Church, and then reflect on some of the ways in which liturgical preaching might feature them. Several homilies will be presented, showing my own efforts to work with the saints in both daily and Sunday homilies.

Earlier I referred to the eclipse of the saints in recent decades. Whether this was a reaction against the type of devotions to saints that threatened to overshadow the unique role of Christ as the one mediator with the Father, or an inability on the part of many believers to see how yesterday's saints had anything to say today, the time now seems ripe for a reevaluation of the role of the saints and their restoration to the communal consciousness. Their various ways of reflecting the light that is Christ can only further illumine and warm a world in which many yearn for the kind of companionship that banishes alienation and nourishes the spirit.

## The Saints and Today's Church

Elizabeth Johnson has written of two ways in which the saints have functioned in the history of the Church: (a) as companions in our journey of faith, joining us as a community of disciples, marked by mutual regard, and (b) as patrons, "friends in high places," using their status as intermediaries and intercessors to speak to God for us in our need.[6] The spatial dimension implied in these two understandings captures an important difference; in the former, the saints are part of a circle with the baptized on earth, all on the same level, whereas in the latter the saints are between God and us, indicating a hierarchical structure with God at the top, us at the bottom, and the saints in the middle relating to us on a patron-client basis. The shift from the former to the latter way of relating to the saints came about in the fourth century. Why the change in perception? Due to losing a sense of being a holy people even while still here on earth, accompanied by a heightened emphasis on Jesus as divine and seated as judge on his heavenly throne, people turned to the saints as intermediaries between Jesus and

---

6. Elizabeth Johnson, *Friends of God and Prophets, A Feminist Theological Reading of the Communion of Saints* (New York: Continuum, 1998); see especially Chapter 4, 71–93.

the rest of us still working out our salvation, approaching them as heavenly power-brokers that pleaded our cause before the throne. They were the holy ones; we, the sinners. Recently, however, a concerted effort has been made to restore the saints to us as companions on our journey. Preachers can participate in this reappraisal by helping the community to see them as family, friends, formators, and signs of our future. A few words about each category.

## The Saints As Family

When the Second Vatican Council refers to the saints as "our brothers and sisters" (Constitution on the Church 50), it is underlining an insight found in the letters of St. Paul: that all who have been baptized are alive in Christ, that they have become coheirs with Christ, members of the one body of Christ, children of God in the power of the Spirit of the risen Lord (Rom 8:29; 1 Cor 12:12-13; Gal 3:26-28). This relationship between believers is not something that ends with death. Our connection with those who have gone ahead of us is not swallowed up when life as we now know it ceases, but those who have died in Christ remain alive in Christ and stay joined with us as members of the same body, animated by the Spirit. In Christ, the family of God remains in communion: one mind, one heart, through the one Spirit.

In the early 1990s, theologian Michael Himes addressed the Catholic Association of Teachers of Homiletics (CATH) and compared the preacher's task to that of a host at a cocktail party. Our role was to greet people and introduce them to the other guests. In his exuberant style, Himes took on the persona of a host and declared to an imaginary parishioner, "Welcome! How wonderful to see you; you must come over and meet Thomas Aquinas. And look, over there by the rhododendron, isn't that Teresa of Avila?" We laughed but the image has stayed with me. It captures one aspect our preaching can accomplish on the feasts of the saints: helping those at the eucharistic assembly see themselves as part of a larger community of believers, past and present, all joining in the great act of praise and thanksgiving.

On further reflection, I would make one minor modification to the image, a change of context: seeing the preacher as a host at a family reunion. Into this setting come all those long lost and distant relatives who have lived in different times, cultures, settings, and circumstances. There are feisty, argumentative people like Martha and Jerome, and conciliatory, soft-spoken ones like Francis de Sales and

Thérèse of Lisieux; great minds like Albert and Thomas, and mystical poets like John of the Cross and Francis of Assisi, reformers like Teresa of Avila and contemplatives like Margaret Mary Alacoque, even politicians, civil like Thomas More and ecclesiastical like Charles Borromeo, courageous young women like Agnes, Cecilia, Lucy in the early centuries, and Maria Goretti in our own time, and gentle young men like Aloysius Gonzaga and Dominic Savio, friends of the poor like Margaret of Scotland and Elizabeth of Hungary, and friends of youth like Angela Merici and John Bosco. They are family, brothers and sisters in the Lord, and, as the Constitution on the Church reminds us, "our communion with the saints joins us to Christ, from whom as from its fountain and head flow all grace and life of the people of God itself" (50).

Thus, it is appropriate to venerate the saints, that is, to respect, reverence and love them. This need not be enacted through the devotional forms of the past, but rather take shape in a deeper practice of love in the daily course of our lives, which makes us turn to them for example, fellowship, and support. They are not patrons to be manipulated into assisting us, but family bound together by the blood of our Redeemer.

### The Saints As Friends

It may be easier to regard the saints as ancestors in the faith and extended family in the Spirit, united through baptism into Christ, than to relate to them as active and engaging friends. Friendship is usually built on sharing common interests, concerns, projects, and a common way of life. Many of the saints are so far removed from our postmodern culture, our political agendas and issues, and even our personal interests that any connection can seem beyond our imagination. What does a thirteen-year old girl celebrated as a virgin-martyr, or a monk who lived out his days in the desert, have to say to our age of cellphones and computers, a time marked by threat of nuclear disaster, ecological destruction, and random violence? Furthermore, the officially recognized saints comprise a rather limited group. When one looks at the calendar of the saints and the list of their annual feasts and memorials in the Sacramentary, this impression of selectivity is further reinforced by the similarity of those we are called to remember. Apart from the saints found in the Gospels, who had the privilege of walking and talking with Jesus, and the early martyrs whose stories of courage in facing torture and death for their commitment to Christ send most of us into a state of unmitigated gratitude for a later birth date, the rest are frequently Church leaders who were male, celibate, and European. The gender ratio is three to one, in favor of men.

Now and again a woman is mentioned, but she is usually either a queen, a contemplative, or the founder of a religious community. Seldom have married woman been canonized, unless they were royalty like Margaret of Scotland or Elizabeth of Portugal, or went on to become founders of religious communities like Frances of Rome and Elizabeth Seton. And few married men are so honored apart from kings like Edward the Confessor, Louis of France, and Stephen of Hungary, or a martyr like Thomas More, Chancellor of England during the reign of Henry VIII. While we do remember Hilary of Poitiers who probably became a bishop while still married, and Frances of Rome whose husband Lorenzo was a model of support for her pursuit of holiness, other than those couples of the New Testament like Joachim and Anne, and Mary and Joseph, it is rare that a married couple is celebrated as saints; Isidore and Maria de la Cabeza alone come to mind.[7]

Given such limitations, preachers have been likely to overlook any sanctoral feasts other than those celebrating major figures like John the Baptist, and apostles like Peter and Paul, perennial favorites like Francis of Assisi or Teresa of Avila, or the patron of one's parish. But I have found that time spent looking into these lives can be quite rewarding, bringing people into my life that I have enjoyed having as companions, even beyond the day the Church honors them each year. And I have come to believe that others might also come to treasure them.

The Pulitzer-prize-winning *Angela's Ashes* recounts the time when the local librarian tells thirteen-year-old Frankie McCourt he cannot leave the library with his books because it is pouring rain, and so she sends him over to read about the saints. The author recalls: "There are four big books, Butler's *Lives of the Saints*. I don't want to spend my life reading about saints but when I start I wish the rain would last forever."[8] Young Frankie becomes enthralled with several of the martrys of the early Church—though perhaps for less than ideal reasons, acknowledging with great enthusiasm, "There are stories about virgins, martyrs, virgin martyrs and they're worse than any horror film at the

---

7. For an interesting presentation of married saints, see John F. Fink, *Married Saints* (New York: Alba House, 1999).

8. Frank McCourt, *Angela's Ashes* (New York: Scribner, 1996) 285.

Lyric Cinema."⁹ Still, in the end he has added St. Christina the Astonishing to his small list of saints "worth keeping," which puts her right behind Francis of Assisi, his patron. She has come into his life, been welcomed, and stays on as a witness to a Power beyond the human.

As so often happens with the people who come to matter in our lives, friendship with a saint often begins accidentally. It can be a chance encounter, a time when a particular saint matches up with a personal sorrow or quest, "connecting" with what is happening at a particular moment in one's life. I can remember as a boy coming upon a comic book that introduced five saints to school children, and there I discovered someone my own age, Dominic Savio, who ended up as part of my life from the sixth grade until I graduated from high school. A saint can appear suddenly as a gift, offering hope, encouragement, another way of thinking about things. Certain saints may be with us for a lifetime, and we are not alone facing either our joys or sorrows. Companionship is one of the great gifts friends bring. The possibility of befriending and being befriended by a saint depends on a willingness to invest time with them, coming to know them through the sources available, biographies, their writings, even their legends. The bonds of friendship can lead to a deeper sense of being connected to the larger community bound together by the Spirit of Christ.

## The Saints As Formators

The work of being formed into the image of Christ is one that continues throughout the life of each individual. The saints continue to minister to God's people by helping to form us in discipleship. True, such work is fundamentally the task of the Holy Spirit who has been placed in our hearts at baptism and whose gifts lead to our being configured into the body of Christ. But as the sacraments remind us, the Spirit works through the matter at hand. These men and women who preceded us and now live in the presence of God may also function as our teachers, leading us more deeply into the mystery of God and calling us to respond in our time as they did in theirs. Herman Wegman writes that "the lives of the saints are not informative or historical, but *performative*. They intend to stir up and stimulate the hearers to imitation, to perpetuate the continuous biography of Christ."[10]

9. Ibid.
10. Herman Wegman, "Successio Sanctorum," trans. Gordon Lathrop, *Time and Community*, ed. J. Neil Alexander (Washington, D.C.: Pastoral Press, 1990) 227.

In recent years I have paid more attention to the writings of the saints, especially those selected as a second reading for the Office of Readings in the Liturgy of the Hours. Of course, there are the expected selections from the writings of such major historical figures as Irenaeus, John Chrysostom, Athanasius, Augustine, Catherine of Siena, Teresa of Avila, and others known for their spiritual writings, but I have experienced a sense of discovery in coming across lesser known voices. Recently the feast of Angela Merici, founder of the Ursuline sisters, revealed a woman whose words might continue to form not only the sisters of her religious community but anyone who reads them and is presently engaged either in ministry to young people or has the care of the young as a responsibility. Her words instill a love for children, a voice that might be needed more today as an alternative to those calling for "child-free environments."[11] Angela's words (after reading them one is tempted to call her "Mama Merici"!) have the warmth of the One who called her, and present her as a worthy companion for leading us to She Who Is. And on August 18, the memoirs of the secretary of Jane Frances de Chantal provide this saint's reflections on those who did not die as martyrs, but nevertheless suffered another kind of martyrdom: the martyrdom of love. "Divine love takes its sword to the hidden recesses of our inmost soul and divides us from ourselves."[12] These writings offer phrases and images that can enrich a homily.

The saints' lives give witness to how others have cooperated with God's grace, helping our hearts to grow in the love of God and neighbor, and encouraging us to continue in our journey of faith. Again the Office of Readings gives us glimpses into the lives of the saints with an immediacy that can be arresting. On January seventeenth, Athanasius portrays Abbot Anthony's wholehearted response to God's call which came to him as a young man of eighteen on hearing the story of Jesus and the rich young man at Mass; on February sixth, the final hours of the Japanese martyrs, Paul Miki and companions, are movingly described by an eyewitness portraying the crucifixion of this group of clergy, religious and laity—including several teenagers and a ten-year-old boy—on a hill outside Nagasaki. The courageous spirits of African martyrs Perpetua and Felicity during martyrdom are powerfully rendered

11. Lisa Belkin, "The Backlash Against Children," *New York Times Magazine* (July 23, 2000) 30–35, 42, 56, 60–63.

12. *The Liturgy of the Hours Supplement* (New York: Catholic Book Publishing Co., 1992) 15–16.

on March seventh; and on September ninth the ministry of Peter Claver to the slaves brought into Cartagena continues to confront us with our tragic legacy almost four hundred years later, while presenting one person's human response to a situation of such inhumanity.

Elizabeth Johnson turned to the book of Wisdom to title her work on the communion of saints, *Friends of God and Prophets*.[13] The pertinent passage speaks of Wisdom's action in the world, drawing all men and women into the mystery of God, thereby forming a community of wisdom:

> Although she (Wisdom) is but one, she can do all things, and while remaining in herself, she renews all things; in every generation she passes into holy souls and makes them friends of God, and prophets (Wis 7:27).

These good friends of God and prophets continue to touch our lives, offering friendship and love, and giving both insight into living out the gospel and a prophetic vision of what might be achieved under the guidance of the Spirit. Allowing them to function as formative influences helps to shape our minds and hearts into the image of Christ. The Constitution on the Church affirms this role when it acknowledges that through the saints "we are taught about the safest path by which, through a changing world and in keeping with each one's state of life and condition, we will be able to arrive at perfect union with Christ, which is holiness" (no. 50).

### The Saints As Our Future

The saints image and beckon us toward our future. They serve as a "sign of the kingdom," so that "we are inspired anew to seek the city which is to come" (no. 50). They are not only our companions in memory but in hope. As companions in memory, they show us how the imitation of Jesus in his saving ministry, sufferings, death, and resurrection, has been lived in the world, linking us through time with the ever active movement of the Holy Spirit. But they do more than speak to us from the past; they are present to us as companions in hope, giving us cause for trusting in the fulfillment of God's promises in Christ, because it has already happened in them.

This awareness of their role as imaging our future comes home at every liturgical celebration when we call them to mind. Such occasions include the litany of the saints at the Easter vigil and at every celebra-

---

13. Johnson, *Friends of God and Prophets*, 40.

tion of baptism and holy orders, the prayer of the faithful during the funeral liturgy which asks God to give this departed one "joy in the company of the saints." Within the celebration of the Eucharist, we acknowledge their presence at the conclusion of most prefaces when we join our voices with those of the angels *and the saints* to proclaim, "Holy, holy, holy . . . ," and during every Eucharistic Prayer when we honor Mary and the saints, asking God for a share in their fellowship and their inheritance of eternal life.

The Constitution on the Church reminds us, "It is especially in the sacred liturgy that our union with the heavenly Church is best realized; in the liturgy, the power of the Holy Spirit acts on us through sacramental signs; there we celebrate, rejoicing together, the praise of the divine majesty. . . . When, then, we celebrate the eucharistic sacrifice we are most closely united to the worship of the heavenly church. . . ." (no. 50). In worship we anticipate our future. For we have assurance that "if we continue to love one another and to join in praising the most holy Trinity—all of us who are children of God and form one family in Christ (see Heb 3:6)—we will be faithful to the deepest vocation of the Church and will share in a foretaste of the liturgy of perfect glory" (no. 51).

## The Saints and the Lectionary

Joan Chittister has remarked that in modern times the saints have become official and bland.[14] If this is so, I would put the blame less on the canonization process than on our failure to seek out their stories, hear their voices through their own words, and when possible, to befriend them. Some need to be rescued from the captivity of hagiography that drains them of the human qualities allowing us to identify with them. With the best of intentions, the sisters of Thérèse of Lisieux edited out of her autobiography any part that made her less than perfect. The admonition of Francis de Sales applies: "There is no harm to the saints if their faults are shown as well as their virtues. But great harm is done to everybody by those hagiographers who slur over the faults." Preachers can do a great service by restoring the saints to the memory of their communities, presenting them in ways that others can hear their voices and appreciate what they achieved in their own time.

14. Joan Chittister, *A Passion for Life, Fragments of the Face of God* (Maryknoll: Orbis, 1996) ix.

But we are not to approach this task solely as historians, or even storytellers, though both tasks are part of the job. We are called to preach the gospel and to enlist the saint of the day in this task. Whenever preaching a homily within the celebration of the Eucharist, I try to remain faithful to the intent of preaching articulated in *FIYH*, that is, to preach a homily that scripturally interprets the human existence of those present. That is our primary responsibility. Still, on the feasts of the saints I feel some responsibility to present the saint, or to make the saint present, to the community so that there is an opportunity to know the saint better. I try to do this by working with and through the saint to have the biblical texts interpret the lives of the listeners. In this way both the community's hunger for meaning and belonging can be satisfied by the homily.

The place of the saint within preaching is constrained, then, by the nature of the liturgical homily as an act of biblical interpretation of life. This means that a homily on the feast of a saint is not to be either a historical lecture on the life and times of the saint, or a storytelling session of interesting and inspiring anecdotes about the saint, but to retain its liturgical function of leading the gathered community to give thanks and praise. The saint is not ignored, or relegated to a few words at the beginning of Mass, but subservient to the obligation to preach the gospel.

We will first consider the liturgical directives for sanctoral celebrations found in the Constitution on the Sacred Liturgy, the General Instruction of the Roman Missal, and the Introduction to the Lectionary. I will then propose four alternatives for featuring the saint, while remaining faithful to the nature of the liturgical homily.

When discussing the liturgical year, the Constitution on the Sacred Liturgy called for memorial days devoted to the martyrs and other saints to be included in the annual liturgical cycle; in these celebrations "the church proclaims the paschal mystery in the saints who have suffered and have been glorified with Christ" (no. 104). Later, this document notes that "the feasts of the saints proclaim the wonderful works of Christ in his servants and offer to the faithful fitting examples for their imitation" (no. 111). The saints, then, are not to be seen apart from the paschal mystery of Christ; they are embodiments of how this mystery has been lived out through history. A caution is given in conclusion: "Lest the feasts of the saints take precedence over the feasts which commemorate the actual mysteries of salvation, the celebration of many of them should be consigned to particular churches, nations, or religious families. Only those should be extended to the universal Church which commemorate saints of truly universal importance" (no. 111).

This concern led to certain classifications in the Calendar of the Saints, ranked in a descending order of importance: (a) solemnities (certain feasts of Mary, Joseph, John the Baptist, Peter and Paul); (b) feasts (other celebrations of Mary, the apostles and evangelists); and (c) memorials, either obligatory or optional, depending on the significance of the saint to the universal Church, or a particular church, region, or religious family. Recently several new memorials have been added to reflect the saints of Asia and Eastern Europe: the Polish concentration camp victim, Maximilian Kolbe (August 14), the Korean martyrs Andrew Kim Taegon, Paul Chong Hasang, and Companions (September 20), the martyrs of Japan, including Lawrence Ruiz (son of a Chinese father and Tagala mother) and companions (September 28), and the Vietnamese martyrs Andrew Dung-Lac and companions (November 24). In the United States, the obligatory memorials of saints like Elizabeth Ann Seton (January 4), John Neumann (January 5), Blessed Kateri Tekawitha (July 14), and Frances Xavier Cabrini (November 13) exemplify a regional emphasis.

The Constitution on the Sacred Liturgy speaks in this same section of the importance of the sacred seasons in the Liturgical Year, calling for their restoration and preservation in a way that "they duly nourish the piety of the faithful as they celebrate the mysteries of Christian redemption, and, above all, the paschal mystery" (no. 107). The constitution clearly affirms the priority of the liturgical seasons over the sanctoral celebrations when it states:

> The minds of the faithful should be directed primarily toward the feasts of the Lord whereby the mysteries of salvation are celebrated throughout the year. For this reason, the Proper of the Seasons must be given due preference over the feasts of the saints so that the entire cycle of the mysteries of salvation may be suitably recalled (no. 108).

To effect this prioritization, certain memorials of the saints become optional during Lent or fall out altogether during Easter week. But this does not have to be taken as an invitation to remove the saints whose feasts occur during the seasons of Advent and Christmas, Lent and Easter, from the consciousness of the community. Again, the question is how can a saint help to celebrate the mystery of Christ in a particular season.

Just as the major feasts of the Lord, then, shall never be overshadowed by the feasts of saints, so too the preeminence of Christ in our preaching should never be overshadowed by any saint. Just as the feasts of the saints reflect the paschal mystery of Christ celebrated in the Liturgy of the Eucharist, so we feature the saints in our preaching to relate this same paschal mystery to the lives of our people. To this end, the story of the saint is at the service of the story of Christ found in the Scriptures, helping it to shed light on the story of the faith community and the world in which we live. This dynamic suggests an approach which considers how the saint can relate both to the biblical texts and to the gathered community.

The relationship between the Scripture texts and the saints varies, ranging from one clearly intended by the authors of the Lectionary to one serendipitously forged—but not forced—by the preacher. First, a word about the Lectionary and the readings assigned for the feasts of the saints. The Lectionary contains a section of readings called the Proper of Saints and then several sections called the Commons (Common for Martyrs, Pastors, Virgins, Saints). The Proper of Saints contains readings selected for certain saints, although it often refers you to the Common of the Saints. The Proper seldom has required readings for the entire Liturgy of the Word; more often it will suggest one reading and then refer to a particular Common. The various Commons offer numerous texts from the Old Testament, New Testament writings of the apostles and Acts, and the Gospels. The preacher can choose texts appropriate to a particular saint.

The General Introduction to the Lectionary for Mass offers a number of guidelines (nos. 83-84). I offer the following summary:

a. When available, biblical passages about the saint or the mystery which the Mass celebrates are provided for saints' celebrations. These are found in the Proper of Saints. This occurs usually on the solemnities and feasts of the biblical saints, for instance, Mary, the apostles and evangelists, the conversion of St. Paul, the birth and beheading of John the Baptist, Mary Magdalene, etc. Even when the celebration is designated a memorial, these readings are to take the place of the weekday readings from Ordinary Time.

b. At other times, there are "accommodated readings, those, namely, that bring out some particular aspect of a Saint's spiritual life or work" (no. 83). Consider the feasts of St. Anthony of the desert (January 17), St. Catherine of Siena (April 29), or St. Jerome (September 30). The use of these readings is not seen as binding, "except for compelling pastoral reasons." More often, references are made to passages found in the various Commons, but these, too, are suggestions, and any reading can be chosen from an appropriate Common. In all celebrations of the saints, the readings may be taken not only from the particular Common to which reference is made, but also from the Common of Holy Men and Women which applies to all categories of saints.

c. The first concern in the selection of the biblical texts is "the spiritual benefit of the faithful"; presiders are not to impose their personal preferences, or "omit too often or without sufficient cause the readings assigned for each day in the weekday Lectionary: the Church's desire is that a more lavish table of the word of God be spread before the faithful" (no. 83).

d. In regard to the relation of readings to the different classifications of the saints' celebrations: on solemnities and feasts, the readings must be those given in the Proper or Commons. In the general Roman Calendar these readings are always assigned. In particular calendars, three readings are to be assigned, unless the Conference of Bishops has allowed for two.

e. On feasts and memorials which have only two readings, the first can either be from the Old Testament or from an apostle; the second from the Gospels. In the Easter season, the first reading is to be taken from an apostle, the gospel from that of St. John.

The result of these guidelines is that the relationship between the saint and the Scripture text(s) will vary: (i) from being closely related or being "accommodated," that is, the text refers to the saint in terms of his or her mission in the Church or a particular aspect of his or her life; (ii) to a more general connection because of typology: saint as martyr, pastor, virgin, holy man or woman; (iii) to no deliberately planned connection at all: the feast or memorial falls on a day when the readings are either those of Ordinary Time or of a particular liturgical season such as Lent or Advent. While the first two categories offer more evident connections between text and saint, the final category does not rule out possible points of connection. As a matter of fact, I have often found the saint to be a helpful mediator between the text and the life of the community on days when saint and readings came together without any planned intent on the part of the Lectionary.

### The Saints and Preaching

Frequently a saint can be an effective vehicle for connecting the word of God and the community. I have found four ways in which the saints may function to relate the biblical texts with the lives of the community. The saint can be considered as (a) a *mirror* of some aspect of the God revealed in salvation history, most notably in Jesus Christ, in a particular text; (b) a *model* of human response to God's grace; (c) a *mentor* to the community; and (d) a *metaphor* for the human condition under God's grace.

These four ways of featuring a saint in a homily are not meant to be exhaustive or exclusive. I am sure there are many other ways to consider how a saint might function in a homily, and a preacher might consider a saint under more than one heading when preparing the homily. But I would suggest limiting the way a saint is featured in a particular homily to the one with the most potential for effecting an encounter between the word of God and the community. What is important to remember is that the saint is at the service of the word of God, leading the community more deeply into understanding some aspect of God's saving action in our lives as proclaimed in the reading. Preachers can enable an encounter, introducing the saint as a companion who joins us on the way, giving us cause to praise and give thanks.

*The Saint As Mirror*: The preacher looks for how the saint reflects some aspect of God, of Jesus Christ, the image of the invisible God (cf. Col 1:15), of the Holy Spirit, concretizing, enfleshing, the God at work in the Scriptures. This approach is rooted in the observation of the Constitution on the Church when addressing the role of the saints in the life of the Church:

> In the lives of those companions of ours in the human condition who are more perfectly transformed into the image of Christ (see 2 Cor 3:18) *God shows, vividly, to humanity his presence and his face.* He speaks to us in them and offers us a sign of his kingdom, to which we are powerfully attracted, so great a cloud of witnesses are we given (see Heb 12:1) and such an affirmation of the truth of the Gospel (no. 50).

Often it is immediately apparent how a saint mirrors Christ. For instance, saints like Margaret of Scotland and Elizabeth of Hungary mirror Christ's love and care for the poor, while Angela Merici reflects his concern for the little ones, the orphans and abandoned children. John of God shows us Christ's compassion for the sick while Alphonsus Liguori shows us his passionate love and dedicated outreach to sinners. But there is a further challenge. A homily on the feast takes care to enlist the saint in the service of the Scriptures. Our authority in preaching is rooted in the word of God; the saints are as much at the service of this word as the preacher. The fundamental task is to deepen the community's awareness of how God, as presented in today's Scripture, is acting in *their* lives, giving them cause to give thanks and praise in the Eucharist. By making use of the saint in this process, we engage them as coworkers in the ministry of the word and bring them and the community together through this ministry.

For instance, the suggested reading from the Proper of the Saints on the feast of St. Francis of Assisi is Galatians 6:14-18 where Paul proclaims, "May I never boast of anything except the cross of our Lord Jesus Christ, by which the world has been crucified to me and I to the world. . . . From now on, let no one make trouble for me; for I carry the marks of Jesus branded on my body." Certainly Francis as one who received the stigmata mirrors Paul's image of "carrying the marks of Jesus branded on my body." Francis reflected the crucified Lord not only in this physical participation in his suffering at the end of his life, but throughout it by his ascetical practices, and in his suffering we glimpse the face of our Redeemer.

Or, take the feast of Alphonsus de Liguori with the suggested reading from Romans 8:1-4, proclaiming that "Christ Jesus has set you free from the law of sin and death." This text allows the preacher to remind us how Alphonsus mirrored Christ the liberator by bringing the freeing message of our redemption in Christ to those imprisoned by the teachings of Jansenism which emphasized human sinfulness and unworthiness to draw closer to God in the Eucharist.

I often have found that a facet of the saint's life or something a saint said or wrote can be linked with a weekday reading. On the feast of St. Angela Merici, founder of the Ursulines, the first secular institute and first order dedicated to teaching schoolchildren, the gospel was Mark 4:21-25. Mark's collection of four wisdom sayings is applied to Jesus' use of the parables and offers the image of a light not being put under a bushel basket but rather on a stand. Exegetical research reveals that this image refers to the parables Jesus told and to Jesus himself; on this feast one can also make a connection with the person of Angela Merici as an image of the Light that came into the world and continues to come. In her own day she mirrored Christ the light and called her sisters to do the same in her care for the "little ones" to whom she dedicated her life.

When Joan Chittister speaks of the saints as "icons" and "fragments of the face of God," she acknowledges the danger of fostering the attitude that "only the perfect give us glimpses of the face of God

. . . ."[15] Preachers can reinforce the outlook that God reigns over a restricted neighborhood, allowing access only to the chosen few, that is,
"the theologically proper, the ecclesiastically docile, the morally safe."
Both Chittister and Robert Ellsberg[16] call us to look beyond the official calendar of saints for those whose sanctity crosses established
boundaries, even religious ones. Chittister calls attention to such figures as Charles de Foucauld as an icon of the "Universal Brother,"
Simone Weil as an icon of the "Face of Truth," Bartolome de las Casas
as an icon of "Justice," Mother Jones as an icon of "God's Righteous
Anger," and John XXIII as an icon of the "Heart of God." Ellsberg reminds us that in addition to those on the official list or "canon," we can
be enriched, and enrich others, by allowing room for such worthy figures as Pastor Andre Trocme of Le Chambon, the artist Georges
Rouault, the nonviolent Hindu leader Mohandas K. Gandhi, the Jewish prophet Abraham Heschel, and even Albert Camus, a professed
nonbeliever.[17] We must be careful not to baptize the latter into the
Christian faith, but it is not difficult to see in them a glimpse of that
same Spirit that animated Christ.

*The Saint As Model.* Whereas the saint as mirror emphasizes the
saint in relation to Christ, the saint as model places them in relation to
us. The saints serve as examples for us to follow, human like us, men and
women who struggled, failed, even sinned, yet remain worthy of imitation in their commitment to Christ and their responsiveness to the
grace of the Holy Spirit. This approach to a saint is probably the most
common one. These men and women continue to encourage and inspire
us when we find ourselves faltering. They put flesh and blood on the life
of grace. Thus, the Constitution on the Sacred Liturgy says that when
we celebrate their feasts, the Church does three things: it "proclaims the
paschal mystery in the saints who have suffered and been glorified with
Christ. It proposes them to the faithful as *models who draw all people to
the Father through Christ*, and through their merits it begs for God's
favor" (no. 104). This second aspect of serving as "models who draw all
people to the Father through Christ" concerns us here.

It is particularly in their concrete struggles that we find models to
admire and imitate. While I had read of Thérèse of Lisieux modeling

15. Ibid., x.
16. Robert Ellsberg, *All Saints: Daily Reflections on Saints, Prophets, and Witnesses
for Our Time* (New York: Crossroad, 1998) 3–4.
17. Ibid., 3.

patient endurance through the practice of her "little way," this remained abstract to me until I heard of her being able to keep faith in God through a sixth-month period when she lay in her bed gasping for breath, choking on her own vomit, yet still able to write of "the incomprehensible depth of God's abiding love." I marvel at the dedication of Albert the Great and Thomas Aquinas who used their intelligence to extend the human search for God in science and philosophy, respectively. I admire and applaud St. Monica's perseverance in prayer and that loving heart that could overlook her son's abandoning her at the dock, and sailing off to Rome without her; this mother's love ultimately moved both God's heart to effect Augustine's conversion and Augustine's own heart which paid her a poignant tribute in his *Confessions*.

Sometimes the saints stimulate us to examine our lives, our society and our Church with a critical eye. I wonder what Paulinus of Nola might say to our own day from his experience of being a married bishop at a time when this was not approved. I wonder what the great reformer Teresa of Avila would say to the present state of so many religious communities. I wonder how Alphonsus de Liguori, who wrote his treatises holding a cold stone to stem the pain of his migraine headaches, would evaluate the pastoral dedication and output of the religious community he founded, the Redemptorists. Or what Thomas More might say to today's members of Congress. In spending time researching who these men and women were, the world they lived in, how they challenged that world, the saints begin to make their own inroads into a preacher's heart and head.

The challenge for preachers is to find ways to link the saint with the Scriptures read at Eucharist, and the community as a *celebrating* community. On the feast of Thérèse, the Jesus of Matthew 18:1-4 places a child before the disciples asking, "Who is of greatest importance in the kingdom of God?" Can Thérèse help bridge the gap between this moment between Jesus and his disciples and how it speaks today to a particular community? Can Hilary of Poitiers who models proclamation of Jesus' divinity at a time "when the world groaned and marveled to find itself Arian"[18] serve as a link between the gospel story about Jesus cleansing a leper (Mark 1:40-45) and some aspect of our lives? Consider St. Martin de Porres, child of a Spanish grandee and a

18. Attributed to St. Jerome; see Leonard Foley, O.F.M., *Saint of the Day: Lives and Lessons for Saints and Feasts of the New Missal* (Cincinnati: St. Anthony Messenger, 1990) 17.

freedwoman of Panama, in seventeenth-century Lima, Peru. At Martin's canonization, John XXIII called him "Martin the charitable" because he was "tireless in his efforts to reform the criminal," and who "would sit up with the sick to bring them comfort, provide food, clothing, and medicine, care for the poor farmhands, blacks and mulattoes who were looked down upon as slaves, the dregs of society." Can Martin help Luke 14:12-14 which presents Jesus addressing the Pharisees who had invited him to dinner about inviting beggars and the crippled, the lame and the blind to the table, speak to those gathered at our eucharistic table?

The saints function as models when they exemplify human response to grace, when we are able to recognize the working of the Spirit in their lives. To appreciate the working of grace, it is often helpful to offer some glimpse of their humanity. Jerome, the most able single translator of the Bible Christianity has known, was both a man who could be viciously sarcastic and even cruel, as when he attacked his former friend Rufinus for his theological stance as well as his physical characteristics, and a man who could be tenderly solicitous, as when he wrote St. Paula, urging her to entrust her granddaughter to his care: "If you send her to me, I shall become her tutor and her nurse. I shall carry her on my shoulders, old man that I am . . ."

Elizabeth Bayley Seton was not only Mother Seton, but, as she wrote in a letter near the end of her life, "I'll be wild Betsy to the end." And the Augustine who could pray, "Lord, make me chaste, but not yet," also revealed his heart when he wrote, "Too late have I loved thee, O Beauty ever ancient, ever new, too late have I loved thee; you called, you shouted, you shattered my deafness." The kindness of Queen Margaret to the people of Scotland made her husband King Malcolm sit by her feet as she read her prayers and cover her prayer books with jewels, and led her son King David to build the little chapel in memory of her that sits on top of the hill within the castle grounds of Edinburgh. And the extravagant generosity of St. Elizabeth of Hungary, daughter of a king and wife of the Landgrave of Thuringia, made her deceased husband's family try to throw her off the royal estate for squandering everything on the poor.

In the complexity of the saints' personalities and the boldness of their actions, we find the world-changing wind of the Spirit blowing and feel the heat of divine fire. Yet, is there a need in our day to go further? In looking to the saints found in the Church calendar as models, Leonardo Boff wrote almost twenty years ago of a need for "political saints." He observes that for the most part the history of the Church "presents few or almost no saints who achieved the synthesis between the mystical and the political as they are understood today."[19] His critique is that the models we often present are more along the lines of offering help than liberating from oppressive structures. "This is the great challenge of our times: to create militants with a truly political holiness."[20]

In a similar vein, Robert Ellsberg writes that we need to expand our understanding of holiness beyond any pattern of the past to what is demanded by the questions, challenges, and needs of the present moment; we need models of "holiness drawn from the worlds of scholarship, political struggle, literary and artistic life, the ordinary worlds in which most people find themselves."[21] To be concrete, we need saints who do not foster disdain for the body, for women, or for the earth; we need models who teach us how to cherish other cultures, ethnic groups, and religious paths.

A balance in presenting the saints is helpful. The saint as mirror reminds us that as God could be glimpsed in their lives, so too in ours. The saint as model can be a cause of encouragement, literally, giving us heart to go up against what can seem insurmountable odds in pursuing the agenda of the kingdom of God. The saints can foster both a sense of the mystery of how God works through each person's uniqueness, implanting a desire to yield to God at work in us, and a spirit of self-confidence to confront the demons of our age and become active coworkers with the Spirit in our world. Both aspects serve to bring a healing, transformational power to bear on the life of the community and, through it, on the world.

*The Saint As Mentor.* Whether as mirror or model the saints can be presented as our mentors, elder brothers and sisters who offer us their guidance. In reading the autobiography of Augustine, the sermons of John Chrysostom, or the writings of Teresa of Avila and Catherine of Siena, we can hear their voices. This experience makes the saint present to us in a different way than hearing *about* them. And it provides another way to present the saint on the feast day. Allow the saint to speak to the community. This can be done in several ways. An obvious one is making use of their own words, when an appropriate link can be made to some aspect of the biblical text, the liturgical action,

19. Leonardo Boff, "The Need for Political Saints," *Cross Currents* (winter 1980–81) 384.
20. Ibid.
21. Robert Ellsberg, "Saints for Today," *New Theology Review* (May 1999) 20.

or both. For instance, the words of John Vianney can be used to lead into the Liturgy of the Eucharist: "Private prayer is like straw scattered here and there: If you set it on fire it makes a lot of little flames. But gather these straws into a bundle and light them, and you get a mighty fire, rising like a column into the sky; public prayer is like that."[22]

Preaching to a group of clergy on the memorial of St. Charles Borromeo, after proclaiming the gospel reading of Luke 15:1-10 (Thursday, Thirty-First Week of the Year) which presents Jesus telling the parable of the shepherd who goes in search of the lost sheep, Borromeo gave me words to remind today's good shepherds of the need to care for their own soul: "Are you in charge of a parish? If so, do not neglect the parish of your own soul, do not give yourself to others so completely that you have nothing left for yourself." In an age of clergy burnout and depression due to overworking, Borromeo's wise words speak directly to the need for attending to one's own spiritual needs. I found them in the reading from the Liturgy of the Hours on this feast. Quite possibly they are part of the last sermon Borromeo gave to his clergy.

The memorial of St. Peter Claver (September 9), the Spanish-born Jesuit who served as a missionary to Colombia, offered another opportunity to link Scripture, liturgy, the words of the saint, and the lives of the community. Claver would go into the infested holds of the ship where conditions were inhuman, bringing medicine, food, water, and even brandy and oranges, to the sick and miserable. He then preached to them of their human dignity and God's love. A connection with the weekday Gospel of Luke 6:6-11, recounting Jesus healing the man with a withered hand, could be made through Claver's words: "We must serve God with our hands before we serve him with our lips." The image of the human hand could further link saint, biblical text, and the liturgy of the Eucharist through the words at the Preparation of the Gifts: "Blessed are you, Lord, God of all creation, through your goodness we have this bread to offer, which earth has given *and human hands have made.* . . ." The memorial of Peter Claver that year served as a reminder that human hands can wither in different ways, in pain or in greed. But Christ's power can restore these hands so that they can do the work of the kingdom. The hands which we raise in prayer and to receive the Eucharist are the hands sent forth to work for the good of others, to bring help and to bring about change.

22. Quoted in Foley, *Saint of the Day*, 186.

A second way to present the saint as mentor is to preach to the community in the saint's name, a first-person preaching employing the persona of the saint. When preparing, the preacher asks what the particular saint might say to this community on this day if he or she were standing before them. This demands careful preparation, since it involves both research and imagination. Knowledge of the saint's life and work can allow the saint to witness to the community through the biblical texts and to connect gospel, a historical life in which the gospel was embodied, and the lives of the present community in a way that leads to praise and thanksgiving in the Eucharist. There is a need for some caution, not to be play-acting in a way that only calls attention to oneself and one's cleverness. But I think an occasional use of this technique can prove to be quite powerful, and bring new life to preachers by allowing them to look through the eyes of another and speak using their voice. When the saint is authentically joined with the word of God, a powerful word might be spoken.

*The Saint As Metaphor.* Aristotle said that "the greatest thing by far is to be a master of metaphor. It is the one thing that cannot be learnt from others; and it is also a sign of genius, since a good metaphor implies an intuitive perception of the similarity in dissimilars."[23] While I do not agree that one cannot learn to work with metaphor, I do see this form of speech as often the gift of our intuitive powers. Metaphor allows us to use the visible to speak about the invisible, to express what is intuited but not directly perceived. It helps us to reveal our inner states of being: "How like a winter has my absence been from thee"; and our most treasured experiences of relationship: "It is a well in the desert, a flowering tree in the wilderness," Narcissus says to Goldmund about their friendship in Hermann Hesse's novel.

Metaphors invite us to play, searching out the similar in what at first sight is dissimilar. "Tell that fox . . . ," Jesus says about Herod. Jesus was a master of metaphor when preaching about the kingdom of God, using images and stories to draw his listeners into contact with God's breaking into the world about them. David Buttrick has said that "Preachers who wish to transform human lives will have to grasp the sheer power of metaphorical language. With metaphors, we can rename the world for faith."[24]

23. Quoted in *The Princeton Encyclopedia of Poetry and Poetics*, ed. Alex Preminger (Princeton, N.J.: Princeton University Press, 1974) 491.

24. David Buttrick, *Homiletic, Moves and Structures* (Philadelphia: Fortress Press, 1987) 123.

We can think of the saints themselves as metaphors. When I refer to the saints as mirrors, the saint is functioning as a metaphor for God revealed in Christ. And some of the stories and images of the saint at work in the world take us into the realm of metaphor. Sometimes preachers may be tempted to dismiss a particular saint because of the lack of factual data to draw on. All that remains are legends or symbolic iconography. By approaching a particular story or presentation of the saint as metaphor, we can enter a field of play where fresh insights are possible.

We discover this possibility in the images surrounding the virgin martyrs, such as Lotto's famous painting of St. Lucy serenely standing behind ten head of oxen that have been brought to take her to a house of prostitution, a punishment for refusing to marry. She had taken a vow of virginity to Christ. The story goes that neither pleas, threats, soldiers, nor oxen could move her. In short, she would not budge! What a marvelous way to express the strength of one of these young women who stood up to the Roman state and refused to accept its limiting role for them: to marry and breed for the empire.

Virgin martyrs like Lucy, Agatha, Agnes, Dorothy, Perpetua and Felicity come to us, offering what Kathleen Norris calls great psychological truth and providing us with sacramental signs of the power of Christ working in human flesh, most especially female flesh, to defy the limits society had placed on them.[25] Their defiance was made possible by their commitment to Christ, chosen as their true spouse. Norris argues persuasively that they witness to a virginity that is a state of being, and reveal a wild power in the hearts of women that, in turn, allows us to glimpse a love stronger than death, whose only source could be the Power that called forth all creation.

The tales of St. Patrick and the snakes, St. George and the dragon, St. Francis and the wolf of Gubbio, as well as such classical paintings as Del Sarto's *St. Agnes,* holding a palm in her right hand, and stroking a lamb with her left, El Greco's *St. Bernardine of Siena,* marked by a thin staff signaling his devotion to the Holy Name of Jesus, and Tiepolo's *Martyrdom of St. Agatha,* eyes glazed in pain, but hands raised in patient expectation—all use the language of metaphor and symbol to proclaim God's power at work in and through human flesh.[26]

25. Kathleen Norris, "The Virgin Martyrs: Between 'Point Vierge' and the 'Usual Spring,'" *The Cloister Walk* (New York: Riverhead, 1996) 186–205.

26. These three works are found with commentary in *The Mystery of God, Saints in Art Through the Centuries* with commentary by Sister Wendy Beckett (San Francisco: Harper, 1996).

The saint as metaphor can sometimes connect in surprisingly effective ways with the Scripture texts and the lives of the people. That is the intent of preaching on the feast. Otherwise we have a history lesson which may be inspiring and hold interest, but not function to lead the community to the Eucharist. Consider the memorial of St. Blase. There is little historical data available about this saint, apart from his being bishop of Sebaste in Armenia and suffering martyrdom in 316. What has come down is the tradition of blessing throats on this day and the legend behind it, telling how the saintly bishop, captured by the emperor's soldiers and on his way to execution, was approached by a mother whose child was choking on some kind of bone. The mother begged the saint to help. At his command, the child coughed up the bone and was saved. Thus the legend. Now the first reaction is to turn the page and leave St. Blase to the past. But the prayer during the blessing of the throat turns us toward Jesus the healer: "Through the intercession of St. Blase, bishop and martyr, may the Lord deliver you from every ailment of the throat and from every other evil."

When it came time to preach on this feast a few years ago, I decided to see whether it was possible to find a link with the biblical texts for the weekday since there were no assigned readings. I found Mark's account of the beheading of John the Baptist (6:14-29) as the assigned gospel for the day—a coincidence worthy of Stephen King!—what with Blase's association with ailments of the throat. Yet as I read it more carefully, the portrayal of Herod in this account caught my attention. Before Mark tells the story of the beheading, he notes that King Herod had come to hear of Jesus because people were talking about him, speculating who he might be: John the Baptist raised from the dead, or Elijah, or a prophet equal to any of the prophets. Hearing all this, Herod himself exclaims, "John, whose head I had cut off, has been raised up!"

Herod's identifying of Jesus as "John raised up" in this account struck me. And because of the legend of the martyred bishop of Armenia, I began to see it in a new way. Herod's reaction and the legend of Blase became linked for me through the metaphor of choking. There is the physical reality of choking and the metaphorical one. Expressions like something being "stuck in my craw" and "I can't swallow that" come to mind. I began to play with the metaphors of choking and swallowing. Herod was choking over what he had done to John; it was more than likely that his decision to have John beheaded haunted him since he had respected John. He simply had not been able to swallow it.

Then I began to think about the community and some of the things that choke us: the hurts we hold onto, the harsh judgments, and prejudices that can cut off the breath of God in us, the work of the Spirit in our lives. And, of course, at the heart of the story of the saint is the witness to the power of Christ working through the bishop, freeing a child from what was choking him, that same power at work in us, freeing us from what threatens to overcome us. Finally there is the obvious link with the Eucharist, coming to Communion as a time for swallowing, both the sacramental body of Christ and the body of Christ of which we are a part. Metaphor often moves out in different directions, weaving saint's story, biblical text, sacramental rite, and life experience of the community.

The saint as metaphor reminds us of the poetic power of every human life, that around each of us images gather to express who we are, both in our human struggles and in our capacity to reflect the power of God at work in us. Metaphors from our tradition can mediate contact with that community of men and women who live in the Mystery that embraces all believers, from which we came and to which we are destined to return.

## Homilies on the Feasts of the Saints

### A. The Saint as Model: St. Catherine of Siena (April 29) / Monday of the Fourth Week of Easter

(The memorial of St. Catherine of Siena, Doctor of the Church, falls during the Easter season. While it has been assigned an optional first reading, I chose to work here with the readings of the Easter season.)

### "Listeners and Learners"
### (Texts: Acts 11:1-18; John 10:11-18)

It always seemed to take Peter a while to learn.
Peter usually did not get "it"—whatever "it" happened to be.
Even when he seemed to get it, he didn't.
When they were up in Caesarea Philippi and Jesus asks, "Who do you
    say I am?"
Peter without blinking an eye says, "You are the Messiah,"
    but when Jesus goes on to say that he must suffer and die,
    Peter says, "Never, never, never."

And when Jesus goes to wash feet on Holy Thursday, Peter says, "Never,
    never, never."
And when Jesus says, "One of you will betray me," Peter says, "Never,
    never, never."
And after Jesus has risen, sent the Holy Spirit, inaugurating a new age,
and Peter has a vision of a bag full of all creatures fit for the banquet hall,
    and where he is told, three times no less, "Come and get it!"
Peter, true to form, says, "Never, never, never."
It took Peter awhile to learn.

Now Catherine of Siena, on the other hand, seems to have been a quick
    learner.
She knew when she was little that she was in love with Jesus,
    and in the battle of the wills with her mother,
    who had a nice handsome suitor all picked out for her Catherine,
    and probably even the names of the first few grandchildren,
    the teenage Catherine won the war.
Jesus himself came to her in a vision and slid a ring on her finger, and
    told her,
    "As the fish is in the sea, so thou art in me and I in thee,"
    a mystical espousal she wrote about in the *The Dialogue.*
If Jesus said she was his, she was.
Catherine listened and learned.
And Catherine did not hesitate to let other people learn what God was
    saying to her—about *them.*
Thus, Catherine bearded the papal lion in his den at Avignon
    and told the pope that as pleasant as the south of France might be
    he really belonged back in Rome.
She was also a gifted spiritual counselor,
    much sought after by the learned, the pious, and those desiring to
    be holy.
Not too long ago, she was declared a Doctor of the Church,
    one of two women—the other being Teresa of Avila, to have this
    honor.
Such honors could easily remove her from us.
But they shouldn't.
She was attentive to the Good Shepherd and heard the call to join in
    his mission.
And, like Catherine, we are sent out to others to meet the needs of the
    world, and to be Church where Church is needed to be.

We are called to be peacemakers in our own day and in our own way,
   as she was in hers.
There were those who tended to dismiss Catherine,
from her mother to the influential and powerful in the papal court
   just as there are those who dismiss the voices of other women in our
   own day.
But I trust that Christ will continue to instruct, to speak to their hearts,
and those who need to listen will eventually learn to hear the voices of
   today's Catherines—and today's Margarets, today's Dianes, and today's
   Annas.
The pattern seems to be that God more often uses the most surprising
   people,—a Peter, a Catherine—just as God uses the most unexpected material—like wafer-thin bread and mediocre wine—to
   overturn our prejudices and conquer our hearts.

## B. *The Saint As Mirror: St. Nicholas (Dec. 6) / Monday of the Second Week of Advent*

(Since this optional memorial falls within the season of Advent
and Advent weekdays have their own proper Mass texts, the readings
are those assigned to the particular day.)

### *"A Glimpse of Our Generous God"*
### (Isaiah 35:1-10; Luke 5:17-26)

The feast of St. Nicholas was a day we honored at home.
When I was a boy, I would hang up a stocking the night before,
And usually I would find several pieces of fruit, some nuts,
   some change wrapped individually in silver foil.
And then there was a piece or two of black coal; *cautionary coal*, if you will.
The coal served as an early warning system in relation to Christmas.
Quite German, to be translated as: "You can always do better."
Our family's version of "Sin no more."
As I got older I realized how liturgically appropriate the whole thing was.
The coal fit in quite well with that motif of repentance that runs
   through Advent:
   John the Baptist calling us to prepare a way for the Lord.
And the rest of the stocking with its fruits and candy and small coins gave
   the more positive side: I was destined for the fruits of redemption.
I was made to celebrate God's ongoing gift of Self to our world.

St. Nicholas, a bishop in today's Turkey, speaks to us of divine generosity.
Did you know the symbol of three golden balls that hangs over pawn-
shops goes back to one of the stories handed down about this saint?
The balls represented the three bags of gold he gave over the years to a
poor father so his daughters would have a dowry and be able to marry.
He gave to those in need, quite fitting for the season that prepares us
for gift giving.
Nicholas images the generosity of God that today's readings speak of.

The heart of the reading from Isaiah 35 proclaims:
"Here is your God,
who comes with vindication;
With divine recompense
He comes to save you."
Isaiah saw God coming to a creation in need and to a people disabled.
He saw God coming to defeat the powers of death that disable us,
and to give good gifts that would restore both creation and us.
For when this God comes, creation would blossom
And all those who are disabled will be healed:
The blind will see, the deaf hear, the dumb speak and the lame leap like
stags.

And Luke's Jesus is also concerned about restoring what is lacking,
giving what's needed.
He looks into the heart and forgives the sin that disables this man.
"My friend, your sins are forgiven you."
Then, in the face of the grumbling by the "pious" folk, he calls the man
to full stature.
"Get up. Take your mat with you, and return to your house."
This is what Jesus does when he comes: he gets us back on our feet.
"At once the man stood erect before them."
Jesus lifts us up from whatever crippling shape sin takes in our lives and
calls us to walk.
The man in the gospel did not just walk away;
he walked the way of the God who ransoms, rescues and redeems.
"He went home praising God."
We are all slouching towards Bethlehem to be born.
Listen again to the prayer that began our liturgy:
"Father, hear our prayers for mercy,
and by the help of St. Nicholas

keep us safe from all danger,
and guide us on the way to salvation."
As we walk to the altar this morning to receive the God who brings
    food and forgiveness, may our hearts leap for joy, knowing our God
    guides us on the way of redemption.

### C. The Saint as Mentor: St. Thomas the Apostle / The Second Sunday of Easter

(In all three cycles of Sunday readings in the Lectionary, Thomas
is featured in the gospel for the second Sunday of Easter. He is a fitting mentor for the Easter season stretching before us.)

### Thomas's Reply

### (John 20:19-31)

Thomas has come down to us as Doubting Thomas.
It has always seemed to me an example of "Make one mistake and they
    never forget it."
I have been thinking what Thomas might say to us today if he were here.
So I decided to write this homily in his voice.
I would ask you to use your imagination this morning and to see before
    you Thomas.

Good Morning, everyone.
Well, you know, I thought they had gotten into the wine.
I mean, we had all crept back into the city between late Friday night
    and early Saturday morning, moving from shadow to shadow.
We returned to the same room we had eaten that last meal with him.
As soon as everyone arrived, we locked the door.
We were scared. They had killed him; surely we would be next.
And so, there we were; no one was talking much, everyone with his own
    thoughts.
We could barely look at each other. Embarrassed, ashamed, a sorry lot.
By Sunday the food was gone and so was the water.
So out I went.

Well, when I came back in, you'd have thought it was like the old days
    when we did a lot of partying.
They were yelling and laughing and crying and no one was making much
    sense.

I thought they had gotten into the wine.

Then, Peter came up and grabbed me by the shoulders, shook me, and
said, "He came back! He was here! All of a sudden he was here! He's
alive."

I must have looked at him like he was out of his head.

He had been the most dejected of us all the past few days;
    now he glowed with excitement.

Before I could say anything, the rest had gathered around and were talking over and through one another and I couldn't make out a thing.

I really thought they had gone out of their heads,
    and I began looking towards the door.

Finally, I said, "Listen, let me tell you this: when I can put my finger
into his hands and my hand into his side, that's when I'll believe."

Well, a week goes by and enough time to come out of whatever fantasy
they were in.

But no one changed the story.

James and John, never particularly patient, began to look at me
    like I needed to have some sense pounded into me.

And then Philip, who could get a bit uppity now and then, the Greek
name and all, and the other James, a stolid, unimaginative fellow, kept
trying to convince me, talking ever so slowly, as if to a child.

But I just kept saying, "Yeah, sure, and last night Moses dropped by,
and we had a jug of wine together, to wash down the manna he
brought."

And then I would say again, also ever so patiently,
    "Look, I'll believe it when I can put my fingers in his wounds and
my hands in his side."

Well, you know the rest.

That Sunday when he came again, I was just dozing off.

And suddenly there he was, standing in the middle of the room.

And he was looking around.

When he caught my eye, he smiled.

"Thomas, come here," he said.

They told me later he said I could put my fingers in his hands and my
hand in his side.

But I never heard those words.

I was up out of my chair at the first syllable of "Thomas" and stumbling
towards him.

I tripped over my own feet.

He *was* alive—he *had* come back.

There was something different about him, but it was him.

"My Lord, My God" came tumbling out of my mouth. (Where had that come from?)

Ever since, people have called me "Doubting Thomas."

Well, that's all right.

As long as you also remember it was I who had talked the rest into going with him back to Bethany when Lazarus got so sick and died;
the hostility and hatred against Jesus was heavy at that time.

And, anyway, you might have doubted too if you had first heard it from that crowd.

You know, people make like I was the only one who didn't believe until I had seen.

But none of the others believed until they had seen him either.

(Well, except for the Beloved Disciple—there's always one!)

If they had believed, would they have been cowering up in that room after the women came with the news?

My question to you is: Do you believe?

It's not a bad thing to believe because of what you see, you know.

You can see signs of the Lord, and of God the Father who raised him, every day.

When you walk outside this time of year and new life is breaking through all about you, how can you not believe, given what you see.

And when you look into the eyes of your wife or your husband,
and see that the love that began years ago is still there, despite the ups and downs, only deeper now—how can you not believe, in light of what you see.

And when you come together here on a Sunday and look at a piece of bread and a cup of wine, and hear the words, "The Body of Christ," "The Blood of Christ," do you believe because of what you see?

The real challenge, of course, is: do you believe when you *can't* see?

When the signs of God have vanished?

When you look at the face of violence, at the ugliness of hatred,
when you feel the heartbreak of a sudden loss,
when sickness comes to your family—to you or to someone you love,
and when you know the pain of death, of losing the person who was your life partner, or your child, or your mother or father, a friend,

when you can't see any light, just darkness . . .
Do you believe then?
Blessed are they who do *not* see and yet believe.
That's the tough part.

All of it's a gift, you know—this believing—all a gift.
I think it's part of the peace he came to give that first Sunday.
If you got it, thank God for it.
If you don't, ask God for it.
After what Jesus went through, I can't imagine your being turned down.
In the meantime, you are not alone, as I wasn't that morning long ago.
There are those around you who believe and walk with you.
Including me . . . and, of course, the Lord, our Lord and our God.

### D. The Saint As Metaphor—SS Michael, Gabriel, and Raphael, Archangels (Sept. 29)

(These figures of power and graciousness continue to speak to us in our desire to touch the transcendent and our need to know God is near. They are rich in metaphorical possibilities for proclaiming the ongoing wonders and ways of God, come to fulfillment in Jesus. The readings for this feast are found in the Proper of the Saints; there is an option for the first reading.)

### Cracking the Code

#### (Texts: Rev 12:7-12; John 1:47-51)

How do you crack the code of this feast?
What do you do with a trio of archangels? In a postmodern age, no less!
Treat it as a superstitious remnant to be jettisoned with other forms of
    outdated piety?
Efforts have been made to modernize them:
Gabriel is honored as the patron of postal workers,
    and Raphael assigned to those involved in health care,
    and Michael is the patron saint of security forces.
But does that really help?
Or does it only make us question all the more their relevance,
    to say nothing of their competence?
It may help to keep in mind the Latin pronunciation of their names:
Gabri-El, Rapha-El, and Micha-El;

(since it calls attention to the final syllable, *El*—one of the Hebrew names
   for God).
Gabri-El: God is strong. Rapha-El: God heals. Micha-El: Who is like
   God?
Or we might change the customary image and see them not with wings
   but as figures of light—like William Tanner does in his painting of
   the Annunciation.
Quite appropriate since light was the first creation.
God said, "Let there be light!" and the angels danced and sang.
Or perhaps we might imagine them as sounds, each a kind of music:
with Gabriel a Mozartean burst of joy,
Raphael more Fauré, a sound that soothes and heals,
and Michael, a Wagnerian crescendo signaling power and might.
But wherever your capacity to imagine takes you,
today's feast calls us to think of each of them.

A good beginning is found in their stories in Scripture.
Gabriel, sent to the young Miriam of Nazareth,
   is wonderfully captured on the bronze door of the basilica in Nazareth.
He is coming into Mary's home at a 90-degree angle,
   penetrating her world, and ours, as God is inclined to do,
   with an invitation to be a carrier of new life, of Life Himself.
Gabriel reminds us that God continues to work through us in bringing
   Christ to birth in the world.
Gabriel reminds us that words of invitation continue to be spoken,
   so that, like Miriam, we will voice our "yes,"
   and then proceed out of our security into the lives of others,
   as she did with Elizabeth.

And Raphael, captured in innumerable artworks as faithful companion
   to Tobias in his quest for a soul mate, and healer of the blindness of
   that young man's father Tobit, brings assurance of an abiding presence whose desire is to heal and journey with us.
At a time when our country has failed to find a way to enact a comprehensive health policy to embrace all who live in our land,
Raphael speaks to us about a God whose will is that people be physically
   cared for, about a God of salvation, of health of spirit, mind, and body.

Particularly relevant these days is Michael.
Two Redemptorist parishes have tremendous statues of Michael.

In the vestibule of St. Michael's, in Baltimore, stands a 20-foot statue
  which used to tower over the neighborhood from the roof.
Michael is brandishing his sword, the warrior archangel we hear of in
  Revelation 12.
In St. Michael's Chicago, the top of the reredos behind the altar portrays
  Michael standing over a cowering Lucifer, the Light-bearer who per-
  versely chose darkness.
Michael, "Who is like God?," speaks of the divine power that can over-
  come evil.
Certainly, there is more to this image than the patron saint of security
  forces.
Michael calls us to join in the battle against all that destroys goodness,
  all that threatens the little ones,
  all that perverts our better angels.
Michael gives us courage when the odds seem insurmountable.

We heard today that curious saying of Jesus:
  "You will see angels ascending and descending on the Son of Man."
The Son of Man is the connecting ladder between heaven and earth.
The Son of Man is now the point of contact for all those angelic powers
  which proclaim the possibility of new life,
  which bring an abiding presence of divine companionship and healing,
  which cast down evil and restore good.
Through our baptism we are joined to this Son of Man, Jesus, Giver of
  eternal life.
And angelic powers can now move through us,
  bringing light and music to our world and its peoples,
  so all may hear the song of salvation, healing and joy that is the desire
  of our God.

### (E) The Saints on Sunday: Thirty-Third Sunday of the Year (A)

(This final example is a Sunday homily in which some uncanon-
ized saints were featured. This Sunday preceded the tenth anniversary
of the martyrdom of six Jesuit priests and two laywomen by the military in San Salvador, November 16, 1989. Holding up these men and
women helped bring the challenge of the gospel into our own day. It is
not only the canonized who continue to speak to us.)

*Dwelling in Wisdom's House*

(Texts: Prov 31:10-13, 19-20, 30-31; 1 Thess 5:1-6; Matt 25:14-30)

Let's begin with the woman who brings the book of Proverbs to a close.
She is praised for being a gem, a jewel, an unfailing prize for her husband.
She's great at making clothes—and is good to the poor and needy—
    and fears the Lord.
She's even more than this when you read the verses omitted from day's
    reading.
She is the boss of the household—assigning tasks to the servants.
And she is quite the businesswoman:
She estimates the value of a field, buys it, and, with her earnings, plants a
    vineyard.
She tackles her work with vigor, her arms are strong.
She sees that her business goes well, and all night long her lamp is
    burning.
She makes linen garments and sells them—a biblical Laura Ashley.
The final lines say: "Give her a reward for her labors
    and let her works praise her at the city gates."

But there is more to her than that: she is a figure of Wisdom—God's
    Wisdom.
Call her Lady Wisdom or Woman Wisdom (if you find the title "Lady"
    too patriarchal).
There is a whole body of literature in the Old Testament called Wisdom
    Literature.
Wisdom is not esoteric knowledge, reserved for a few, but it is to be
    sought by all.
We are all called to be wise—remember last week's parable of the wise
    virgins.
Wisdom has to do with life in the world, and it is a gift from God,
a call from God to live a certain way.
And so we have this figure of the wise woman at the end of the book
    of Proverbs, who tends her household, who cares for the needy and
    poor, who fears the Lord, who has a loving reverence and obedience
    to God's will.
She is the embodiment of God's Wisdom, and in her house we are
    called to dwell.

Jesus tells us a story about the wise and unwise.

Like the gospel last week, this one speaks to a Church waiting for the
  Lord to return.
Last week we were told to keep awake like wise virgins and be ready
  when he comes.
This week we are told what to do while we are waiting.
There are two servants who get praised because they take the riches
  entrusted to them and wisely invest them—and the one servant who
  does nothing.
When the third man buries his, he gets the ax and is tossed into the
  darkness.
Now we might tend to favor the underdog, to feel sorry for the poor guy.
And so we may believe him when he says to the master:
  "I know how harsh you are. You reap where you don't sow
  and gather where you don't scatter."
But the fact is the master is not harsh with the others; he doubles their
  wealth.
His anger flares because the man did nothing with what he was given,
  except bury it.

Now we can hear this as a cautionary tale about being responsible with
  our talents, leading us to examine what gifts we have and how we
  employ them.
But the treasure involved here can be understood as even more particular.
We are talking here about the special gift God has given to us in Jesus:
the gift of the gospel, the Good News, the teaching of Jesus, the Wisdom
  of God.
And the question is: what have we done with that this year?
Did we wrap it up and put it aside? Or did we invest it in life, our lives?
What have we done with the teachings of Jesus, the words of Jesus we
  hear every week?

This coming week on November 16th, we remember the six Jesuits and
  the two women who were so brutally murdered ten years ago in San
  Salvador, machine-gunned on the lawn.
Ignazio Ellacuria, Ignazio Martin-Baro, Amando Lopez, Juan Moreno,
  Joaquin Lopez-Lopez, Segundo Montes, and their cook, Elba Ramos,
  and her sixteen-year-old daughter Celine—both had stayed the night
  there because they thought it was safer than returning home.
Ignazio Ellacuria was president of the University of Central America;
  he was the main target.

The other five Jesuits were theologians, one an expert in catechetics, and
a psychologist.

They were marked as sympathizers with the leftist rebels,
feared by the military because they championed the teachings of social
justice rooted in the gospel.

They were working for a negotiated settlement between the government
and the rebels.

These men were champions of the poor, and they denounced the reign
of terror that the military excelled in.

These men took seriously the teachings of Jesus in the Gospel of
Matthew:

"Blessed are the poor in spirit, those who mourn, the peacemakers,
those who hunger and thirst for justice . . ."

They took seriously Jesus' call to follow him, to care for the least and the
lowly.

These women were there because one of them was a loyal worker and
caretaker, and a careful mother, not wishing her daughter to be in
danger.

She had stayed the night with her daughter because this was a place of
safety, a good place to be on a dangerous night.

All were like the Wise Woman, their hands open to the poor, reaching
out to the needy.

Their deaths marked the end of the 1980s, as the death of Bishop
Oscar Romero and four American women: Ita Ford, Maura Clark,
Dorothy Kazel and Jean Donovan, marked the beginning of that
decade.

All martyrs of El Salvador who chose to live out the wisdom of God
in the struggle for justice and peace.

We are called to take to heart the wisdom of Jesus that we have heard this
year,

wisdom grounded in the teachings of Jesus in this Gospel of Matthew.

We are called to build our house on the rock of the words and deeds of
Jesus, our teacher of wisdom, who will come to judge us on the basis
of whether we feed the hungry, give drink to the thirsty, clothe the
poor, visit the imprisoned.

We are called to take the wisdom of this Gospel and to invest it in life,
not to wrap it up and bury it.

Jesus gathers us around a table every week and feeds us and says:
"Be Eucharist in the world.

Take your body and your blood, and give it to others, spend it for others.
Then you will dwell in the house Wisdom has built for all her children.

May we make our home with Wisdom,
    let her clothe us and nourish us and send us out into the world,
    and at the end of our days let us return to dwell with her in peace
    and joy forever.

## Summary

Some time ago I was reading the morning paper and a local psychotherapist was being quoted. I remember her words: "the disease of our generation is loneliness." More recently, I came across Robert D. Putnam's book, *Bowling Alone: The Collapse and Revival of American Community*;[27] it offers a presentation of the decline of civic engagement on the part of many Americans in terms of our ever-lessening participation in politics, Church life, parent-teacher organizations, and other civic arenas. With this situation comes a decline in the connections between people that foster trust and a cooperative spirit that extends beyond one's own limited sphere, and a decline in "social capital" that is the resource of much social outreach to those in need. Preaching on the feasts of the saints can work in response to both of these issues. It can speak to that part of our lives where we feel isolated and lonely by reminding the community of that much larger community in today's world to which we belong. And our preaching can awaken their imagination with the memories of those men and women who continue to serve as glimpses of the face of God and models of human response to grace.

Such preaching can also help to stimulate a hunger for belonging to this wider community of holy ones, by holding up these men and woman who in their own time were forces serving the good of the least and most abandoned. Storyteller and theologian John Shea wrote a poem called "Friends in high places." It begins by picturing the saints "in stained-glassed glory," locked into their traditional poses of prayer and intercessory acts, and concludes with them climbing down, scrambling through the pews, lifting the processional cross from its stand and making for the door, "pausing only long enough to smile and wave at us to join them." They invite us to join this larger community of light and participate in works of light needed in our world today.

27. Robert D. Putnam, *Bowling Alone: The Collapse and Revival of American Community* (New York: Simon & Schuster, 2000).

To foster the role of preaching on the feasts of the saints as one responding to the hunger for belonging, let us keep in mind:

(a) The first purpose of the liturgical homily during the Eucharist is to enable the community to give thanks and praise during the Liturgy of the Eucharist and to motivate them to live out the gospel in daily life. To this end, the preacher provides a biblical interpretation of the life of the community that binds it in a common vision.

(b) In doing this, the saints can play an active role, serving as mirrors, models, mentors, and metaphors within the human community graced by God. Preachers can bring the community to encounter the saints on their feasts, helping to forge friendships and deepening our sense of what it means to be God's family. In doing this, they also serve to connect the people with the saints on a more intimate level, if only once a year, and to satisfy the hunger to be part of a community that is both supportive and challenging.

(c) For this to happen, preachers need to immerse themselves in three worlds: the world of the listeners, the world(s) of the biblical texts, and the world of the saint, respecting each in its own right, but looking for connections between them. The saints are to serve the Word of God, and in doing this, we come to know them as our family and friends.

(d) In bringing the saints into the homily, a few brush strokes can be enough to make them present. While we might learn a great deal in researching them, the use of this material is to be done with economy. Often, a moment from their lives, or a thought memorably expressed is enough to illuminate and link the biblical text with our lives in the eucharistic setting. In short, don't be seduced by the saint. The saints serve the proclamation of the gospel. We preach Christ.

(e) For further reading:

- *Butler's Lives of the Saints*. 12 vols. (Collegeville: The Liturgical Press, 1995–2000).
- Robert Ellsberg, *All Saints: Daily Reflections on Saints, Prophets, and Witnesses for Our Time* (New York: Crossroad, 1998).
- Leonard Foley, O.F.M., ed., *Saint of the Day: Lives and Lessons for Saints and Feasts of the New Missal* (Cincinnati: St. Anthony Messenger, 1990).
- Elizabeth A. Johnson, *Friends of God and Prophets, A Feminist Theological Reading of the Communion of Saints* (New York: Continuum, 1998).

Chapter 5

# Preaching Through the Saints and the Hunger for Belonging: II—Mary

*"The Madonna is not happy when she is placed before her Son."*

(John XXIII)

*"Mary wants to get off the pedestal.
She wants to be a vital human being."*[1]

(Kathy Denison, *Time*)

*"As Saint Ambrose taught, the Mother of God is a type of the church in the order of faith, charity, and perfect union with Christ."*

(The Constitution on the Church, no. 63)

### Saint Mary and the Challenge of Preaching the Marian Feasts

Even though there are many churches called St. Mary's, do we really think of her that way? *Saint* Mary. Do you pray to *Saint* Mary? Do you have devotion to *Saint* Mary? I wonder if, on some level, we fear that this title does not sufficiently do justice to her privileged role in salvation history? The Eucharistic Prayers refer to her as Mary, the virgin mother of God. Our feasts generally refer to her either as Mary, Mother of God, or Our Lady (of Lourdes, of Mount Carmel, of Sorrows), or, quite simply, Mary (Birth of . . . , Presentation of . . . , Queenship of . . .), with one occasion using a more specific title, the Immaculate Conception. While St. Mary is certainly appropriate, since

1. "Handmaid or Feminist?", *Time* (Dec. 30, 1991) 62.

she is the first of the saints of the new covenant, still it does not satisfy. Just as her intimacy with her Son goes back to the moment of his conception, so her companionship with the Church goes back to the moment of its birth on Pentecost. For the first companions of the Lord, she was Mary, mother of Jesus, mother of the Lord, spouse of Joseph, cousin to Elizabeth, fellow disciple, companion in the journey of faith.

When it comes to Mary, mother of Jesus, preachers are called to foster an ongoing relationship. Next to her son, she is the most acknowledged person in the liturgical life of the Church. With few exceptions, we encounter the various apostles, martyrs, virgins, mystics, holy men and women, once a year on their feast day, or perhaps as key figures during a particular liturgical season—John the Baptist in Advent and Peter, Thomas, and Mary Magdalene during Easter come to mind. But with Mary, the mother of Jesus, it is a different story, or, more accurately, there are many stories, events, and occasions that invite the community of believers to stop and contemplate this woman's unique role in salvation history, her special place in the affections of those who acknowledge her son as Lord and Redeemer, and the implications of her life and ongoing role in the life of the Church for our own lives. Looking at the Liturgical Year, one finds fourteen days designated either as solemnities, feasts, or memorials of Mary, in addition to her strong presence during the Advent and Christmas seasons, on Good Friday and Pentecost, and even on liturgical days redesignated as celebrations of the Lord, such as the Annunciation and the Presentation in the Temple. So, attention must be paid. It is fitting that preachers reflect on how we present Mary, Mother of the Redeemer, to the community of the Redeemed.

Furthermore, we are living at a time when interest in Mary also appears to be undergoing a renaissance among Catholics and Protestants. In the last decade, works on Mary have included historian Jaroslav Pelikan's *Mary Through the Centuries*, theologian George Tavard's *The Thousand Faces of the Virgin Mary*, and liturgist J. D. Crichton's *Our Lady in the Liturgy*.[2] Sally Cuneen's personal quest has provided *The Search for Mary, the Woman and the Symbol*, storyteller Megan McKenna has given us *Mary, Shadow of Grace* and poet-essayist Kathleen Norris

---

2. Jaroslav Pelikan, *Mary Through the Centuries: Her Place in the History of Culture* (New Haven: Yale, 1996); George H. Tavard, *The Thousand Faces of the Virgin Mary* (Collegeville: The Liturgical Press, 1996); J. D. Crichton, *Our Lady in the Liturgy* (Collegeville: The Liturgical Press, 1997).

has recently offered *Meditations On Mary*.[3] "Mary, the first theologian" was the focus of the October 1999 issue of the Protestant quarterly, *Theology Today*. Add to these cover stories in *Time* (December 30, 1991), *Life* (September 1996), and *Newsweek* (August 25, 1997), and even a 1999 television movie, *Mary of Nazareth*. One can say at the very least that there must be a market for Mary.

Yet, for all this, as a teacher of homiletics, I have found that the major feasts of Mary evoke little passion among preachers, often creating more apprehension than enthusiasm, especially among beginning preachers. There seems to be an uncertainty about what one should say about Mary, and a questioning about the value and even credibility of much that has been handed down, and how it can be related to people living in today's culture. How do we make sense of such doctrines as the Immaculate Conception and the Assumption as well as the Queenship of Mary and the apocryphal Presentation in the Temple? To quote the old Rodgers and Hammerstein song, "How do you solve a problem like Maria?"

In this chapter, I would like to do three things that might assist preachers: (a) consider five ways of relating to Mary that predominate among those writing and thinking about her today; (b) review the criteria for a sound Marian devotion provided by Paul VI in his 1974 apostolic exhortation, *Devotion to the Blessed Virgin Mary* (*Marialis Cultus*), as applicable to the preaching we do on Marian feasts; and (c) apply the four ways of preaching on the feast of a saint to the various Marian feasts, thereby encouraging preachers to present Mary as a companion on the journey of faith who draws us more deeply into the community of all believers.

## Images of Mary, Past and Present

Every generation has not only called her blessed but has also found ways to relate to her that have made her accessible to all ages and cultures and fostered an abiding recognition of her as "a sign of certain hope and comfort to the pilgrim people of God" (Constitution on the Church, no. 68). In our own day, five images of Mary continue to have prominence:

3. Sally Cuneen, *In Search of Mary, The Woman and the Symbol* (New York: Ballentine, 1996); Megan McKenna, *Mary, Shadow of God's Grace* (Maryknoll: Orbis, 1994); Kathleen Norris, *Meditations On Mary* (New York: Viking, 1999).

1. *Mary, Mother of Jesus.* This is the biblical designation for Mary; it is the reason she will be honored and venerated until the end of time. This relationship is at the heart of all the Marian feasts and is explicitly recognized in the opening prayer of most liturgies. Mary is who she is for us because she was the mother of Jesus. As the mother of Jesus, she is the mother of the Son of God, the crucified Savior, the risen Lord, Emmanuel, in whom God has acted for our salvation. Because of this role in salvation history, she came to be designated the Mother of God (*Theotokos*; literally, "God-bearer" or "Forth-bringer of God") at the Council of Ephesus in 431. Because the biblical witness and sound doctrine must be at the heart of all preaching on the Marian feasts, let us briefly review it.

The first appearance of Mary in the Bible stresses the divine initiative. In Matthew 1:20-21, the angel tells Joseph not to be afraid to take Mary as his wife, "for the child conceived in her is from the Holy Spirit. She will bear a son, and you are to name him Jesus, for he will save his people from their sins." In Luke 1:35 the angel tells Mary, "The Holy Spirit will come upon you, and the power of the Most High will overshadow you; therefore the child to be born will be holy; he will be called Son of God." These fundamental assertions place Mary in proper relationship to the mystery of the Triune God. Her unique role renders her "blessed among women" and "the Mother of my Lord" as Elizabeth proclaims (Luke 1:42). Thus, this basic affirmation of Mary as Mother of God is christological. We identify her in terms of her relationship with Jesus, as the Mother of Christ, Mother of the Lord, Mother of God.

Believers have related primarily to this image of Mary over the centuries; it has engaged the imaginations of poets, artists, musicians, and preachers. "This is the carnal rose that re-enfolds heaven into earth," quotes Geoffrey Hill in his poem to "Our Lady of Chartres," delicately imaging her role in the mystery of the incarnation.[4] Furthermore, in bearing Jesus, she became the mother of all who believe in him. While it was Paul VI who favored the title "Mother of the Church," this recognition is also given in the patristic age when she was called the "New Eve," mother of all the living, an image itself rooted in her presence at the cross in John's Gospel, from which tree came forth eternal life. Alongside the "New Adam," she ushered in the new creation and was henceforth considered the spiritual mother of all those united in the Mystical Body of Christ.

4. See *Upholding Mystery: An Anthology of Contemporary Christian Poetry*, ed. David Impastato (New York: Oxford, 1997) 269.

2. *Mary, Model of Faith.* Of the Synoptic Gospels, it is Luke who makes the greatest case for the ongoing imitation of Mary by all believers. Luke's presentation reveals her as one who hears the word of God and responds wholeheartedly to it: "Here I am, the servant of the Lord; let it be with me according to your word" (Luke 1:38). Her cousin Elizabeth's greeting recognizes Mary's response when she cries out, "Blessed is she who believed that there would be a fulfillment of what was spoken to her by the Lord" (Luke 1:45). Mary attentively listened to the shepherds' report of what the angels had spoken about her son, and "treasured all these words and pondered them in her heart" (Luke 2:19). Luke's Mary witnesses the encounter between her infant son and his people, represented by the wisdom figures of Simeon and Anna, hearing the words about her child's destiny as "a sign that will be opposed," and her own participation in that sword-like suffering (Luke 2:34-5). Eamon Carroll notes that, due to the Second Vatican Council's use of the so-called "difficult sayings" from the public life, that is, the incidents of the true kinsman (Mark 3:31-5; Matt 12:46-9; Luke 8:19-21) and the enthusiastic woman (Luke 11:27-28), "texts which formerly some had interpreted as being critical of Mary, were now read as praise for the Mother of Jesus, applying them to her as one who does God's will (Mark/Matt), and who hears the word of God and keeps it (Luke)."[5] Finally, there is Luke's last image of Mary, waiting once again on the Spirit (Acts 1:14), this time with the apostles and other disciples in the upper room in Jerusalem, joined with them in prayerful expectation, in readiness for that overshadowing that will bring to birth the new body of Christ, the Church. Mary's role is to be in their midst, praying and waiting with them for God's action through the Spirit.

John's Gospel also offers us Mary as the woman of faith, presenting her at Cana as one whose request is based on a true intuition of faith, not merely on their biological relationship (2:1-11), and whose presence at the foot of the cross furthers this theme by presenting both Mary and the beloved disciple as representing the community of true believers (12:25-7). Pheme Perkins notes that Mary's position here is equivalent to that of the beloved disciple, not yet above it. Together they serve as the heart of that community Jesus came to establish, having perceived his "hour of glory" and responded to it in spirit and truth.[6] In the Fourth Gospel, Mary is present at the beginning and the

---

5. Eamon Carroll, *Understanding the Mother of Jesus* (Wilmington: Glazier, 1979) 13.

6. Pheme Perkins, "Mary in Johannine Traditions," *Mary, Woman of Nazareth: Biblical and Theological Perspectives*, ed. Doris Donnelly (New York: Paulist, 1989) 114.

end of Jesus' ministry, as faithful disciple and as a witness to "the hour" when the glory of God was fully revealed.

3. *Mary, Prophet of God's Justice.* The foundational text for honoring Mary as prophet is Luke 1:46-55 with her bursting into that great biblical aria, the Magnificat. Here she joins with all those prophetic voices in Israel's history which proclaimed Yahweh as the God who saves, lifts up and does great things for the lowly, and who is the hope of the oppressed and the downtrodden. Whereas Matthew's genealogy (1:1-16) puts Mary in the role of an "outsider," chosen to play a pivotal role at a key moment in Israel's story just as Tamar, Rahab, Ruth, and Bathsheba did, Luke's portrayal of Mary singing her canticle places her within the sisterhood of women of great courage and faith, alongside such figures as Miriam, Hannah, Deborah, Judith, and the mother of the Maccabees. Mary of Nazareth, her heart and body having received the Word of God, moves out into the world to serve, attentive to the counsel of the Spirit. In this moment of proclamation she is the courageous herald of the power of God, faithful witness to the hope of fulfillment, and subversive agent opposing the unjust status quo of the rich and self-satisfied.

Both liberation theology and feminist biblical scholarship have taken up this image of Mary. Leonardo Boff writes that even though traditional Christianity "has rendered the critical, liberating content of the Magnificat impotent, today's Church must take up its urgent task and develop a prophetic image of Mary—an image of Mary as the strong determined woman, the woman committed to the messianic liberation of the poor from the historical social injustices under which they suffer."[7] In a similar vein, theologian Sydney Callahan refers to Mary as "the mother of Christian feminism" who enlists us in the liberation of women because "in so many instances women remain the poorest of the poor, unjustly subjected to gender discrimination, sexual abuse, and violence."[8] The words of Mary's Magnificat confront any situation where social, political, economic, or sexual oppression remains. God is for the poor, especially for the poorest of the poor who most often are women in today's world.

4. *Mary, the Female/Feminine Face of God.* A further contribution of feminist theology has been to bring to the consciousness of the com-

7. Leonardo Boff, *The Maternal Face of God* (San Francisco: Harper and Row, 1987) 189.

8. Sydney Callahan, "Mary and the Challenges of the Feminist Movement," *America* (Dec. 18, 1993) 7.

munity how the image of Mary has done over the centuries what the image of the three Persons of the Trinity was unable to do; she has functioned as the carrier of the "female face" of God. Elizabeth Johnson writes that "images of God as female, arguably necessary for the full expression of the mystery of God but suppressed from official formulations, have migrated to the figure of this woman."[9] One of the most radical expressions of this movement is found in the work of Leonardo Boff who sees Mary as the embodiment of a hypostatic union with the Holy Spirit.[10] But while this is the most extreme example,[11] throughout our history there has been a tendency to attribute to Mary the divine compassion, mercy, and tenderness of God. Johnson concludes that the challenge in our age is to retrieve these divine aspects, lifting them from Mary, and directly attribute them to God as female. In this way God will be proclaimed in a fullness presently lacking, "letting God be imaged as a female acting subject," and Mary will be restored to her full stature as "a genuine woman whose life was a journey of faith."[12]

A similar approach is to speak of Mary as the *feminine* face of God, the one who "reveals to us the feminine dimensions of the Christian God."[13] One problem with this approach is that the meaning of "feminine" is so culturally determined. The justified complaint of feminist authors is that what is often referred to as "feminine" is the male idea of what constitutes femininity, that is, the "patriarchal feminine." Mary Gordon has written of her experience of Mary back in the 1960s when "Mary was a stick to beat smart girls with. Her example was held up constantly: an example of silence, subordination, of the pleasure of taking the back seat." Gordon's response was to reject this but found herself "denied a potent female image whose application was universal."[14] Johnson, again, is helpful when she calls for female images of God rather than speaking of feminine dimensions or traits, arguing that both male and female images are needed, that both are capable of imaging

9. Elizabeth Johnson, "Mary and the Image of God," *Mary, Woman of Nazareth*, ed. Doris Donnelly, 26.

10. Boff, *The Maternal Face of God*, 93.

11. For a critique of Boff's position, see Tavard, *The Thousand Faces of the Virgin Mary*, 261–63.

12. Johnson, "Mary and the Image of God," 28.

13. Andrew Greeley, *The Mary Myth, On the Femininity of God* (New York: Seabury, 1977) 217.

14. Mary Gordon, "Coming to Terms with Mary," *Commonweal* (Jan. 15, 1982) 11.

the holy mystery, neither able to exhaust it. Such female imagery that would constitute "ultimate metaphors" for the Divine Mystery could include God as Mother, as Divine Compassion, as Female Saving Power, as Immanent Presence, and as Recreative Energy.[15]

I agree with the goal of offering female imagery to complement the male imagery that has long been dominant in the Christian imagination. This is in line with the example of Scripture itself, which speaks of God in a variety of metaphors, animate and inanimate, human and nonhuman, masculine and feminine.[16] And I can understand the desire to remove from Mary the burden of carrying the God image, of functioning as the "feminine face of God" and restoring her to the community as one who walked in faith and continues in her role as mother of the faithful. Still, I do not think men and women will cease finding in Mary one who images God, as every holy man and woman does in a unique way.

In discussing the role of the saints in the last chapter, it was noted that the Constitution on the Church spoke of the saints' lives, inasmuch as they are "more perfectly transformed into the image of Christ," as the place where "God shows, vividly, to humanity his presence and his face" (no. 50). For two millennia Mary has been first and foremost among the saints in this role of manifesting God's "presence" and "face" to all the generations of the faithful that have come after her. Our challenge is to help others recognize whom we are ultimately seeing at work when we marvel at her whom "all generations call blessed," and to remember, as two of the solemnities in her honor remind us—the Immaculate Conception and the Assumption—that she remains the first recipient of the salvation won for us by Christ.

5. *Mary, Woman.* The earliest reference to Mary is found in Paul's letter to the Galatians which refers to Jesus as "born of a woman" (Gal

---

15. Johnson, "Mary and the Image of God," 48–54.

16. Sandra Schneiders notes the numerous human metaphors for God in the Old Testament, including such role metaphors as potter, builder, shepherd, hero, warrior, physician, midwife, homemaker, judge, and king, in addition to such relational metaphors as mother, husband, and father. And while Jesus in the Gospels imaged God as father, he also offered parables that presented God as a bakerwoman kneading the leaven of the reign of God, and as a woman who rejoiced to find the coin she had lost. Furthermore, he referred to himself not only as the Son of Man who would suffer and die and be raised, but also as a mother hen who longed to cuddle her chicks under her wing. See Sandra M. Schneiders, *Woman and the Word: The Gender of God in the New Testament and the Spirituality of Women* (New York: Paulist, 1986) 20–50.

4:4). While so much of even today's popular religious art presents an image of Mary as the Fairy Queen, the "lovely Lady dressed in blue," she is first of all a woman, born into a specific time, place, and culture. She lived in an occupied country where violence and poverty were part of the landscape. Johnson calls attention to our "debt to third world women theologians who have noticed the similarities between Mary's life and the lives of so many poor women even today. . . . Mary is sister to the marginalized women who live unchronicled lives in oppressive situations. It does no honor to rip her out of her conflictual, dangerous historical circumstances and transmute her into an icon of a peaceful, middle-class life robed in royal blue."[17]

The Gospels set this woman before us in a deliberate fashion, providing a memorable series of vignettes: a young, unmarried woman invited to be part of God's plan for our salvation who responded in a thoughtful, questioning, and finally decisive manner; a pregnant woman, overshadowed by the Spirit, who traveled to attend to an aged, pregnant cousin, and responded to her words of greeting in a hymn of faithful confidence and radiant joy; a young mother who ponders both the child in her arms and the words spoken about him by shepherds from the fields, astrologers from the East, and the pious elders of Israel; an exhausted fugitive who had to escape an enraged king and flee to a foreign land to protect her child; an anguished parent searching out a lost boy in a crowded city; a caring guest whose faith implored her son to act out of the appointed time; a woman of sorrow who stands by her crucified son as he endures an excruciatingly painful death; and, finally, a woman of prayer sitting with the community, once again waiting on the Spirit to bring about a new birth through wind and fire. Mary's life as portrayed in Scripture was a human life, an ongoing journey in faith. Before she was the recipient of the many titles given her over the centuries, she was the woman of Nazareth: virginal, married, child-bearing, widowed, sorrowing, aging, dying. Her seven ages correspond to the universal experience of humanity.

Marian studies today offer us many ways of thinking about Mary; the above are not exhaustive. They can help us to focus on the woman identified as "an icon of human possibility," and a "woman for all seasons."[18] To further aid our preaching about her, we can consider the

17. Elizabeth A. Johnson, "Mary of Nazareth: Friend of God and Prophet," *America* (June 17–24, 2000) 13.

18. Cuneen, *Search for Mary* . . . 307ff.; Pelikan, *Mary Through* . . . 215ff.

contribution of Pope Paul VI in his exhortation, Devotion to the Blessed Virgin Mary (*Marialis Cultus*).

## Paul VI and Marian Devotion: Four Guidelines and a Principle

In Devotion to the Blessed Virgin Mary, Paul VI places the renewal of Marian devotion within the context of the Second Vatican Council's liturgical reforms. The second part of his exhortation on Marian devotion offers specific guidance "to help the development of devotion that is motivated in the Church by the Word of God and practiced in the Spirit of Christ" (Introduction). Such guidance is particularly helpful for the preacher. We find articulated first the key theological principle expressing Mary's relationship to the Trinity, to Christ, and to the Church, followed by four guidelines that develop the implications of this principle (nos. 25–39).

Pope Paul begins by setting out the foundation for Mary's relationship with the Trinity: "In the Virgin Mary everything is relative to Christ and dependent upon him. It was with a view to Christ that God the Father from all eternity chose her to be the all-holy Mother and adorned her with gifts of the Spirit granted to no one else" (no. 25). At the same time, devotion to Mary must recognize her unique mission within the mystery of the Church, helping us realize that "both the Church and Mary collaborate to give birth to the Mystical Body of Christ since 'both of them are the Mother of Christ, but neither brings forth the whole (body) independently of the other'" (no. 28). Mary serves as a model for the Church both in bringing Christ to bodiliness and to action in the world, and she serves as a sign of hope for sharing in the salvation made possible for all through Christ's death. To keep a proper balance in speaking of Mary in relation to both the Trinity and the Church, Pope Paul offers four guidelines that can help preachers avoid some areas that have proven problematic in the past.

1. *The Biblical Guideline*. Paul VI writes that it is not enough that Marian devotions make "diligent use of texts and symbols skillfully selected from the Sacred Scriptures" but also "the texts of prayers and chants should draw their inspiration and their wording from the Bible, and above all that devotion to the Virgin should be imbued with the great themes of the Christian message" (no. 30). If the prayers and chants should make use of the words, symbols, and themes of Scripture, how much more preaching. Mary's presentation in Scripture as one blessed because she heard the Word of God and kept it, as one who

is mother and sister and daughter in the eschatological family founded in the saving death and resurrection of her son Jesus, is the resource for ongoing reflection and meditation by all preachers. Mary engages us from within these texts as one who is the recipient of God's grace, rejoicing in God her Savior and going forth to be of service. She is seen first and last as one waiting on the Holy Spirit; between the Annunciation and Pentecost, she is presented always in relationship to her Son, never for her own sake. This is particularly important for those feasts of a more devotional nature whose imagery tends to present her as standing alone, for instance, Our Lady of the Rosary (October 7) or Our Lady of Lourdes (February 11). The biblical imagery keeps her in proper relationship with the Father, Son, and Holy Spirit, and with the community of believers.

The biblical witness also keeps preaching in check by avoiding the excesses of either an overly saccharine approach that further removes her from our lives or an exaggeratedly contemporary approach that tries to make her into something she was not, either by divinizing or humanizing her beyond the evidence at hand.[19] Pope Paul's call to root Marian devotion in the great biblical themes of the Christian message, like God's initiative in the work of salvation, and God's care for the lowly and the poor, is clearly pertinent to preaching on the feasts of Mary. A supplementary resource can be found in the work of artists and sculptors and their depiction of pertinent biblical scenes and various images of Mary. Such presentations can help to provide a fresh take on scenes that have become "frozen" in our imaginations. I think of the differences between Lotto's and Tanner's paintings of the Annunciation, the various contemporary images of Mary by such artists as Meinrad Craighead and John Giuliani, and the controversial exhibit by Robert Gober which featured a traditional statue of Mary with a culvert pipe running through it. The work of artists often helps us to see her from a fresh perspective.

2. *The Liturgical Guideline.* Preaching on the Marian feasts should also be in harmony with the focus of the liturgical action and season,

---

19. On the divinizing side, Andrew Greeley has noted that in the fourteenth-century presentations of Mary that made her more important than Jesus or God were "often not the Mary of Mother-love but the Mary . . . of enormous and dangerous spiritual power who could be especially punitive when she was offended." See "The Faith We Have Lost," *America* (Oct. 2, 1993) 26; on the humanizing side, I think of a television movie some time ago that presented Joseph and Mary as the Romeo and Juliet of the Galilee region.

derive inspiration from it, and orient people toward it (no. 31). Preaching within the Eucharist functions as an integral part of the liturgy, that is, its purpose is to serve as the connecting link between the Liturgy of the Word and the Liturgy of the Eucharist. Keeping in mind the particular Marian feast and its relation to the paschal mystery, such preaching is grounded in the particular scriptural and liturgical texts, and disposes the community to move from being attentive hearers of the word of God to giving thanks and praise for what has been and is being done for them in Christ, then to participation in the reception of the Eucharist, and, finally, to ethical behavior that fosters the coming of the reign of God in our world. In this way preaching on the Marian feasts remains an integral part of the rite.

Preaching mindful of its liturgical setting will help make the community conscious that Mary stands with us as a member of the communion of saints, as a sign of hope, and as one who intercedes for us, as we pray to the Father in the Eucharistic Prayer: "Make us worthy to share eternal life with Mary, the virgin Mother of God . . ." (Eucharistic Prayer 2) and "May he (Christ) make us an everlasting gift to you and enable us to share in the inheritance of your saints, with Mary the virgin Mother of God, with the apostles, the martyrs . . . and all your saints on whose constant intercession we rely for help" (Eucharistic Prayer 3). Careful study of the liturgical texts proper to each Marian feast, especially the opening prayer of the day and the preface, can help provide a clear focus for the preaching. That the liturgical prayers are addressed to God reminds us that Mary stands with us as a recipient of God's grace. These prayers situate Mary first of all as one in whom God has worked for our salvation and then recommend her as one who intercedes for us. Consider the alternate collect on the solemnity of the Annunciation, which addresses God who has "revealed the beauty of your power by exalting the lowly virgin of Nazareth and making her the mother of our Savior," then concludes by saying, "May the prayers of this woman bring Jesus to the waiting world and fill the void of incompletion with the presence of her child." Such prayers realize the theological principle of keeping Mary in proper relation to the Triune God and the community of believers.

Preaching on the Marian feasts can also help to lead the community more deeply into the celebration of the liturgical seasons: the solemnity of the Immaculate Conception in Advent, the solemnity of Mary, Mother of God, during the Christmas season, and the solemnity of the Annunciation during Lent or the Easter season. Such events celebrated conscious of the season also keep Mary's place in the life of the Church connected to the central mysteries of Christ: the incarnation and the paschal mystery of his suffering, death, and resurrection. The liturgical guideline, then, complements the biblical one by presenting Mary in relation to the great events and themes of salvation history, always first and foremost the recipient of God's saving grace.

3. *The Ecumenical Guideline.* As Marian devotion is to be "in accord with the deep desires and aims of the ecumenical movement" (no. 32), so too the preaching on Marian feasts is to be sensitive to ecumenical concerns. Paul VI notes how Catholics share Mary as a subject of devotion with the Orthodox and the Anglicans, and that we share her words of praise in the Magnificat with the Churches of the Reform. But he then goes on to warn that in fostering devotion to Mary "every care should be taken to avoid any exaggeration which could mislead other Christian brethren about the true doctrine of the Catholic Church" (no. 32). For all Christians, Christ is the one mediator, the source and center of the Church's communion, the Lord and Savior. Mary must not be placed over and against Christ as was done during the medieval period with its attribution of the kingdom of justice to Christ and the kingdom of mercy to Mary. And there must be a proper understanding of Mary's spiritual motherhood of the faithful: "For Mary did not and cannot engender those who belong to Christ, except in one faith and one love: for 'Is Christ divided?' (1 Cor 1:13)" (no. 33). Preaching does not hesitate to proclaim Mary as one who continues to love even beyond death, as she continues to behold new sons and daughters who have become part of the body of Christ, her son in the flesh.[20] Mary does not cease to love the brothers and sisters of Jesus, nor to intercede for them as a mother would for all her children, "for she is inseparably linked with her son's saving work" (Constitution on the Sacred Liturgy, no. 103).

4. *The Anthropological Guideline.* This last guideline keeps Mary within the circle of the community of believers as fully human, as one with whom we can identify. Mary as presented in some devotional literature, Pope Paul recognizes, "cannot easily be reconciled with today's life style, especially with the way women live today" (no. 34), noting such contemporary realities as women's equality and co-responsibility with men in caring for the family, and their achievements in the political, social, and cultural arenas of our day. In light of such factors,

20. See Carroll, *Understanding the Mother of Jesus*, 57.

Mary's life may seem too constricted to have any contemporary relevance. But Mary is not to be approached as one to be imitated precisely in the type of life she led, but rather "for the way in which, in her own particular life, she fully and responsibly accepted the will of God (cf. Luke 1:38)" (no. 35).[21] In her journey of faith, she listened, questioned, pondered, sang, worried, showed concern for others, and grieved. To keep sight of her humanity in no way shortchanges her unique role in God's plan, but rather makes her more accessible for those who experience the life of faith as a challenge. Paul VI asserts that the modern woman will find in Mary one who exercised decision-making power in "an event of world importance," who opted for virginity as a "courageous choice" made not as a rejection of marriage but as a sign of total love for God, and who was neither "timidly submissive" nor "one whose piety was repellent to others" (no. 37). Rather, Mary was "a woman who did not hesitate to proclaim that God vindicates the humble and the oppressed, and removes the powerful people of this world from their privileged positions (cf. Luke 1:51-3)" (no. 37). Mary of Nazareth remains as a strong woman who knew poverty, exile, and suffering, a woman for others who is "the perfect model of the disciple of the Lord" (37).

How preachers speak about Mary can do much to counter the often nonbiblical, nonliturgical presentations of the past. Sound preaching offers a portrait of a biblical figure of heroic stature who put her trust totally in the living God. She continues to stand in this new millennium as one worthy of honor and praise. She encourages all of us to hear God's call to bring Christ into the world in our bodies, to dwell in the awareness that together we form the body of Christ, and to participate in the continuing work of the liberation of the world from all that enslaves and destroys. Paul VI has provided guidance for all preachers on the feasts of Mary. We will now consider how the Marian feasts allow preachers to present Mary.

## Preaching on the Marian Feasts

There are fifteen Marian feasts in the General Roman Calendar explicitly dedicated to Mary, the Mother of the Lord, and several others in which she plays a primary role. Some are clearly rooted in the biblical story, whereas others are grounded in a combination of theological,

21. Ibid., 47.

devotional, and historical factors. When preaching on her feasts, we do not put Mary in the place of Christ. Rather, we attempt to discover how we can work with and through her in the task of interpreting the community to itself as the locus for God's ongoing work of salvation. Mary can function in the same ways the other saints do on their feasts: as model, mirror, mentor, and metaphor. I will briefly consider the various celebrations in relation to each heading. I do not mean to limit a particular day to one heading. Mary may be presented in various ways on the same occasion, although I would suggest choosing one for the sake of coherence and clarity.

(a) *Mary as Model.* Jessica Powers' poem "The Visitation Journey" contrasts the Mary that popular religious art has frequently portrayed—Lady Mary in a blue silk gown, riding gently over hill and dale on a bright spring day, with birds singing and flowers bowing—with her own terse vision: "Rather, I see a girl upon a donkey/ and her too held by what was said to mind/ how the sky was or if the grass was growing./ I doubt the flowers; I doubt the road was kind/ . . . a girl riding upon a jolting donkey/ and riding further and further into the truth."[22] In the poet's view, Mary's journey covers more than geographical distance. And it is one all are invited to make: to ride further and further into the truth of who God is and what God has done for us in Christ, into the truth of who we are and what we are called to be. Mary is a model of responding to God's grace and the Spirit's good counsel on this particular feast (May 31) as she goes forth to be with Elizabeth and to utter the prophetic song that proclaims the agenda of God and her willing part in it.

Mary as a model of saying "yes" to God, of becoming a willing participant in the saving plan that began with the incarnation, is at the heart of such feasts as Mary, Mother of God (January 1), the Annunciation of the Lord (March 25), and the Dedication of St. Mary Major (August 5), which is the commemoration of the church built by Pope Sixtus III to honor the Mother of God shortly after the declaration of Mary as Theotokos at the Council of Ephesus in 431. From the moment of her "yes," Mary begins her growth into the image of the New Eve, woman of the new creation, mother of Jesus and of all the living. But this "yes" does not set her apart from the rest of us; it places her ahead of us. "Yes" is what we are all called to say, as the mystic Caryll Houselander reminds

---

22. Jessica Powers, *Selected Poetry of Jessica Powers*, ed. Regina Siegfried and Robert F. Morneau (Kansas City, Mo.: Sheed and Ward, 1989) 67.

us, so that we might fulfill the universal vocation of bearing Christ in our bodies and giving him to the world. "Nothing but things essential for us are revealed to us about the Mother of God; the fact that she was wed to the Holy Spirit and bore Christ into the world."[23]

(b) *Mary as Mirror.* On the solemnities of the Immaculate Conception (December 8) and the Assumption (August 15), we can see in Mary the mirror of God's saving and gracious action. On both occasions she mirrors the touch of God in human life, from its beginning until the end. While these feasts have often been thought of as setting her apart from the rest of us, Karl Rahner notes in speaking of the Immaculate Conception that "the eternal Father could not intend anything for the mother of his incarnate Son, without intending it for us too, and giving it to us in the sacrament of justification."[24] In her Immaculate Conception, Mary reflects what has happened for all of us in baptism, the ratification of our being surrounded by God's love from the very beginning; and in her Assumption she mirrors our final destiny in Christ, to be raised up into the communion of all the saints with Christ who reigns.[25] The gospels for the two feasts emphasize what God has done in her. Preaching on these feasts calls us to know more deeply the gift of God's salvation given in Christ, and expressed in the body of Mary, our mother and sister in faith.

George Tavard writes that the Mary of folk piety often is a "mirror of the attributes of God," especially of God's ubiquity and healing power. "Our Lady of Everywhere reflects the God who is everywhere by creative presence and power. Our Lady of Everything Good reflects the benevolent God who is at the same time supreme power and supreme goodness."[26] Such mirroring can be found in feasts like the Immaculate Heart of Mary (the Saturday following the Second Sunday after Pentecost, and the day after the feast of the Sacred Heart of Jesus), the mother's heart reflecting the compassionate love of her Son's. On the feast of Our Lady of Sorrows (September 15, the day after the feast of the Triumph of the Cross), Mary the suffering mother at the cross mirrors the Son who was lifted up for our salvation.

---

23. Caryll Houselander, *The Reed of God* (New York: Sheed and Ward, 1944) xii.

24. Karl Rahner, *Mary Mother of the Lord*, trans. W. J. O'Hara (New York: Herder and Herder, 1963) 49.

25. Ibid.; see, especially the chapters on the Immaculate Conception (42–52) and the Assumption (83–92.)

26. Tavard, *Thousand Faces*, 248.

The feast of the Queenship of Mary (August 22) seemingly takes us a long way from the humble maid of Nazareth and the sorrowful mother standing by the cross. But rightfully understood as Mary's ongoing participation in both the glory and ongoing work of her son, any tendency to set Mary in isolation from the saving work of Christ and to reinforce the medieval idea of parallel kingdoms where Mary dispenses mercy, while Christ dispenses justice, can be avoided. While the feast only came into the liturgical calendar at the end of the 1954 Marian year, J. D. Crichton points out that the Church had long celebrated Mary as Queen, seeing in her exaltation "the dazzling 'reward,' so to say, of Mary who gave herself totally to her son and his saving work."[27] The gospel text proposed for this feast is the account of the Annunciation (Luke 1:26-38) where the angel invites her into God's plan. We can see this celebration as the culmination of God's work in Mary throughout her life until her coming to full communion with her Son after death, already given expression in the celebration of the Assumption, and here taking her position by his side where, as the Constitution on the Sacred Liturgy reminds us, she is "linked with his ongoing saving work" (no. 103). Preachers can also be helped on this feast by attending to the emphasis given on the solemnity of Christ the King, particularly by the Gospels chosen for that feast, as to what kind of kingdom Christ presides over: a kingdom of service (Matt 25:31-46), truth (John 18:33-37), and compassion (Luke 23:35-43). It is in this light that we can also celebrate the Queenship of Mary.

Other feasts such as Our Lady of Lourdes (February 11) and Our Lady of Guadalupe (December 12) present Mary as a mirror of God's healing power and God's love for the poor. We can encounter the problem already mentioned of preaching about Mary alone on these feasts. In their imagery, both feasts present her as the crowned Queen of heaven, and both present her standing alone (though Our Lady of Guadalupe is pregnant.) Preachers must take care not to give the impression that this feast is only about Mary's power to bring healing to the sick and freedom to the oppressed. But insofar as the biblical texts are at the center of our preaching, these feasts proclaim God who continues to do great things for those who believe and who stands with the poor and will be their vindication. And the opening prayers also help to set the appropriate tone, as on the memorial of Our Lady of Lourdes

---

27. Crichton, *Our Lady in the Liturgy*, 87. This work is very helpful for preachers, providing comments on the biblical and liturgical texts of all the Marian feasts.

when the Church asks that through the prayers of Mary, strength may be given to rise above our human weakness.

(c) *Mary as Mentor.* Certain feasts allow preachers to present Mary as one who guides us more deeply into the paschal mystery. As our mother, she is also our mentor, instructing us in the ways of her Son. As Our Lady of Sorrows (September 15), she draws us into the contemplation of and participation in the suffering and death of Jesus (John 19:25-27), and as Our Lady of the Rosary (October 7), she calls us to prayer (Acts 1:12-14), pondering the saving mysteries that surround the incarnation, death, and resurrection of the Redeemer. The feast of Our Lady of Mount Carmel (July 16), commemorating the origin of the Carmelites in the twelfth century, presents her as the true daughter of Zion (Zech 2:14-17) who invites us to "hear the word of God and keep it" (Matt 11:27-28). And on the feast of her birth (September 8), she teaches us through the Matthean genealogy and the annunciation to Joseph (Matt 1:1-16, 18-23) that God worked through the most broken circumstances to bring about the birth of the Messiah, empowering the weak and lowly, confounding the wise and powerful. Mary as mentor calls us to ponder and pray, to go forth in service, to wait patiently on the Lord to act, to trust in the working of the Spirit, and to participate in the sufferings of her Son.

(d) *Mary as Metaphor.* Mary was made for metaphor and she has proved a most gracious recipient over the ages. The litany of Loretto generously employs them: Mirror of justice, Seat of wisdom, Vessel of honor, Tower of David, Tower of ivory, House of gold, Ark of the covenant, Morning star. Throughout the ages, Mary has been saluted by preachers and spiritual writers in a manner worthy of impassioned troubadours. She has untied the Church's prosaic tongue and liberated it into poetry. Mary Gordon reminds us that we must continue to find words and images to name her role in our own day, that "one must travel the road of metaphor, of icon, to come back to that figure . . . who has moved the hearts of men and women. . . ."[28] One feast in particular invites the preacher to play in its metaphorical field, the Presentation of Our Lady in the Temple (November 21), based on a legend found in the Protoevangelium of St. James. Originating in the East with the dedication of the Church of St. Mary in Jerusalem in 543, it invites preachers to identify the God of Israel who came to dwell in the Temple (Zech 2:14-17) with the God who is Emmanuel

28. Gordon, "Coming to Terms . . . ," 12.

who comes to dwell in the body of Mary. Artists have portrayed the three-year-old Mary joyfully going to live in the Temple, leaving her parents without a backward glance. While historically impossible, it is poetically perceptive. The image of this young girl, soon to be the temple of the living God, listening to and learning from the temple made of stones, invites all the faithful to ponder their own identity as the temple of the Spirit and body of Christ.

## Homilies on the Feasts of Mary

### (a) The Feast of the Immaculate Conception: Mary as Mirror

"The grace of God rains down upon us all"

(Texts: Gen 3:9-15, 20; Eph 1:3-6, 11-12; Luke 1:26-38)

While at the National Shrine recently, I gazed up at the ceiling.
And, though I had seen it many times before,
the mosaic of the Pentecost event caught my attention.
In the lower center are Mary and several disciples,
  representing the community on the day of Pentecost,
  with additional figures scattered around the perimeter.
It was the falling tongues of flame that captured my imagination.
Flame after flame is falling from above, many more than the figures
  below.
The mosaic witnesses to the abundance of the Spirit,
  God's generosity showering divine life and love.
This image helps us to enter into an understanding of today's feast.
Mary's Immaculate Conception reflects the generosity of God to all
  creation.
Most of my life I have thought of today's feast as trumpeting Mary's
  uniqueness.
As a youth, I was taught that this feast celebrated the unique privilege
  God bestowed upon Mary because of her future role as the mother
  of Jesus. Period.
As a good Catholic boy, with a grandmother and mother devoted to
  Mary, I had no difficulty accepting that God would do this.
There was a logic in thinking that the Sinless One would come forth
  from a sinless mother, thereby necessitating that from the first mo-
  ment of her conception Mary was free from all stain of original sin.

The catechism of my youth carefully explained that this was due to the
  anticipated merits of the saving death and resurrection of Jesus.
And so as a child I joined in praising God for this special gift to Mary.
After all, she was God's mother.

Only later did I begin to appreciate how it could put a divide between
  her and us.
Perhaps it started with the woman who said to me one Mother's Day
  as she was going into church,
"I do hope you're not going to preach about Mary today.
She makes us all feel so guilty.
She never yelled at her child, or lost her temper,
  or did anything that was other than perfect.
How could she, being preserved from sin?"
For many people the feast seemed to separate, even isolate, Mary from
  them.
It emphasized how different she was from the rest of us.

In his history of American Catholicism, Charles Morris wryly comments that Pope Pius IX's major reason for proclaiming the dogma
  was to emphasize how depraved the rest of humanity was, and, con-
  sequently, how unfit for self-government.
The Pope agreed with his predecessor Gregory XVI who said it was in-
  sanity to believe in liberty of conscience, or freedom to worship, or
  a free press.
Which brings us back to that mosaic in the National Shrine.
If this feast is to touch our lives as more than an invitation to spiritually gaze at what God has done for, in, and through Mary, it will do
  so only when it serves to remind us that God's grace, given to Mary
  so she might fulfill her role in the divine plan, has also been given to
  each of us for exactly the same reason.

This is not to diminish what God has done for Mary.
But it is also not to diminish what God has done for each of us.
In both instances, God has acted for our salvation through Jesus, Lord
  and Messiah.
God rains down the Spirit on all,
  but the Spirit enters and shapes the life of each of us differently.
God's plan for Mary was unique, but God also has plans for us.
Karl Rahner says this feast reminds us that God gives the beginning
  which contains the whole.

God gives to each of us the beginning we were born into and we can
do little about that.

But God also traces the plan of every life in divine wisdom and redemptive love.

As we heard in the letter to the Ephesians today,

"God chose us in Christ before the world began, to be holy and blame-
less, to be full of love; likewise God predestined us through Jesus
Christ to be adopted children . . ."

The grace that rained down on Mary at the moment of her conception
has fallen upon us in our day.

But the readings also remind us of something else equally important.

In the beginning, God gave us freedom.

Today we have scenes of two beginnings presented in the Scriptures.

Both beginnings were initiated by God.

We might think of the God of Genesis as one who only forbids:

"Don't eat from that tree. If you do, you will die."

But before God was the God of prohibition, God was the God of the
call, and the God of permission.

God called Adam and Eve into life, then called them to care for the
garden.

God permitted them to eat from all the trees in the garden—except one.

There's the prohibition: "You can eat all but this one tree."

God then left them in freedom.

And in that freedom, they chose what looked like autonomy;
they wanted to know like God, to know good and evil.

And what did they come to know? All they found out was that they
were naked.

God invited them to live on God's terms; in their freedom, Adam and
Eve said, "No."

They wanted life on their own terms, independent of God.

A second beginning happened in Nazareth. Again, God took the initiative.

This time an invitation to a young woman named Mary, human like us.

God invited her into the divine plan.

Then God waited. God waited on a human response.

God paused and all creation was still.

And Mary pondered.

It must have been the most dramatic pause in the history of the world.

Mary began creation again when she freely said, "Yes."

On this feast, *we* are invited to ponder the mystery of God's grace and
our freedom.
The Spirit continues to rain down all around us, but we can walk between
the drops.
God waits on *us* each day. And so does our world—
waiting on our choice: to be bearers of light or bearers of darkness.
God pauses and waits.
God waits for our Yes this day and we give it when we approach the table.
We say Yes to taking within us the body of Christ,
and to being the body of Christ in the world.
May today's Yes spring forth from the depths of our hearts.


*(b) Feast of Our Lady of Sorrows: Mary as Model*

## "Standing with Mary, Being Defined by Her Child"

### (Text: John 19:25-27)

Often, it seems true to say that parents define a child.
After meeting the parents of another, in some way, the child "makes
sense."
A sense of "Ah, I see."
You see that certain qualities have been handed down.
It might be a tendency to neatness, or a way of pausing, or a certain
kind of smile.
Parents define, or to be more cautious, *help* to define their child.

The gospel, as in so many other ways, turns this upside down.
When we come to Mary, the child defines the parent.
This short portion from John's Gospel is part of the passion,
a seven-part movement, a chiasmic pattern,
and this is the fourth segment, the center of the pattern.
After this segment, Jesus says, "It is finished, completed."
So what is happening in these few verses has import, especially since
this is the heart of the Fourth Gospel, the crucifixion and death,
the "hour" Jesus has been waiting for, the hour of glory.

John first presents four women at the foot of the cross.
Then he focuses our attention on one of them: Mary, the Mother of Jesus.
And he brings out from the side the Beloved Disciple.
In this setting of crucifixion, Jesus defines who his mother is forever.
In light of "the hour," he calls her "Woman."

"Woman, behold your son."
She is the new Eve, sprung from the side of the new Adam,
    the beginning of a new creation.
And she is entrusted to the Beloved Disciple—and to all beloved disciples
    as the mother of a new family, the community of disciples:
"Son, behold your mother."

She is with us today, standing with us at this Eucharist,
    as we enter into the dying and rising of Jesus.
She calls us to listen to her son, to heed him, to do what he tells us.
Every Eucharist we mention her name during the Eucharistic Prayer:
    "make us worthy to share eternal life with Mary the virgin Mother
    of God. . . ."
And, at every Eucharist, we are reminded that we, like her,
    have been called to be defined by this child: in our work, in our prayer,
    in our life.
And we are to live another paradox: that we are defined not solely by
    our past, from where we have come and from the deeds we have al-
    ready done, but we are to be defined by our future, by where we are
    heading, as we move ever so gradually into the fullness of life in
    Christ.
So whatever sorrows have marked our lives thus far
    will be transformed into the glory which God has planned for those
    who are faithful.
Like the mother of sorrows we are destined to reign in heaven with
    Jesus, our Lord.


*(c) The Feast of Our Lady of the Rosary (A Vesper Service)—Mary as
Mentor*

"An Invitation to Ponder and Pray"

(Texts: Acts 1:12-14; Luke 2:15-19)

This Marian feast may not be called a biblical one in the strict sense.
There is certainly no basis in the Bible for the title, Our Lady of the
    Rosary.
I suppose we would classify it as a devotional feast.
For many people the rosary has been a lifelong companion, a form of
    devotion, and an honored way of praying to Mary to intercede for us.
For all the times I have turned to it on plane takeoffs and landings,

(reminiscent of the nun who told Kathleen Norris she prays best in the dentist chair) and cherish it as much for its ability to calm me as well as its power to help the pilot, it has also served more important purposes.

When I was growing up in Baltimore during the '50s, the family rosary was part of life.
In those days all of us—grandparents, parents, children—knelt down together after supper, and prayed for the conversion of Russia.
In the early '70s, I can remember traveling through the night after receiving a call that my stepfather had had a serious heart attack, fingering the rosary during that five-hour drive.
And in the spring of 2000, I prayed it with my mother as she lay dying.
The rosary has been there to lead me into the heart of the mysteries of our faith.
The association of Our Lady with the rosary goes back to a thirteenth-century legend that Mary appeared to St. Dominic and gave it to him with instructions on its use.
As for the feast day itself, it only goes back to the sixteenth century, 1571 to be exact.
A group of devoted believers called the Rosary Confraternity was in Rome, praying the rosary, on the day that the Christians won a great naval victory over the Muslim Turks at the Gulf of Lepanto.
Pope Pius V, a former Dominican, attributed this victory to praying the rosary.
(Believers have a history of drafting God into the armed forces, always on *their* side, so I suppose it was inevitable that it would happen to Mary.)

However, while there is no biblical basis for the title, Our Lady of the Rosary, there is certainly a biblical basis for what the feast calls us to.
The two brief texts we heard tonight present Mary in terms that are quite congruent with the devotional practice of "saying the rosary."
At one end of her story we have Mary presented to us as the woman who ponders.
She ponders the words of the shepherds who tell her what happened to them that very night in the fields; "she treasured these things and reflected on them in her heart."
And there is no reason to doubt she would have pondered the words of the angel who came to her that day in Nazareth, and the words of the wise men who came to adore.
The biblical tradition is that she was a woman who pondered.

And the biblical tradition also presents us with the final image of Mary
at prayer.
Here, with the Eleven, and some women and Jesus' brothers,
she was "devoted to constant prayer," waiting for the Spirit.
A woman who ponders and prays—that is the biblical Mary.

So, while this feast is not biblical in the strict sense,
it is biblical in a more important sense.
Rather than calling on us to visualize Mary as a Christian Athena
who once guided the cannon fire and arrows at Lepanto and can
now be enlisted into whatever form our contemporary battles are
taking,
it calls on us to join with her on pondering and praying over the mystery
of her Son's birth, suffering and death, resurrection and ascension.
Mother Mary mentors us into mystery.
She leads us and joins us in joyfully pondering the goodness of our loving
God, the goodness that took flesh in the fruit of her womb, and continues to come to birth in the ongoing work of the Spirit in the world.
She leads us to look at the suffering and death that won for us our salvation, to see in the hour of the cross the hour of glory, the full reve-
lation of her Son as the image of the invisible God who is our Father.
And she leads us into the mystery of glory, already achieved in her Son
and in her own flesh, with its promise for our own lives.
Today we honor Mary as holy Mary, mother of God
and ask her to pray for us sinners, now and at the hour of our death.
Today we can pray, in union with Mary, to our God:
"Make us partners (with Christ) in his suffering,
and lead us to share his happiness and the glory of eternal life."
Amen.


## Summary

On the first anniversary of the beginning of the Second Vatican
Council, Pope Paul VI prayed: "O Mary, make this church . . . recognize you as its Mother and Daughter and elect Sister, as its incompa-
rable model, its glory, its joy, and its hope."[29] The many ways of naming
this woman, so central to our faith story, can help us to know more
fully the ways God has and continues to interact with all those who

29. Quoted in Tavard, *Thousand Faces of Mary*, 205.

have been baptized in Christ. Mary of Nazareth remains for us both Mother of God and St. Mary. Through the preaching that occurs on her feasts, the community can come to appreciate more fully both the unique role of this woman and the common calling and gift she shares with all of us: redemption in and through Jesus Christ.

When preaching on the Marian feasts, these suggestions may be helpful:

(a) Ponder the image that the feast presents. What aspect of the heart does it speak to and invite you to address?

(b) How does the feast relate to the assigned or suggested Scripture readings? Spend time with each text, looking for ways to link the text, Mary and the community in light of the gospel proclamation the texts contain.

(c) How does the feast, along with the Scriptures, encourage you to present Mary: mirror of God's attributes, model of human response, mentor to the community, metaphor of grace? If more than one, which would be most beneficial for the community at Eucharist?

(d) For further reading:

- Raymond E. Brown and others, *Mary in the New Testament* (Philadelphia: Fortress, 1978).
- J. D. Crichton, *Our Lady in the Liturgy* (Collegeville: The Liturgical Press, 1997).
- Jim McManus, C.Ss.R., *All Generations Will Call Me Blessed* (New York: Crossroad, 1999).
- George H. Tavard, *The Thousand Faces of the Virgin Mary* (Collegeville: The Liturgical Press, 1996).

# Chapter 6

# Cultivating the Preacher's Hunger: "To Make the Lord Known and Loved"

*"All who believe in Christ should feel as an integral part of their faith, an apostolic concern to pass on to others its light and joy. This concern must become, as it were, a hunger and thirst to make the Lord known, given the vastness of the non-Christian world."*

(John Paul II, *Redemptoris Missio* 40.3)

*"It is undeniable that the priest's life is fully taken up by the hunger for the Gospel and for faith, hope and love for God and his mystery, a hunger which is more or less consciously present in the people of God entrusted to him."*

(John Paul II, *Pastores Dabo Vobis* 28)

For five chapters we have considered the homily as "a necessary source of nourishment of the Christian life" (General Instruction of the Roman Missal, no. 41), capable of feeding three particular hungers of the human heart. For preachers to satisfy the hunger people have for wholeness, meaning, and belonging, there must be within preachers themselves both a hunger for the gospel in their own lives and a hunger to make the Lord known by preaching the gospel to all others. To nourish the hearts of others includes tending to one's own. This chapter will suggest four areas preachers might cultivate, four loves that lie at the heart of preaching: a love for words, for Scripture, for people, and for Jesus Christ. When these loves are tended, preachers are most likely to know how to feed "the hunger for the Gospel and for faith, hope and love for God and his mystery, a hunger which is more or less consciously present in the people of God entrusted to him" (*Pastores Dabo Vobis* 28).

## A Love for Words

"In the beginning was the Word," the author of the Fourth Gospel tells us. And we might add, "And in the beginning were words." The authors of Genesis confirm this truth in both creation accounts. The first account by the Priestly author offers the majestic seven days, when the world and language began: "Then God said, 'Let there be light'; and there was light." And so it continues for six days. God speaks and life comes forth. Out of chaos, the word of God brings order, beauty, and life in all its diversity, and then gives divine approval: "God saw everything that he had made, and indeed, it was very good" (1:31). Words are not restricted to God. In the second creation account (2:4-25), after creating man and putting him in the garden to till it, God speaks directly to Adam as "you." The human creature is drawn into the world of words from the beginning.

Through language, God creates a world of choice and consequences: "You may freely eat of every tree of the garden, but of the tree of the knowledge of good and evil, you shall not eat, for in the day you shall eat of it, you shall die." Then, God enlists the human creature in the creative power and play of language. God brings all the animals of the field and all the birds of the air to man "to see what he would call them; and whatever the man called every living creature, that was its name" (Gen 2:19). Unfortunately, no words come down to us about this naming of the animals and birds. But it is significant when the first human utterance occurs. Only when God has made woman and brought her to the man, and the man looked at this new creation, only then do we get the first human utterance, and it is a cry of wondrous joy: "This at last is bone of my bones and flesh of my flesh; this one shall be called Woman, for out of Man, this one was taken" (2:23). The first words express praise and gratitude to the Creator God, and a clear recognition of the equality of the one given as companion. Adam's first effort at oratory confirms the definition of the human creature as *homo loquens* (the speaking person).

Words are our inheritance and our legacy. They create, name, confirm, and welcome, as well as confine, negate, confuse, and expel. They have the power both to express and conceal the heart and mind. Dreams are given shape and visions make their first move toward realization through words. A preacher must revel in this first gift of God to the world: language. Through language God revealed who God was, our Creator calling us to live in love, to be listeners to the divine word, and to take part in the ongoing work of creation. For preachers, words must become a passion. To love words means to approach them with respect, to enjoy their company, to spend time with them, to court them, to listen to them. We can learn from others here.

Lewis Carroll teaches us how to play with them, "Twas brillig and the slithy toves did gyre and gimble in the wabe . . . ,"[1] to take pleasure in the sheer sound of speech, to create words and drop them into the stillness of the world. There is the sheer beauty of putting certain sounds together the way Gerard Manley Hopkins does when he writes about "The Windhover": "I caught this morning morning's minion, kingdom of daylight's dauphin, dapple-dawn-drawn Falcon, in his riding of the rolling level underneath him steady air. . . ."[2] Such sounds send a listener soaring. Words bring us back to the joy of Eden and the thrill of naming what is before us.

Judith Viorst's words bring a smile of remembrance of crushes in the past, as when her determined young speaker exclaims in "The Lizzie Pitofsky Poem":[3] "I can't get enoughsky//Of Lizzie Pitofsky.// I love her so much that it hurts," and a smile of recognition of love in the present, as when the married narrator speaks in "Alone": "Alone I could own both sides of the double bed/ And stay up reading novels half the night . . . ," then goes on, after listing the joys of being alone and not "bothered" or "inconvenienced" by another, to conclude: "And no one would be here. I would be alone// And I would hate it."[4] Words reveal the universal feelings that lay deep in our hearts and reveal us to ourselves.

But words give us more than a sudden flash of insight or a peek from a provocative point of view. When words come together to form worlds, we realize their greatest power. The art of the poet and the novelist, the storyteller and the playwright, invites us to be schooled in human wisdom, to navigate into new worlds. "Where does the heart go to be educated?" we might ask. Archetypal psychologist James Hillman answers that we go to story: "From my perspective as depth psychologist, I see that those who have a connection with story are in better shape and have a better prognosis than those to whom story must be

---

1. Lewis Carroll, "Jabberwocky," in Leland H. Roloff, *The Perception and Evocation of Literature* (Glenview, Ill.: Scott, Foresman and Co., 1973) 55–56.

2. Gerard Manley Hopkins, *Poems and Prose,* selected by W. H. Gardner. (New York: Penguin, 1963) 30.

3. Judith Viorst, *If I Were in Charge of the World and Other Worries: Poems for Children and Their Parents* (New York: Atheneum, 1981) 13.

4. Judith Viorst, *When Did I Stop Being 20 and Other Injustices* (New York: Simon and Schuster, 1987) 37.

introduced . . . to have 'story awareness' is *per se* psychologically thera-
peutic. It is good for soul."⁵

We go to those who lead us into the heart's maze of passageways,
guiding us through its intricate turns and sudden changes of direction,
preventing our becoming disoriented and discouraged. Some mentors
that immediately come to mind include the poets Shakespeare, Milton,
Emily Dickinson, T. S. Eliot, Robert Frost, Denise Levertov, Billy
Collins, Jane Kenyon, and Toi Derricotte. All offer knowledge of the
heart. They also provide a realization of how much can be done with
little—the lesson of the multiplication of the loaves, in a different key.
They call us to love, honor, and respect the power of words. "Be careful with words, even the miraculous ones," warns Anne Sexton, "they
can be both daisies and bruises."⁶

The words of poets remind us how sturdy words are, holding up an
edifice like Homer's *Iliad* and *Odyssey* or Dante's *The Divine Comedy*.
And poets, in particular, reveal how important it is to work carefully
with words, taking time to make the right choices, turning them over
and looking closely at them, shifting them from here to there, searching for the right "fit." Words can be obstinate, possessive, and stubborn,
demanding that their users submit humbly to their meaning, accepting
certain limitations and boundaries so that communication can occur.
Words do this in self-defense, countering confusion and carelessness,
resulting from a sloppy use of language. A character who is a profes-
sional writer in Tom Stoppard's play *The Real Thing* speaks harshly
about another author as "a lout with language," then goes on to say:

> Words don't deserve that kind of malarkey. They're innocent, neutral,
> precise, standing for this, describing that, meaning the other, so if you
> look after them you can build bridges across incomprehension and
> chaos. . . . They deserve respect. If you get the right ones in the right
> order, you can nudge the world a little or make a poem which children
> will speak for you when you're dead.⁷

The words of storytellers and playwrights also take us into worlds
that reveal us to ourselves. In his short story, "Night," Andre Dubus⁸
takes us to the shoreline of eternity, as we stand by a nameless woman

5. James Hillman, "A Note on Story," in *Loose Ends* (spring 1975) 1.

6. Anne Sexton, "Words," in *The Awful Rowing Toward God* (Boston: Houghton
Mifflin, 1975) 71.

7. Tom Stoppard, *The Real Thing* (London: Faber and Faber, 1983) 54.

8. Andre Dubus, *Dancing After Hours* (New York: Vintage, 1997).

who wakes next to her husband and, without turning, knows that he has died during the night. In four short paragraphs we come to know the measured joy of a life together and the final, terrible blow suffered when death comes into the room, however softly. There is Athol Fugard's play, *"Master Harold"* . . . *and the boys*,[9] situated in a tea room on a rainy afternoon in Port Elizabeth, South Africa, during the years of apartheid, where words spoken in frustration, hurt, and anger prove as devastating as a bomb tossed through the window. Fugard's young, white protagonist, Hallie, son of the owners, dealing with a home situation he does not have the strength to bear, eventually tells a cruel racial joke to Sam, a black man who has been both mentor and father figure. The power of words to injure lingers as we witness the final moments of the play when a devastated Sam waltzes around the room with Willie, the other black worker, re-creating a world where collisions do not happen.

A love for words only comes from spending time with them, coming to know and appreciate their infinite variety. Hillman tells us that words are like angels; they are "powers which have invisible power over us. They are personal presences which have whole mythologies: genders, genealogies (etymologies concerning origins and creations), histories, and vogues; and their own guarding, blaspheming, creating, and annihilating effects."[10] A sense of a word's history can be found by looking up its lineage, its roots—an enlightening experience, especially when it contains one of those graphic images deep inside, which suddenly springs up before you. I can remember when I realized that the word *rend*, as in the opening words of the prophet Joel on Ash Wednesday, "Rend your hearts, not your garments," was related to the word "rind," that tough, hardened skin that has to be peeled away. The word then carried its message to me more clearly. "We need to recall the angel aspect of the word, recognizing words as independent carriers of soul between people," Hillman suggests.[11]

There are three mentors who might instruct us preachers in the use of language; I have already mentioned the poet and the storyteller/playwright. I now turn to the third: the orator. One of the oldest

---

9. Athol Fugard, *"Master Harold"* . . . *and the boys* (New York: Penguin, 1982).

10. James Hillman, *Revisioning Psychology* (New York: Harper Colophon, 1975) 9.

11. Ibid. For an approach to preaching that draws on the archetypal psychology of James Hillman, see James A. Wallace, *Imaginal Preaching: An Archetypal Perspective* (New York: Paulist, 1995), especially ch. 2.

arts is rhetoric, "the use of all the available means of persuasion in any given situation."[12] Traditionally, in ancient Greece and Rome, oratory was to be found in three settings: the law courts, the political arena, and the settings of civic celebrations. The goals of oratory consisted, respectively, in moving the listeners to act in behalf of justice (legal or forensic oratory), determining what course of action was most expedient for the common good (deliberative or political oratory), and arousing praise for virtue or blame for vice (ceremonial or epideictic oratory). The early Church debated whether rhetoric was an appropriate tool for preachers, fearing the loss of apostolic simplicity and integrity in favor of the "tricks" of the rhetorician's trade. St. Jerome had a dream in which Christ appeared to him and accused him of being a Ciceronian instead of a Christian. But eloquent defenders like John Chrysostom in the East and Augustine in the West saved the art and placed it within the service of the gospel.

Augustine defined the preacher as an "ecclesiastical orator" whose preaching was to teach, delight, and persuade listeners of the truth of the gospel and to put it into practice. Ultimately, he wanted people "to be moved rather than taught, so that they may not be sluggish in putting what they know into practice and so that they may fully accept those things which they acknowledge to be true."[13] The legacy of Augustine continued until the time of the Reformation when a renewed insistence on returning to apostolic simplicity in preaching again came to the fore. Often rhetoric has functioned as a marginal figure in homiletics, employed but not necessarily respected or trusted.

In our own day the traditional well-honed speech, characterized by an artistic use of Aristotle's three modes of persuasion—namely, *logos* (the quality of reasoning within the speech), *pathos* (the effort to put the listeners into a certain frame of mind or state of emotion) and *ethos* (the appeal of the speaker's character as this is presented within the speech)—has given way to nightly news sound bytes, Sunday morning punditry, and late-night talk show "probing." The role of the orator in society has greatly diminished. It is rare, apart from the televised funerals of people more often honored for being celebrities than embodiments of wisdom, to have a large group of people listen to any

12. Aristotle, *Rhetoric*, trans. W. Rhys Roberts (New York: Modern Library, 1954) 24.
13. Quoted by Beverly Zink-Sawyer in "'The Word Purely Preached and Heard': The Listeners and the Homiletical Endeavor," *Interpretation* (October 1997) 343.

public speaking as part of the normal routine of life. When we think of national oratory that has stirred our hearts as well as touched our minds, we usually reach back for the words of Martin Luther King, John and Robert Kennedy or, further yet, to Winston Churchill and F.D.R. Even so, there have been some oratorically skilled speakers in the past twenty-five years, as William Safire[14] reminds us, who have practiced effectively the art of oratory: political figures like Ronald Reagan, Jesse Jackson, Mario Cuomo, and Barbara Jordan, public figures like scientist Carl Sagan, author Elie Wiesel, and humorist Art Buchwald. If there is any one place people might still experience some degree of oratory, I would hope to find it in preaching.

Preaching the word of God begins with a love and respect for words themselves. Such a love for language can be stimulated in many ways. Turning to artists, past and present, can help to foster a sense of the power of language to instruct, delight, and move. Reading the works of respected preachers like Walter Burghardt, S.J., whose homilies reflect the influence of the orator, and Robert P. Waznak, S.S., whose work witnesses to the poet-storyteller at work[15] can incite and stimulate a desire for developing the craft of working well with words. Finally, listening to good speakers, seeking them out, wherever they might be found, in churches or lecture halls, at public readings or sessions of storytelling, can help form a sense of the life giving power of language.

## A Love for Scripture

A preacher's love for words leads to a desire to offer the best words to our listeners, which, in turn, leads us to an ever-growing love for God's word. This begins by listening to the scriptural texts given in the Lectionary, for "the principle source for preaching is naturally Sacred Scripture, deeply meditated on in personal prayer and assimilated through study and adequate contact with suitable books."[16] In the

---

14. See William Safire's *Lend Me Your Ears: Great Speeches in History* (New York: W. W. Norton and Co., 1992) for a wonderful collection of examples of oratorical excellence.

15. Some of Walter Burghardt's collections of homilies include: *When Christ Meets Christ: Homilies on the Just Word* (New York: Paulist, 1993) and *Let Justice Roll Down Like Waters: Biblical Justice Homilies Throughout the Year* (New York: Paulist, 1998); Robert P. Waznak, S.S., *Like Fresh Bread: Sunday Homilies in the Parish* (New York: Paulist, 1993).

16. Congregation for the Clergy, *The Priest and the Third Millennium: Teacher of the Word, Minister of the Sacraments, and Leader of the Community* (Vatican City, 1999) 19.

opening chapter I stressed the importance of the ancient practice of *lectio divina*; I would like to return to it now as a most valuable way to grow in love of Scripture. Michael Casey, prior of Tarrawarra Abbey in Australia, states in his book *Sacred Reading*: "*Lectio divina* is more than the perusal of 'spiritual books.' *Lectio divina* is a technique of prayer and a guide to living. It is a means of descending to the level of the heart and of finding God."[17] There is no one way of falling in love with the word of God, but I cannot imagine it happening unless proximity is involved. Unless you draw near to the "object of affection," approaching the text as a "thou," you are likely to relate to it as an object, treating it only as a carrier of meaning from the past, which is found most quickly by consulting biblical commentaries. The problem with going to commentaries right away is that you short-circuit your own encounter with the text.

The way of *lectio divina* was set down in the twelfth century by Guido II, prior of Chartreuse, as a way of approaching sacred writings by moving through four steps: reading, meditation, prayer, and contemplation. A slow, prayerful reading leads to reflection on how the text speaks to one's own life, then to prayer to carry out the insights gained, and finally, to silent contemplation of the truth arrived at. This process does not happen in strict sequence, or necessarily at one sitting. A flow between reading, reflection, and prayer is an important part of this process. I would like to expand on this and offer a ladder of five steps for homiletical preparation, indicating some ways that I have found helpful for drawing near to the biblical text.

1. *Attend to the Word.* To attend (*ad/tendere*) to the word of God carries the image of leaning (*tendens*) toward (*ad*); leaning in with one's body, drawing close in an intimate way. This begins with a reading marked by attentive listening. Reading the biblical texts to oneself in a quiet place is a good beginning. Better yet is to read it aloud, restoring the word to sound, moving it from the world of print to the world of orality. Through his studies over the years, Walter J. Ong, S.J., has provided us with a sense of the profound differences brought about in the individual and in society by the transition from an oral culture to a literate one, and then to an electronic culture. The world of literacy offers us the word in space; it is the world of letters (from the Latin *littera*) of the alphabet, storing information in manuscripts, books, li-

17. Michael Casey, *Sacred Reading: The Ancient Art of Lectio Divina* (Liguori, Mo.: Liguori/Triumph, 1996) vi.

braries and computers. The dominant sense in this world is sight; we go and "look things up." When we understand, we say, "I see." Literacy brings with it complexity of verbal expression, depth of meaning, and a sense of possessing objective knowledge. The word becomes objectified, an "it," standing out there on its own, far away from the time and culture that originally produced it.

In contrast, the world of orality is the word in time, spoken now, then gone; the moment matters. The word is a presence and a power, the word as "thou." The spoken word carries not just thought but feelings. The oral world is the domain of the storyteller, the orator, and the poet, and its primary sense is sound. Restoring the word to sound is an act of resurrection; black marks on the page become living words, sounded forth from one person to another, "turning ink into blood." The oral word forms community between speaker and listener. How appropriate that we begin our homiletic preparation by sounding the word, confined in the tomb of print, sending it forth with the breath of life.

The writer Eudora Welty remembers the intimate experience of reading as a child. "Every time I was first read to, then started reading to myself, there has never been a line that I didn't hear. As my eye followed the sentence, a voice was saying it silently to me. It wasn't my mother's voice, or the voice of any person I can identify, certainly not my own. It is human but inward, and it is inwardly that I listen to it. It is to me the voice of the story or the poem itself."[18] St. Benedict wanted each monk to have his own book and a place where he could say its words aloud. The first line of Benedict's rule calls on its readers to be careful listeners: "Listen, my son, to the master's instructions, and attend to them with the ear of your heart."

During preaching workshops, I ask participants to block their ears and read the lesson aloud so that they can hear their voice saying the words. It does not have to be very loud; but read slowly, savoring the text and its sounds, sensing its rhythm and how it moves, allowing the words to work their way into one's consciousness, memory, and imagination, pausing often, allowing each phrase to "sink in." Listen not only for the thought but allow your imagination to feel its way into the world of the text, and your body to respond to the words and their rhythm. Listening to your voice as it resonates within your body provides an experience of what Ong calls *interiority*.[19] "Sound . . . reveals

18. Eudora Welty, *One Writer's Beginnings* (Cambridge, Mass.: Harvard, 1984) 11.
19. See Walter J. Ong, *The Presence of the Word: Some Prolegomena for Cultural and Religious History* (New York: Clarion, 1970) 117–22.

the interior without the necessity of physical invasion. . . ."[20] Paradoxically, sound brings the word further "in"; Ong reminds us that "our bodies are a frontier, and the side which is most ourselves is 'in.'"[21] Oral performance heightens the consciousness of our "inner-ness," taking the word off the page and bringing it inward. Attentively sounding a text offers an intimacy not found when reading silently to oneself. Reading silently brings the voice of the text to us, but not with the same intensity and immediacy. The word as sound first penetrates the reader, then proceeds from the inner being of the reader and enters the "inner-ness" of other listeners, uniting speaker and hearers in the moment of listening, and thus, "it forms men [sic] into groups. It is the expression and incarnation of community."[22]

2. *Responding to the Word.* Listening to the word of God evokes some response. There may be a question, a reaction of uncertainty, disagreement, even a lifting of the heart in response to the biblical passage. The response may be intellectual, emotional, kinetic. You may want to read a particular line or paragraph more than once, slowly and deliberately. Usually it helps to read from the Bible what immediately precedes and follows a biblical text in the Lectionary, going beyond the assigned verses. And if verses are dropped out, you would do well to attend to them. Take your time. It is not necessary to "cover" all three readings at once. Give each text its due. Then, move on to the next reading.

After reading a text several times, respond to it in writing. Writing helps to keep focused, enabling a reader to penetrate more deeply into the thoughts and feelings of the text, and entering into a dialogue with them. Thomas Merton was often asked why he wrote so much for a man who had taken a vow of silence. His response was "Writing is a form of contemplation." Writing slows a person down; whereas if you only "think about" something, it is more likely your mind will jump from one thought to another.

Natalie Goldberg gives helpful suggestions to preachers. In *The Wild Mind,*[23] she suggests four rules to help writers "break through," to get thought flowing. After picking a topic to write about and deciding on a definite period of time, she suggests: 1. Keep your hand moving.

20. Ibid., 118.
21. Ibid.
22. Ibid., 310.
23. Natalie Goldberg, *Wild Man: Living the Writer's Life* (New York: Bantam, 1990) 1–5.

2. Lose control. 3. Be specific. 4. Don't think. These same rules can be used in writing a response to a biblical text. Rule 1 breaks through the wall of having to write the perfect first sentence. Just start writing, and keep writing whatever comes in response to the text. This is not for publication—or proclamation. Just write and do not stop to correct. The second rule follows: lose control, say what you want. We can begin censoring our thoughts right away. Keep the hand moving and allow the thoughts and reactions to flow freely without judging them. Reactions like "this is stupid" or "this is silly" do not belong at this stage. Be open to whatever the text sparks in you; this might well be the very reaction it is sparking in the people in church.

Then, rule 3, make the words of your response as concrete and specific as possible. Use the language of the poet and the storyteller, be graphic, concrete, colorful. Look for images over concepts, feelings over judgments. "When I heard this, I felt like . . ." or "That reminded me of the time when . . ." Write in terms of your senses: sight, hearing, touch, taste, smell. The final admonition, "Don't think," means go with what comes first, do not overanalyze. Goldberg suggests going with first thoughts rather than second or third. Again, the purpose at this stage is avoiding the tyranny of the one's inner editor who is quick to call for perfection and to be dismissive of anything less than articulate, fully developed responses. This four-step exercise is not aiming at even a first draft of a text. It is just opening your mind and heart to get a first reaction. It begins the process of personal engagement, putting you in dialogue with the text. You may be surprised what comes forth.

I have found doing this exercise with a lectionary selection from St. Paul has been eye-opening for many preachers. First of all, we rarely spend much time with Paul since most preaching centers on the gospel. But give Paul some of your time for a few weeks and see what can happen. Those instructions and exhortations might break out of their imprisonment as a secondary reading and touch life. Goldberg adds several other rules in addition to the four major ones: Forget about punctuation, spelling, correct grammar. Go where it is uncomfortable, "for the jugular," she advises (yours, not the people's!). Finally, feel free to do the worst writing of your life. This is not for publication; it is a warm-up, but it can get the fires burning.

As I have indicated, a writing response can work well with the epistles, and with texts from Wisdom literature and the prophets. All have a single voice. With a narrative, you might use the same four rules in responding to one of the characters in the story. Look at all the characters, even secondary ones; pay close attention to your reactions. What would you like to say to or ask them? Another possibility: write from the perspective of one of the characters, tell the event from his or her perspective, what this character saw, felt, thought. After finishing this exercise, take a break, stretch, walk around. Get some distance. If you have been writing for ten or fifteen minutes, things can get intense. Then, go back and read what you have written. You might also go back to the text and read it again. Is there something you missed the first time, something your reaction did not take into account? In your response to or as a particular character, is there a question raised or a reaction that disturbs or surprises you? You might want to do this exercise from at least two different perspectives that can be found in the story, and make one that of a secondary character. Note how they differ?

3. *Praying with the Word.* This may very likely be already happening. Prayer can easily occur during the first two steps. Prior Casey says that *lectio divina* is not meant to be a "method" implemented mechanically. Prayer does not suddenly occur at the third stage. "Rather, prayer accompanies us as we open the book and settle our mind, as we read the page and ponder its meaning."[24] And contemplation is not the "outcome of the process," but a "gift from God . . . given in God's time not as a 'reward' for work done, but as an energizing component within the total context of life."[25] These first two steps we have been discussing, attending to the word and responding, can often move us into meditation, prayer, or a wordless, contemplative silence in the presence of the One who wishes to speak to our hearts.

There is value, I believe, in engaging in these exercises in solitude. You can take your time, proceeding at your own pace. But also consider doing them with others, with a group of other preachers, or a group of parishioners. To gather and engage with others in these steps can lead to a deeper appreciation of the many ways a text can be heard, and the variety of questions a text can raise, questions that may never have occurred to you. Most especially, reading the Scriptures and responding to them with others can lead to a deep sense of community and support that comes when two or more gather in Christ's name.

4. *Studying the Word.* Some authors separate study from the practice of *lectio divina.* Pastor Ernest J. Fiedler encourages study at an-

24. Michael Casey, *Sacred Reading,* 61.
25. Ibid., 59.

other time,[26] but biblical scholar Eugene H. Peterson holds for the necessity of exegesis as part of the process:

> Exegesis is an act of love. It means loving the one who speaks the words enough to want to get the words right. It is respecting the words enough to use every means we have to get the words right. Exegesis is loving God enough to stop and listen carefully. It follows that we bring the leisure and attentiveness of lovers to this text, cherishing every comma and semicolon, relishing the oddness of this preposition, delighting in the surprising placement of this noun. Lovers don't take a quick look, get a "message" or a "meaning" and then run off and talk endlessly with their friends about how they feel.[27]

Scholars have written about "a divide between biblical studies and preaching."[28] The importance of taking into account the contributions of biblical scholarship in preaching has been given strong emphasis in the Pontifical Biblical Commission's document *The Interpretation of the Bible in the Church* which reminds preachers that "study of the Bible is . . . the soul of theology. . . . This study is never finished; each age must in its own way newly seek to understand the sacred books."[29]

The primary value of study is that commentaries, both on the individual books of the Bible and on the Lectionary, help to place current biblical scholarship at the service of preaching, keeping us faithful to the intent of the text and preventing our going off on a tangent that results more in a Rorschach response than in the "sharing the fruits of our contemplation with others" that Thomas Aquinas called for.[30] Again,

26. Ernest Fiedler, "Lectio Divina: Devouring God's Word," *Liturgical Ministry* (spring 1996). The author puts study outside of the area of *lectio divina* saying that "beyond their literal sense, the words of Scripture carry a profound spiritual resonance" (68). His view appears similar to the Reformers' insistence on "what they called the 'perspicacity' of Scripture, that the Bible is substantially intelligible. It is essentially open to our understanding without recourse to academic specialists or a privileged priesthood. . . ." See, also, Eugene H. Peterson, "Eat This Book: The Holy Community at Table with the Holy Scripture," *Theology Today* (April 1999) 8.

27. Peterson, "Eat This Book," 10.

28. Stephen Farris, "Limping Away with a Blessing: Biblical Studies and Preaching at the End of the Second Millennium," *Interpretation* (October 1997) 358–70; see also Paul Scott Wilson, "Biblical Studies and Preaching: A Growing Divine?" *Preaching as a Theological Task: World, Gospel, Scripture*, Thomas G. Long and Edward Farley, eds. (Louisville: Westminster/John Knox, 1996) 137–47.

29. Pontifical Biblical Commission, "The Interpretation of the Bible in the Church," *Origins* (Jan. 6, 1994) 497.

30. St. Thomas Aquinas, *Summa Theologiae* II–II, q. 188, a. 7.

the Pontifical Biblical Commission notes the distinct contribution that exegetes have made which must then be brought into conversation with theological research, spiritual experience, and the discernment of the Church. "Exegesis produces its best results when it is carried out in the context of the living faith of the Christian community, which is directed toward the salvation of the entire world."[31] Study of the text is an essential step for growing in our love of Scripture, whether it is done as part of the *lectio divina* method or outside of it.

5. *Playing with the Text.* I do not mean to sound frivolous here. Johan Huizinga's definition of the human person as "homo ludens," as well as anthropologist Victor Turner's placement of "play" at the heart of ritual, point to recent evaluations of this fundamental element of human culture.[32] We are a playful species by necessity. Play is necessary not only for forming social bonds, but it lays the groundwork for creative thinking, helping us to see our world in a new way. There has always been a certain degree of "playing" with the biblical text. Jewish midrash plays by filling in the gaps in a story, creating insights from what lies between the lines of the text. We find another kind of play in the Christian patristic era which delighted in discovering the four senses of a text: the literal, the allegorical, the tropological/moral, and the anagogical. Preaching moved back and forth among the various levels of theological insight, allowing for an interplay of these meanings.

In our own day, we hear of the need for "actualization" and "inculturation" of the text; both call for a creative engagement. The former allows the Bible "to remain fruitful at different periods" by getting to the essential meaning of a text, while the latter "looks to the diversity of place," ensuring that "the biblical message take root in a variety of terrains."[33] Actualization aims to discover what the text has to say at the present time, a pertinent meaning drawn from a text that, by its nature as a literary work, bears a surplus of meaning; inculturation then facilitates some aspect of a text's meaning being shared with a particular culture. Part of the latter's challenge is translation, but equally important is interpretation "which should set the biblical message in more explicit relationship with the ways of feeling, thinking, living and self-

31. Ibid., 520.

32. Johan Huizinga, *Homo Ludens: A Study of the Play-Element in Culture* (Boston: Beacon, 1955) and Victor Turner, *From Ritual to Theatre: The Human Seriousness of Play* (New York: Performing Arts Journal Publications, 1982); see especially his essay "Liminal to Liminoid, in Play, Flow, and Ritual," 20–59.

33. Pontifical Biblical Commission, "Interpretation of the Bible in the Church," 521.

expression which are proper to the local culture."[34] "Here lie dragons" might be cautioned in all these endeavors, but the dragons are not necessarily destructive. All these efforts call for the use of the imagination. Through the imagination, actualization and inculturation proceed to link the texts of the past with the life of the present.

Certain preachers in our time have modeled a responsible playing with the text, such as theologian John Shea in his retelling of the parables. What Shea achieves honors both their original meaning and a contemporary understanding. His playful reworking of the stories of the Samaritan Woman (John 4:1-42) and the Prodigal Son (Luke 15:11-32) serves as a model of evocative, truthful, and moving storytelling.[35] Frederick Buechener also plays creatively with biblical stories and characters; see his work *Peculiar Treasures* for brief treatments of over one hundred and twenty biblical characters.

## A Love for the People

At the end of the Fourth Gospel, the risen Lord takes Simon Peter for a walk down the beach (John 21:15-19). Jesus has just served an early morning breakfast for some of the apostles who had been fishing all night (another feeding story), and he invites Simon to walk with him. Jesus asks, "Do you love me, Simon, son of John?" And Simon answers, "Yes, Lord, you know that I love you." Three times Jesus asks, and three times, with growing exasperation, Simon answers. Each time Jesus responds with basically the same command: "Feed my lambs." "Tend my sheep." "Feed my sheep." This post-resurrection call to ministry in the Fourth Gospel echoes the command given during the miraculous feeding in the Synoptic tradition, "*You* feed them." Donald B. Cozzens in his analysis of *The Changing Face of the Priesthood* makes the connection between tending God's people and the preaching of the parish priest: "Tending the word is the purest form of tending to the people of his parish. Saved himself by this word, he swallows and dares to do what he was ordained to do, he dares to preach."[36]

34. Ibid.

35. The retelling of the Samaritan Woman at the Well was published in *New Catholic World* (Nov.–Dec. 1982) 248–9; the retelling of the parable of the Prodigal Son from three perspectives is found as "Let Them Be Who They Will Be," *The Spirit Master* (Chicago: Thomas More, 1987) 229–36.

36. Donald B. Cozzens, *The Changing Face of the Priesthood* (Collegeville: The Liturgical Press, 2000) 84.

Love is rooted in knowledge and understanding. In order to love the people, a preacher has to know and understand them. And this begins with listening to them. This is the other side of the equation for preachers: listening to the people as attentively as to the Scriptures. *Fulfilled In Your Hearing (FIYH)* goes so far as to say that "attentive listening to the Scriptures and to the people is, in essence, a form of prayer, perhaps the form of prayer most appropriate to the spirituality of the priest and preacher" (10). Preachers must listen for the word of God in the Scriptures, but we also must listen for the word of God in the experience of our brothers and sisters. "We listen to the Scriptures, we listen to the people, and we ask, 'What are they saying to one another? What are they asking of one another?'" (10).

While direct listening is the most rewarding, it can also be helpful to listen to other listeners who have recorded what they are hearing: Tom Brokaw has given us the voices of "the greatest generation";[37] Tom Beaudoin has provided us with insight into Generation X and its spiritual quest;[38] William Finnegan has journeyed into four struggling communities and given us access into several lives of today's less fortunate teenagers;[39] and Jonathan Kozol has shown an attentiveness to the poor children of Mott Haven that helps us to see life through their eyes in the late 1990s.[40] One of the greatest listeners to children in the last half century is the psychiatrist Robert Coles.[41]

Listening to sociologists like Robert N. Bellah,[42] Dean Hoge,[43] James Davidson,[44] and Andrew Greeley,[45] and their reports on the be-

37. Tom Brokaw, *The Greatest Generation* (New York: Random House, 1998).

38. Tom Beaudoin, *Virtual Faith: The Irreverent Spiritual Quest of Generation X* (San Francisco: Jossey-Bass, 1998).

39. William Finnegan, *Cold New World: Growing Up in a Harder Country* (New York: Random House, 1998).

40. Jonathan Kozol, *Ordinary Resurrections: Children in the Years of Hope* (New York: Crown, 2000).

41. See Robert Coles, *The Moral Life of Children* (Boston: Houghton Mifflin, 1986) and *The Spiritual Life of Children* (Boston: Houghton Mifflin, 1990).

42. Robert N. Bellah and others, *Habits of the Heart: Individualism and Commitment in American Life* (Berkeley: University of California Press, 1985).

43. Dean Hoge and others, *Vanishing Boundaries* (Louisville: Westminster/John Knox Press, 1994).

44. James D. Davidson, Andrea S. Williams, Richard A. Lamanna, Jan Stenftenagel, Kathleen Maas Weigert, William J. Whalen, and Patricia Wittberg, *The Search for Common Ground: What Unites and Divides Catholic Americans* (Huntington, Ind.: Our Sunday Visitor, 1997).

45. Andrew M. Greeley, *The Catholic Myth: The Behaviors and Beliefs of American*

liefs and practices at work within our culture allows us to hear the questions, desires, dreams, and fears that touch the lives of believers in our contemporary society. Equally crucial for our day is to listen to the voices of the new immigrants coming to our land from South and Central America, Eastern Europe, Africa, and Asia, and to learn about the experiences that brought them here and that are presently shaping their lives and the lives of their children. Love of the people is rooted in knowledge and understanding, and both of these begin with listening.

Only after listening is it time to preach. We express our love for God's people when we offer them *a person of faith speaking. FIYH* reminds us that "ultimately, that's what preaching is all about, not lofty theological speculation, not painstaking biblical exegesis, not oratorical flamboyance. The preacher is a person speaking to people about faith and life" (15). And that word which we eventually speak must be a word that is true, just, and loving. When we are careful to speak the truth, not out of arrogance or harshness, but out of compassion and a desire to proclaim a word that offers hope, then we are servants of the Word. Preaching has to involve a certain amount of risk-taking, of addressing issues and confronting evils when it would be much easier and attractive to turn aside, to substitute generalities instead of naming the contradictions within the life of the larger cultural community and the smaller Christian community.

The word we speak must be a "just word." Walter J. Burghardt, S.J., and Ray Kemp have formed a team with other dedicated men and women during the last decade that has called preachers to personal conversion reflected in a deeper commitment to preaching God's justice. Preaching justice is a matter of fidelity to the basic relationships in life—the relationship with God, with others, and with the earth; it is a call to live out the covenant which we entered by our baptism into the mystery of Christ, and which calls for an ongoing transformation of the human heart in a way that touches every aspect of life. Such a conversion must happen within the preacher. "Ultimately I am the word, the word that is heard,"[46] says Burghardt. Preachers must embody the just word in their flesh or it remains just a word.

---

*Catholics* (New York: Collier Books, 1990); *The Catholic Imagination* (Berkeley: University of California Press, 2000).

46. Walter J. Burghardt, *Preaching: The Art and the Craft* (New York: Paulist, 1987) 137.

To love the people is to put one's heart into preaching. Alphonsus de Liguori, founder of the Redemptorists, wrote to his religious community of preachers, "He only who speaks from the heart, that is, who feels and practices what he preaches, shall speak to the hearts of others."[47] And the great Protestant preacher Charles Spurgeon centuries later wrote, "Above all the preacher must put heart work into his preaching. He must feel what he preaches. It must never be with him an easy thing to deliver a sermon."[48] To love the people is to be alive for them. There is a story Thich Nhat Hanh[49] tells about St. Francis of Assisi walking in midwinter and coming upon an almond tree. He went up to it and said, "Speak to me of God." And the tree blossomed. The only fitting witness to the living God is aliveness.

Love makes the word alive. And a loving word is a life-giving word. More than that it is salvific. The Nobel prize winning poet Czeslaw Milosz challenges preachers as well as poets when he asks: "What is poetry which does not save / Nations or people?"[50] If our preaching does not draw our people to the Source of life, if it does not bring salvation to our people, we have failed to love them.

## A Love for Jesus Christ

Paddy Chayefsky wrote a wonderful play in the early 1960s called *Gideon.* The main character can be found in the book of Judges (6:1–8:35), that reluctant warrior from the tribe of Manasseh who, with only three hundred men, routed an army of thirty thousand Midianites. In the play, immediately after the unexpected victory over Midian, the Angel (God) who had commissioned an unwilling Gideon for the job, appears again, only now to a Gideon beside himself with delight at what he has achieved. In the course of their conversation, Gideon asks God if he loves him. After responding affirmatively the Angel goes on to speak of those he has loved, finally coming to Moses, "the one I loved best" because he was "a monumentally impassioned man." Then the Angel says to Gideon:

47. St. Alphonsus de Liguori, *The Dignity and Duties of the Priest; or Selva* (Brooklyn: Redemptorist Fathers, 1927) 267.

48. Quoted by David Holwick, "You Are Gifted," (Unpublished Text, Sept. 14, 1997) 5.

49. Thich Nhat Hanh, *Living Buddha, Living Christ* (New York: Riverhead, 1995) 43.

50. Czeslaw Milosz, "Dedication," *The Collected Poems: 1931–1987* (Hopewell, N.J.: Ecco Press, 1988) 78.

It is passion, Gideon, that carries man to God. And passion is a balky beast. Few men ever let it out of the stable. It brooks no bridle; indeed, it bridles you; it rides the rider. Yet it inspirits man's sessile soul above his own inadequate world and makes real such things as beauty, fancy, love, and God and all those other things that are not quite molecular but are. Passion is the very fact of God in man that makes him other than a brute. I must own, Gideon, yours was an old and cold and settled soul, and I huffed and puffed quite a bit before I found the least flame of passion in you.[51]

The same flame is needed today. Walter Burghardt has spoken of the need for "fire in the belly."[52] But this is nothing new. Perhaps in our own time it is aggravated by a style of communication that is either casual, off-handed, and cynical, as with the late-night talk shows, chatty, banal, and mindless as with the daytime talk shows, or neutral, objective in tone, and affectless, as with the more high-minded news programs. Perhaps overexposure to all this has made so many preachers so dispassionate. Or is it that we have bought into the conversational style of delivery so much that any show of passion becomes embarrassing? I am not calling for the equivalent of red-hot, oratorical, heavy breathing. But a periodic flash of flame would be welcome.

The need for fire in preachers has long been recognized. We can feel it in Paul's words to the Corinthians that "I cannot help myself; it would be an agony for me not to preach" (1 Cor 9:16, in NEB translation which is much stronger than the almost passive NRSV translation: "for an obligation is laid on me, and woe to me if I do not proclaim the gospel!"). And it was Paul who wrote to his protégé Timothy: "Stir into flame the gift of God bestowed when my hands were laid on you" (2 Tim 1:6). Pope Gregory the Great wrote that "the one whose heart is not on fire will not inflame."[53] Centuries later, Francis of Assisi recorded that "the servant of God should be so aflame in his life and his holiness that he would reprove all wicked men by the light of his example and by the words of his conversation."[54] And John Wesley gave us a most wonderful statement when he exclaimed, "When I preach, I set myself on fire and the people come and watch me burn."[55]

---

51. Paddy Chayefsky, *Gideon: A New Play* (New York: Random House, 1961) 67.

52. Walter J. Burghardt, *Long Have I Loved You: A Theologian Reflects on His Church* (Maryknoll, N.Y.: Orbis, 2000) 127–9.

53. Quoted by Alphonsus de Liguori, *Dignity and Duties*, 267.

54. *St. Francis of Assisi, Writings and Early Biographies: Omnibus of Sources*, ed. Marion A. Habig (Chicago: Franciscan Herald Press, 1983) 447.

55. Quoted in Phyllis McGinley's *Saint-Watching* (New York: Viking, 1961) 220.

What is it that makes this fire in a preacher? It is a passionate love for Jesus Christ. The most indispensable love in the life of the preacher is this love for Christ. Without it, there may be profound research, stirring thought and emotion, a virtuoso delivery, and even applause, but the danger is very real that preaching will eventually degenerate into an exercise of the ego, aiming to please, or entertain, or no longer even aiming. What keeps the preacher alive is a love for Jesus, a deep, personal, and intimate love. It is what sends the preacher searching for the right words, pursuing the understanding of the Scriptures and all the other texts that give substance to preaching, and which grounds and sustains the preacher's love for the people so that it can grow and develop in the face of ministry's many challenges and even the inevitable disappointments and failures in most of our human relationships. It is this love for Jesus Christ that is the foundation for the preacher's perseverance in struggling to present people with a language to express their faith, to open up more deeply the meaning of the word of God, and to unite them with the God who is Father, Son, and Holy Spirit, forever at work enticing all into the fire of divine love.

As we began with the story of Jesus feeding the multitudes, let us conclude by looking back at it once again. This time we go to Mark's second feeding account (8:1-9) where Jesus is feeding the Gentiles. And he takes the initiative, not the disciples. Unlike the disiciples in the first account who noted the people's hunger but called on Jesus to dismiss them, Jesus moves immediately to feed them, saying he cannot send them away at this point because they are so hungry, they might collapse on the road. After all, they have come from a great distance. Significantly, this feeding takes place "on the third day" which is always a reference to the resurrection. It is on the third day that Jesus is moved to care for the crowd. And this response of the Lord continues until this very day. The risen Christ continues to feed us whenever we gather to celebrate "the third day." And it is this Jesus Christ we are called to love and make known: Jesus Christ whose risen life flows outward to embrace the world in all its hungers; Jesus Christ who feeds us with his presence, and his word, and the sacrament of his Body and Blood; and Jesus Christ who stands there, and turns toward us, and urges us again and yet again, "*You* feed them."

# Index